CIMA

ENTERPRISE

PAPER E1

ENTERPRISE OPERATIONS

This Kit is for exams in 2011.

In this Kit we:

- Discuss the **best strategies** for revising and taking your E1 exam
- Show you how to be well prepared for the **2011 exams**
- Give you **lots of great guidance** on tackling questions
- Demonstrate how you can **build your own exams**
- Provide you with **three** mock exams

PRACTICE & REVISION KIT

FOR EXAMS IN 2011

LEARNING MEDIA

First edition 2010
Second edition January 2011

ISBN 9780 7517 9453 3
Previous ISBN 9780 7517 7518 1
eBook ISBN   9780 7517 8708 5

British Library Cataloguing-in-Publication Data
A catalogue record for this book
is available from the British Library

Published by

BPP Learning Media Ltd
BPP House, Aldine Place
London W12 8AA

www.bpp.com/learningmedia

Printed in the United Kingdom

Your learning materials, published by BPP
Learning Media Ltd, are printed on paper sourced
from sustainable, managed forests.

We are grateful to the Chartered Institute of
Management Accountants for permission to
reproduce past examination questions. The
answers to past examination questions have been
prepared by BPP Learning Media Ltd.

A note about copyright

Dear Customer

What does the little © mean and why does it matter?

Your market-leading BPP books, course materials and
e-learning materials do not write and update themselves.
People write them: on their own behalf or as employees
of an organisation that invests in this activity. Copyright
law protects their livelihoods. It does so by creating rights
over the use of the content.

Breach of copyright is a form of theft – as well as being a
criminal offence in some jurisdictions, it is potentially a
serious breach of professional ethics.

With current technology, things might seem a bit hazy
but, basically, without the express permission of BPP
Learning Media:

- Photocopying our materials is a breach of copyright

- Scanning, ripcasting or conversion of our digital
  materials into different file formats, uploading them to
  facebook or emailing them to your friends is a breach
  of copyright

You can, of course, sell your books, in the form in which
you have bought them – once you have finished with
them. (Is this fair to your fellow students? We update for a
reason.) But the e-products are sold on a single user
licence basis: we do not supply 'unlock' codes to people
who have bought them second-hand.

And what about outside the UK? BPP Learning Media
strives to make our materials available at prices students
can afford by local printing arrangements, pricing policies
and partnerships which are clearly listed on our website.
A tiny minority ignore this and indulge in criminal activity
by illegally photocopying our material or supporting
organisations that do. If they act illegally and unethically
in one area, can you really trust them?

Contents

	Page

Finding questions and using the Practice and Revision Kit

Question index	iv
Topic index	vi
Using your BPP Learning Media Practice and Revision Kit	vii

Passing E1

Revising E1	viii
Passing the E1 exam	ix
The exam paper	xi
What the examiner means	xiii

Planning your question practice

BPP's question plan	xiv
Build your own exams	xviii

Questions and answers

Questions	3
Answers	61

Exam practice

Mock exam 1

•	Questions	175
•	Plan of attack	183
•	Answers	185

Mock exam 2

•	Questions	195
•	Plan of attack	203
•	Answers	205

Mock exam 3 (November 2010 exam)

•	Questions	215
•	Plan of attack	225
•	Answers	227

Question index

The headings in this checklist/index indicate the main topics of questions, but questions often cover several different topics.

Questions set under the old syllabus's *Organisational Management and Information Systems (OMIS) exam* are included because their style and content are similar to those that appear in the Paper E1 exam.

		Marks	Time allocation Mins	Page number Question	Answer
Part A: The Global Business Environment					
1	Objective test questions: Global business environment	20	36	3	61
2	Various global business environment topics	30	54	4	62
3	McBride Gibbon	30	54	4	65
4	G Banking Group (5/10)	25	45	5	68
5	F Food	25	45	5	71
6	HU3	25	45	6	73
7	Gus	25	45	6	75
8	FutureGreen	25	45	7	77
Part B: Information Systems					
9	Objective test questions: Information systems 1	20	36	8	79
10	Objective test questions: Information systems 2	20	36	9	80
11	S&C software project (OMIS 5/06 – amended)	30	54	10	81
12	S1K (Specimen paper)	25	45	11	84
13	New system	25	45	12	87
14	System implementation	25	45	12	89
15	K1S (OMIS 5/08 – amended)	25	45	13	91
Part C: Operations Management					
16	Objective test questions: Operations management 1	20	36	14	93
17	Objective test questions: Operations management 2	20	36	15	94
18	Capacity, supply and demand	30	54	17	95
19	W Company (5/10)	25	45	18	98
20	TQM and sourcing	25	45	19	101
21	YO and MX (OMIS 5/07 – amended)	25	45	20	104
22	Electro	25	45	21	106
23	DOH (OMIS 5/08 – amended)	25	45	22	108
Part D: Marketing					
24	Objective test questions: Marketing 1	20	36	23	110
25	Objective test questions: Marketing 2	20	36	24	111
26	V (OMIS – 5/05 amended)	30	54	25	112
27	CW (Specimen paper)	25	45	26	115
28	Marketing action plan (OMIS 11/05 – amended)	25	45	27	118
29	Consumer purchasing	25	45	28	120
30	Marketing, segmentation and ethics (OMIS 11/06 – amended)	25	45	28	123
31	4QX (OMIS 11/07 – amended)	25	45	29	126

	Marks	Time allocation Mins	Page number Question	Answer

Part E: Managing Human Capital

	Marks	Time allocation Mins	Question	Answer
32 Objective test questions: Managing human capital 1	20	36	30	128
33 Objective test questions: Managing human capital 2	20	36	31	129
34 Corporate upheaval (OMIS 11/08 – amended)	30	54	32	130
35 HR division and strategy (OMIS 11/05 – amended)	25	45	33	133
36 Human resource plan and activities (OMIS Pilot Paper – amended)	25	45	34	135
37 Training and development (OMIS 5/07 – amended)	25	45	35	137
38 Motivation and reward (OMIS 5/06 – amended)	25	45	36	140

Mixed Section A multiple choice questions

	Marks	Time allocation Mins	Question	Answer
39 Multiple choice questions: General 1 (5/10)	20	36	37	143
40 Multiple choice questions: General 2 (Specimen paper)	20	36	39	144
41 Multiple choice questions: General 3	20	36	41	145
42 Multiple choice questions: General 4	20	36	43	146
43 Multiple choice questions: General 5	20	36	45	147
44 Multiple choice questions: General 6	20	36	47	148
45 Multiple choice questions: General 7	20	36	49	149

Mixed Section B questions

	Marks	Time allocation Mins	Question	Answer
46 Various topics 1 (5/10)	30	54	51	150
47 Various topics 2 (Specimen paper)	30	54	52	156
48 Various topics 3	30	54	53	160
49 Tracey plc scenario	30	54	54	162
50 Zodiac plc scenario	30	54	55	164
51 Hubbles scenario (OMIS – Pilot Paper)	30	54	56	167
52 OK4u scenario (OMIS 11/08 – amended)	30	54	57	169

Mock exam 1

Questions 53-56

Mock exam 2

Questions 57-60

Mock exam 3 (November 2010 exam)

Questions 61-64

Planning your question practice

Our guidance from page xiv shows you how to organise your question practice, either by attempting questions from each syllabus area or by **building your own exams** – tackling questions as a series of practice exams.

Topic index

Listed below are the key Paper E1 syllabus topics and the numbers of the questions in this Kit covering those topics.

If you need to concentrate your practice and revision on certain topics or if you want to attempt all available questions that refer to a particular subject you will find this index useful.

Syllabus topic	Question numbers
Appraisal	38, 50, 52, ME1 Q4
Balance of trade	2
BPR	19
Branding	28, ME3 Q4
BRIC economies	4, ME3 Q2
Business environment	3, 6, ME1 Q3, ME3 Q3
Business organisations	7, 18
Business to Business (B2B) and Business to Consumer (B2C) marketing	48
Capacity management	18, ME3 Q3
Change management	14, ME2 Q2
Competitive environment	2
Consumer behaviour	18
Corporate governance	5, 8
Corporate political activity	3
Corporate social responsibility	2, 3, 8, 26, 52, ME1 Q3, ME3 Q4
Country risk	3
Cross-cultural management	3, 7
Development and training	34, 37, 48, ME2 Q3
E-business	26, ME3 Q3, ME3 Q4
Global business	2, 3, 5, 6
Human resource management	4, 12, 21, 26, 34, 35, 36, 38, 49, 51, 52, ME1Q4, ME2 Q2, ME3 Q3
Information system changeover	11, 12, 13, 14
Information system implementation	11, 12, 13, 14, 49, ME2 Q3
Information system outsourcing	50
Information systems	11, 12, 13, 14, 48, 49, 50, ME2 Q2, ME3 Q2
Information systems and business strategy	11, 15, 49
Inventory management	18, 22, ME1 Q2
Lean techniques	22, ME3 Q2
Market segmentation	30, ME1:Q2, ME2:Q4
Marketing	26, 27, 28, 29, 30, 31, 49, 51, ME2 Q2, ME3 Q4
Marketing environment	30, 31, ME1 Q2, ME2 Q4, ME3 Q4
Marketing mix	26, 27, 28, 49, 51, 52, ME3 Q4
Offshoring	3, 4, ME1 Q2, ME3 Q2
Operations strategy	18
Outsourcing	3, 4, ME1 Q2, ME3 Q2
Political risk	3
Pricing	28, ME3 Q4
Product development and lifecycle	ME2 Q2
Quality management	21, 22, 23, ME2 Q2
Stakeholders	3
Supply chain management	18, 19, 20, 21, 52
Total Quality Management (TQM)	21, ME3 Q2

Using your BPP Learning Media Practice and Revision Kit

Tackling revision and the exam

You can significantly improve your chances of passing by tackling revision and the exam in the right ways. Our advice is based on feedback from CIMA. We focus on Paper E1; we discuss revising the syllabus, what to do (and what not to do) in the exam, how to approach different types of question and ways of obtaining easy marks.

Selecting questions

We provide signposts to help you plan your revision.

- A full **question index**

- A **topic index**, listing all the questions that cover key topics, so that you can locate the questions that provide practice on these topics, and see the different ways in which they might be examined

- **BPP's question plan**, highlighting the most important questions

- **Build your own exams**, showing you how you can practise questions in a series of exams

Making the most of question practice

We realise that you need more than questions and model answers to get the most from your question practice.

- Our **Top tips** provide essential advice on tackling questions and presenting answers

- We show you how you can pick up **Easy marks** on questions, as picking up all readily available marks can make the difference between passing and failing

- We include **marking guides** to show you what the examiner rewards

- We refer to the **BPP 2010 Study Text** for detailed coverage of the topics covered in each question

Attempting mock exams

There are three mock exams that provide practice at coping with the pressures of the exam day. We strongly recommend that you attempt them under exam conditions, as they reflect the question styles and syllabus coverage of the exam. To help you get the most out of doing these exams, we provide guidance on how you should have approached the whole exam.

Our other products

BPP Learning Media also offers these products for practising and revising the E1 exam:

Passcards	Summarising what you should know in visual, easy to remember, form
Success CDs	Covering the vital elements of the E1 syllabus in less than 90 minutes and also containing exam hints to help you fine tune your strategy
i-Pass	Providing computer-based testing in a variety of formats, ideal for self-assessment
Interactive Passcards	Allowing you to learn actively with a clear visual format summarising what you must know

You can purchase these products by visiting www.bpp.com/learningmedia

Revising E1

The E1 exam

This will be a time-pressured exam that combines a variety of different types of question. It is very important that you do not spend too long on the objective test and shorter written questions at the expense of understanding and appreciating the issues involved in the longer written questions that make up half the marks on the paper.

Topics to revise

You need to be comfortable with **all areas of the syllabus** because any question may span a number of syllabus areas. Question spotting will absolutely **not work** on this paper. It is better to go into the exam knowing a reasonable amount about most of the syllabus rather than concentrating on a few topics.

The global business environment

- The major economic systems of the world and the emergence of new economies
- The role of government in shaping the business environment and market regulation
- The importance of corporate governance and corporate social responsibility

Information systems

- The role of information systems and how they are implemented and evaluated
- Types of information system and their role in enabling change
- The importance of protecting information systems and aligning them with business strategy

Operations management

- How to manage inventory, production capacity, demand and supply chains
- The importance of quality and methods of quality measurement and management
- Information systems used in operations management

Marketing

- Marketing orientations, the marketing environment and social responsibility issues of marketing
- Targeting market segments with an appropriate marketing mix through various marketing methods
- Branding and not-for-profit marketing

Managing human capital

- Human resource management theories and HR planning
- Good human resource practices from recruitment to dismissal
- Training, development and the role of appraisals

Question practice

Question practice under timed conditions is essential in order to get used to answering exam questions in **limited time** and to practise the different skills involved in answering each type of question.

Passing the E1 exam

Displaying the right qualities

The examiner expects you to display the following qualities.

Qualities required	
A good understanding	Questions will often test your grasp of **generally accepted** management thinking in the main syllabus areas, there will often be some **flexibility** allowed, there may be **no** single right answer.
Business awareness	You will be tested in different questions on your ability to **identify** and **understand** the **management implications** of the problems you are faced with.
Evaluation and recommendation	You must be able to **analyse** a situation, **generate** and **evaluate** a range of **options** and be ready to **recommend** a **reasonable** course of action.
Communication skills	A **challenging** aspect of E1 is that you have to adapt to the **four types** of question (MCQ, OT, short-answers and scenario questions of unlimited length).
	To answer the short **Section A** and **Section B** questions you should **carefully structure your response** (use bullets or short sentences) and only answer the question set.
	When answering **Section C** questions you should remember that **markers assess your overall answer** as well as counting points made.
	Limited answers that make **basic points** score poorly, **pass answers add realistic insights**, but **only strong answers** offer **clear, purposeful explanations** that earn the big marks. Ensure your answers have enough depth to score well.

Avoiding weaknesses

You will enhance your chances significantly if you ensure you avoid these mistakes:

- Failure to read the question
- Lack of application of knowledge to scenario
- Failure to pick up scenario details eg size of company, morale of workforce, the business environment
- Confusion of scenario details from different questions
- Time management – spending excessive time on strong areas or too long on areas you struggle with
- Poor English, structure and presentation
- Poor knowledge of basic concepts and definitions
- Exceeding 50 word/one page limits
- Repeating the same material in different parts of a question
- Brain dumping everything you know about the topic area being tested – seeing a familiar word in a question and going off on a tangent

Using the reading time

We recommend you spend the first ten minutes of reading time scanning the paper and identifying the main topic areas covered. The second ten minutes, we suggest you spend looking at the compulsory Section A questions and marking your answers on the question page. Answers can be transferred to your answer booklet once writing time commences. **DO NOT** write in you answer booklet until you are given permission to do so.

Choosing which questions to answer first

Choosing which questions to answer first is a matter of preference. You should practise different methods during your revision to decide which one suits you best.

One option is to do Section C questions once you have tackled Section A as these questions are longer and require more thought and planning. An alternative method is to do the questions in the order they appear on the exam paper that is, Section A, Section B and then Section C. The **most important** thing to remember is to spend **no longer** than 36 minutes on Section A, 54 minutes on Section B and 90 minutes on Section C!

Discussion questions

Remember that **depth of discussion** is important. Discussions will often consist of paragraphs containing 2-3 sentences. Each paragraph should have a short header and:

* **Make a point**
* **Explain the point** (you must demonstrate **why** the point is important)
* **Illustrate the point** (with material or analysis from the scenario, perhaps an example from real-life)

Gaining the easy marks

The first few marks are always the easiest to gain in any question. This applies particularly to Section B. Spend the same amount of time on each part of the Section B question. This will give you a good chance of passing each part of the question, and comfortably passing the question overall.

Section C questions carry a lot of marks. Make sure you read the requirement carefully and apply your knowledge to the situation outlined in the scenario.

The exam paper

Format of the paper

		Number of marks
Section A:	Expected to be 10 compulsory multiple choice questions worth 2 marks	20
Section B:	6 compulsory short-written questions worth 5 marks each	30
Section C:	2 compulsory longer written questions worth 25 marks each	50
		100

Time allowed: 3 hours plus 20 minutes reading time.

Section A will always contain some multiple choice questions, but other types of objective test question may be included as well. Short scenarios may be provided to which a group of questions relate.

Section B questions will be short-answer written questions which may or may not be based around a scenario. This section will require breadth of syllabus knowledge and also good time management skills.

Section C questions will be longer written questions based around a scenario. They will require knowledge, some application, and discussion surrounding the issues raised.

Breadth of question coverage

Questions in all sections of the paper may cover more than one syllabus area.

Important!

This exam information page sets out what to expect from your E1 exam in terms of exam format and style, however it is possible for exam papers to vary slightly over time.

For example:

Section A may include just MCQ or OT questions rather than a mix. None or all questions could be based around a scenario.

Section B questions may be based around a scenario, or may not.

By practising a range of question styles you will be prepared to take anything which comes up.

Specimen paper

Section A

1   Ten compulsory multiple choice questions drawn from all areas of the syllabus.

Section B

2   HR planning, quality costs, SERVQUAL, Six Sigma, stakeholders, political risk.

Section C

3   Marketing, segmentation, ethical concerns.

4   Information systems and operations, system implementation problems, training.

May 2010

Section A

1   Ten compulsory multiple choice questions drawn from all areas of the syllabus.

Section B

2   IS outsourcing, IS/IT and HR, promotions and distribution channels, marketing mix, internal recruitment options, non-financial motivators.

Section C

3   BRIC economies, offshoring, redundancies.

4   Strategic supply chain management, BPR and process maps, code of ethics.

November 2010

Section A

1   Ten compulsory multiple choice questions drawn from all areas of the syllabus.

Section B

2   Outsourcing, emerging economies and multinationals, ICT transformation, lean processes, TQM.

Section C

3   HR practices, planning HR strategy, e-HR.

4   Ethics and CSR, marketing mix and branding, Internet marketing.

The November 2010 paper is Mock Exam 3 in this Kit.

What the examiner means

The table below has been prepared by CIMA to help you interpret exam questions.

Learning objective	Verbs used	Definition	Examples in the Kit
1 Knowledge			
What you are expected to know	• List	• Make a list of	13(b)
	• State	• Express, fully or clearly, the details of/facts of	
	• Define	• Give the exact meaning of	
2 Comprehension			
What you are expected to understand	• Describe	• Communicate the key features of	11(e)
	• Distinguish	• Highlight the differences between	32.5
	• Explain	• Make clear or intelligible/state the meaning or purpose of	27(a)
	• Identify	• Recognise, establish or select after consideration	27(c)
	• Illustrate	• Use an example to describe or explain something	29(c)
3 Application			
How you are expected to apply your knowledge	• Apply	• Put to practical use	
	• Calculate/compute	• Ascertain or reckon mathematically	
	• Demonstrate	• Prove the certainty or exhibit by practical means	
	• Prepare	• Make or get ready for use	49(f)
	• Reconcile	• Make or prove consistent/ compatible	
	• Solve	• Find an answer to	
	• Tabulate	• Arrange in a table	
4 Analysis			
How you are expected to analyse the detail of what you have learned	• Analyse	• Examine in detail the structure of	23(a)
	• Categorise	• Place into a defined class or division	
	• Compare and contrast	• Show the similarities and/or differences between	
	• Construct	• Build up or complete	
	• Discuss	• Examine in detail by argument	11(c)
	• Interpret	• Translate into intelligible or familiar terms	
	• Prioritise	• Place in order of priority or sequence for action	
	• Produce	• Create or bring into existence	
5 Evaluation			
How you are expected to use your learning to evaluate, make decisions or recommendations	• Advise	• Counsel, inform or notify	
	• Evaluate	• Appraise or assess the value of	21(a)
	• Recommend	• Propose a course of action	20(c)

Planning your question practice

We have already stressed that question practice should be right at the centre of your revision. Whilst you will spend some time looking at your notes and the Paper E1 Passcards, you should spend the majority of your revision time practising questions.

We recommend two ways in which you can practise questions.

- Use **BPP Learning Media's question plan** to work systematically through the syllabus and attempt key and other questions on a section-by-section basis

- **Build your own exams** – attempt the questions as a series of practice exams

These ways are suggestions and simply following them is no guarantee of success. You or your college may prefer an alternative but equally valid approach.

BPP's question plan

The plan below requires you to devote a **minimum of 35 hours** to revision of Paper E1. Any time you can spend over and above this should only increase your chances of success.

 Review your notes and the chapter summaries in the Paper E1 **Passcards** for each section of the syllabus.

 Answer the key questions for that section. These questions have boxes round the question number in the table below and you should answer them in full. Even if you are short of time you must attempt these questions if you want to pass the exam. You should complete your answers without referring to our solutions.

 Attempt the other questions in that section. For some questions we have suggested that you prepare **answer plans or do the calculations** rather than full solutions. Planning an answer means that you should spend about 40% of the time allowance for the questions brainstorming the question and drawing up a list of points to be included in the answer.

 Attempt Mock exams 1, 2 and 3 under strict exam conditions.

Syllabus section	2010 Passcards chapters	Questions in this Kit	Comments	Done ☑
The global business environment	1, 2	1	Answer in full. These objective test questions are focussed on specific parts of the syllabus and enable you to build up speed in answering this type of question.	☐
		4	Answer in full. This question, taken from the May 2010 exam, tests your knowledge of the BRIC economies and offshoring.	☐
		6	Identify the environmental factors in part (a) and the six strategies in part (b).	☐
		7	Answer in full. This question tests your recall of types of business organisation and the issues surrounding the use of expatriate staff.	☐
		8	Answer in full. A good general question on corporate governance and corporate social responsibility.	☐
Information systems	3, 4	9	Answer in full. These objective test questions are focussed on specific parts of the syllabus and enable you to build up speed in answering this type of question.	☐
		11	Answer in full. This question covers many aspects of systems implementation and the importance of aligning systems with business strategy.	☐
		12	Answer in full. This Specimen Paper question covers the role of IT/IS in operations and also covers systems implementation issues.	☐
		13	Produce a question plan for the three parts, listing each point that you need to make.	☐
		14	Produce a question plan for each part, listing each point that you need to make.	☐
Operations management	5, 6, 7	16	Answer in full. These objective test questions are focussed on specific parts of the syllabus and enable you to build up speed in answering this type of question.	☐
		18	Answer in full. Planning operations carefully in order to meet actual demand is an important aspect of manufacturing. Use this question to help your understanding of this area.	☐

Syllabus section	2010 Passcards chapters	Questions in this Kit	Comments	Done ☑
		20	Answer part (b) in full. Prepare answer plans for (a) and (c).	☐
		23	Answer in full.	☐
			This question requires you to apply your knowledge of quality management by spotting quality issues in a scenario.	
Marketing	8, 9, 10	24	Answer in full.	☐
			These objective test questions are focussed on specific parts of the syllabus and enable you to build up speed in answering this type of question.	
		26	Answer in full.	☐
			A number of marketing issues are examined in this question. In particular, the use of the internet, the marketing mix and ethical issues.	
		27	Answer in full.	☐
			This Specimen paper question includes aspects of the marketing mix and also tests your knowledge of segmentation and targeting.	
		28	Answer parts (b) and (c) in full. Prepare a plan for part (a).	☐
		31	Answer in full.	☐
			An unusual question that requires an explanation of how to calculate income potential – an area often overlooked by students.	
Managing human capital	11, 12	32	Answer in full.	☐
			These objective test questions are focussed on specific parts of the syllabus and enable you to build up speed in answering this type of question.	
		34	Answer in full.	☐
			A cunning question that warms you up with simple 'advantages and disadvantages of...' questions – and then delivers a tricky final part requiring an explanation of Maslow's theory by reference to the scenario!	
			Avoid theories such as this at your peril!	
		36	Produce a question plan for the three parts, listing each point that you need to make.	☐
		37	Answer in full.	☐
			This is an interesting question which gives you an opportunity to explain how training and development has wider benefits to the organisation.	
		38	Answer in full.	☐
			A very full question that examines the detail that you are expected to know concerning appraisals and reward schemes. Beware of part (b) concerning Herzberg's theory – you were warned of theory questions such as this earlier!	

Syllabus section	2010 Passcards chapters	Questions in this Kit	Comments	Done ☑
Mixed multiple choice questions		39 to 45	Answer in full. These questions cover a range of syllabus areas very quickly. You will practise switching your mind between them, enabling you build up speed in answering this type of question.	☐
Mixed Section B questions		46 to 52	Answer in full. As with the mixed objective test questions, you will practise switching your mind between different syllabus areas. However these questions will also hone your skill in keeping your answers short and focussed – exactly what you need to cope with time pressure in the actual exam.	☐

Build your own exams

Having revised your notes and the BPP E1 Passcards, you can attempt the questions in the Kit as a series of practice exams, making them up yourself or using the mock exams that we have listed below.

	Practice exams					
	1	2	3	4	5	6
Section A						
1	39	40	41	42	43	44
Section B						
2	47	46	48	11	18	26
Section C						
3	5	17	30	28	20	21
4	21	31	9	37	15	38

Whichever practice exams you use, you must attempt **Mock exams 1, 2 and 3** at the end of your revision.

QUESTIONS

2

THE GLOBAL BUSINESS ENVIRONMENT

Questions 1 to 8 cover The Global Business Environment, the subject of Part A of the BPP Study Text for Paper E1.

1 Objective test questions: Global business environment   36 mins

1.1   What is the main financial objective of public sector organisations?

    A   Profitability
    B   Efficient use of resources
    C   Avoidance of loss
    D   Maximisation of charitable donations   **(2 marks)**

1.2   Which two government policies support an emerging nation's import-substitution strategy?

    A   Import tariffs and import quotas
    B   Import quotas and currency devaluation
    C   Import tariffs and industry subsidies
    D   Currency devaluation and industry subsidies   **(2 marks)**

1.3   The European Union (EU) is an example of:

    A   A free trade area
    B   A customs union
    C   A common market
    D   A transition economy   **(2 marks)**

1.4   According to monetarist theory, the primary effect of increasing the money supply is to:

    A   Increase prices
    B   Increase reserve requirements
    C   Increase the volume of exports
    D   Increase demand for imports   **(2 marks)**

> Each of the sub-questions numbered **1.5** to **1.7** below require a brief written response. Each sub-question is worth 4 marks. The response should be in note form and should not exceed 50 words.

1.5   Explain the differences between economic liberalisation and economic nationalism.   **(4 marks)**

The following scenario is related to sub-questions 1.6 and 1.7.

Emerland is an undeveloped nation. The government wishes to develop the economy and industry but is concerned that by doing so its markets may become dominated by foreign monopolies.

As an adviser to Emerland's government:

1.6   Explain in general terms how the government may influence Emerland's economy.   **(4 marks)**

1.7   Explain how the government may prevent foreign monopolies taking over Emerland's industries.

    (4 marks)

    (Total = 20 marks)

> If you struggled with the MCQ and OT questions in Q1, go back to your BPP Study Text for Paper E1 and revise Chapters 1 and 2 before you tackle the longer questions on the Global Business Environment.

2   Various global business environment topics   54 mins

Required

(a)   Explain how factor conditions in Porter's diamond contribute to the competitive advantage of a nation.

(5 marks)

(b)   Identify and discuss the arguments in favour of free trade.   **(5 marks)**

(c)   Describe the main issues an organisation needs to consider when deciding whether to outsource its information technology (IT) function.   **(5 marks)**

(d)   Explain how macroeconomic factors can affect a nation's balance of trade.   **(5 marks)**

(e)   Discuss the effects that deregulation may have on a nation's manufacturing industry.   **(5 marks)**

(f)   Describe the key drivers for corporate social responsibility within a developing economy.   **(5 marks)**

(Total = 30 marks)

3   McBride Gibbon   54 mins

McBride Gibbon (MG) is a successful, large manufacturing company which designs and manufactures children's toys. The company's activities all take place in its home country of Blueland which is one of the world's most developed industrial nations.

A key reason for MG's success is its ethical stance. All of its products are made from environmentally friendly and sustainable materials – a point that is well advertised on its products and marketing documents. All of its suppliers have to conform to MG's ethical standards before they can trade with it.

The company also considers itself socially responsible and will quickly recall any products that are found to have defects or that are dangerous. This is because it recognises the need of parents to be sure that the toys they give to their children are completely safe.

MG recently published a social responsibility policy which highlighted the company's excellent treatment of its employees and the fact that it supports community based activities in the locations where it has factories.

As a consequence of its ethical stance, MG's cost base is considerably higher than other toy manufacturers. Shareholders are increasingly demanding that the company's cost base is reduced so that it can generate more profit and pay them greater dividends. This has led the Chief Executive Officer, Graham McBride, to find a cheaper location to manufacture the toys.

The country of Redland has been identified as a possible location to establish a new manufacturing base. It is a newly emerging industrial nation which has a large number of its citizens unemployed and historically low labour costs. The country is run by a military government which overthrew a democratically elected parliament a year ago. The country has a very high inflation rate and the value of the national currency is currently unstable, but it is rich in the natural resources MG needs to manufacture its products.

Graham McBride is unsure what the best course of action for MG is, however he has heard of outsourcing and offshoring as possibilities. As a consultant, he now looks to you for advice.

Required

(a)   Explain how the interests of MG's shareholders conflict with other groups of stakeholder.   **(5 marks)**

(b)   Explain the drivers of social responsibility in developing nations.   **(5 marks)**

(c)   Explain the concept of political risk and identify the main political risks of Redland.   **(5 marks)**

(d)   Explain the term 'transnational vertical integration' and how MG could use outsourcing or offshoring as part of a cost reduction plan.   **(5 marks)**

(e)   Explain the term 'corporate culture' and the cultural constraints on organisations which operate globally.   **(5 marks)**

(f)   Explain the actions MG could take in order protect itself from the risks involved in relocating its manufacturing operations to Redland.   **(5 marks)**

(Total = 30 marks)

4   G banking group (5/10)   45 mins

The G Banking Group recently reported that it was offshoring (moving) its back-office operations from European country D to India where it already has some significant operations. Centralising most back-office operations in India is part of the Group's plan to grow its international banking business. (India is one of the fast emerging economies in the so-called BRIC group of Brazil, Russia, India and China).

According to a G Banking Group spokesperson, the move would involve cutting about 500 jobs from its operations in country D but generating a similar number of new jobs in India where it already employs 3,000 people. The spokesperson was, however, quick to add that some call centres would still remain in country D.

One banking analyst commented that the Group's current Chief Executive Officer (CEO) was 'more aggressive' and 'less sentimental' about moving back-office jobs than his predecessors. The National Secretary of the Banking Union described the cuts as 'disgraceful' and argued that it showed a lack of concern for the difficult employment situation faced by many young people in country D.

In response to such criticism, the CEO explained that banking was becoming increasingly global and that unless the Group responded to the global challenges facing it, it would be unable to survive into the future. The CEO went on to assure employees that it would assist those affected by the relocation of its operations in every way possible.

Required

(a)   Describe the key factors involved in the emergence of the BRIC economies.   **(10 marks)**

(b)   Explain the advantages and the associated problems for the G Banking Group of offshoring its back-office operations to an emerging country.   **(10 marks)**

(c)   Identify the role that the Group's Human Resources Division can play when dealing with employees who cannot be redeployed following the offshoring of its back-office operations.   **(5 marks)**

(Total = 25 marks)

5   F food   45 mins

F Food is a listed company that operates a successful chain of fast food restaurants in North America. It is currently looking to expand its operations into Asia, believing that there is significant growth potential.

F Food plans to use existing expatriate management staff in the new management roles in the Asian operations, but it will introduce a new management programme for local employees once the operations are established.

F Food currently operates a bonus scheme to senior management and directors, based on achieving a specified level of profit in the previous quarter. The CEO is a dominant figure and controls all board decision making.

Required

(a)   Identify and explain the main organisational (including cultural considerations) and management issues that F Food must consider as part of its plans to expand into the Asian market. (Note: your answer to part (a) should **not** refer to the issue of whether management staff are local or expatriate.)   **(10 marks)**

(b)   Following a spate of recent corporate scandals, F Food wishes to improve its corporate governance. Explain why the CEO and the bonus scheme present a risk to corporate governance. Also explain how an audit committee and an appropriate remuneration policy can help corporate governance.   **(10 marks)**

(c)   Discuss the relative advantages to F Food of using local staff and of using expatriate staff in the new management roles.   **(5 marks)**

(Total = 25 marks)

6 HU3   45 mins

HU3 manufactures components for computers and is based in the country of Lowland. Its products are not the best quality, however they normally work and scrap and rework are within what is expected in Lowland's industry.

The company wishes to expand its operations and enter the fiercely competitive computer market in the nearby country of Highland. Due to competition, the quality of products produced in Highland are far superior to those in Lowland. Highland's industry is also far more technologically advanced. Highland does however share a common culture and societal values with Lowland.

The computer market in Highland is continually expanding. This is partly due to the government creating a stable economy – inflation, interest and exchange rates have barely changed in the last few years. The government also created legislation that offers employees a high level of protection (greater than Lowland) and more incentives, such as government grants and a favourable tax regime to attract investment. The government also created a research and development zone to support industry in the country. However, for ecological reasons, certain areas of the country will not allow further industrial development.

HU3 is keen to expand its operations into Highland to take advantage of the expanding market. However the board of directors are concerned about a number of factors which will affect the success of the expansion. In particular they believe the lack of quality in its products leave it unable to compete.

Required

(a)   Identify and explain the environmental factors that HU3 should consider when deciding whether or not to expand into Highland.   **(12 marks)**

(b)   Briefly explain the term 'competitive advantage' and suggest six strategies HU3 could use in order to improve the quality of its products and compete in Highland's market.   **(13 marks)**

(Total = 25 marks)

7 Gus   45 mins

Gus is an inventor who has recently designed and built a prototype device which solves an everyday problem. He has kept the details of his invention secret and no other individual or organisation was involved in product development or funding.

The product solves such an obvious problem that Gus is fairly sure it will be a success, although he is very inexperienced in business. Gus recently inherited a large amount of money and has plenty of funds with which to set up a business organisation that will take the prototype to market, but he does not wish to risk personal liability.

Gus wishes to set up production of the product in the country where he was born (a developing nation). Products would then be shipped around the world. He would like to set up a corporate head-quarters in the developed country where he currently lives.

Gus is struggling to decide how the production facility in the developing nation would best be managed. The main concern Gus has over this ethical decision is whether or not the local population are educationally advanced enough to cope with managing the operation. He is therefore considering sending over expatriate staff from the corporate headquarters to oversee production. This would mean local staff would only be used to perform low-level, routine production tasks.

As an adviser to Gus, you have been asked to help him make the main business decisions he faces. In particular, the most suitable legal structure for his business and the management of the production facility in the developing nation.

Required

(a)   Explain four types of profit seeking organisation and recommend one that is most appropriate to Gus.

(13 marks)

(b)   Explain six issues that Gus should consider when deciding whether or not to use expatriate staff in the overseas operation.   **(12 marks)**

(Total = 25 marks)

8 FutureGreen
45 mins

FutureGreen is a UK based company that manufactures a range of environmentally friendly products with an everyday use around the home. It has been in business for five years as a private limited company and has seen the scale of its operations and profitability grow rapidly.

The owners are keen to continue the growth of the organisation and are considering floating on the London Stock Exchange during the next two years, to raise cash to fund expansion.

FutureGreen's owners are all committed to the cause of protecting the environment and consider the business to be socially responsible as all of its operations are designed to be environmentally friendly. Equally, however, they are in business to make a profit and senior managers are set demanding performance targets. However problems have recently emerged concerning the identification of which manager is accountable for what aspect of organisational performance.

With the planned future expansion and floatation in mind, the owners have asked you, a consultant, for some advice.

Required

(a)   Explain the term 'corporate social responsibility', and identify and explain four types of social responsibility relevant to FutureGreen. **(11 marks)**

(b)   Explain the term 'corporate governance' and the benefits to FutureGreen of developing a corporate governance policy based on the Stock Exchange Combined Code. **(14 marks)**

(Total = 25 marks)

INFORMATION SYSTEMS

Questions 9 to 15 cover Information Systems, the subject of Part B of the BPP Study Text for Paper E1.

9   Objective test questions: Information systems 1   36 mins

9.1   Many large organisations have established a computer intranet for the purpose of

   A   Providing quick, effective and improved communication amongst staff using chat rooms
   B   Providing quick, effective and improved communication to staff
   C   Providing quick, effective and improved communication to customers
   D   Providing quick, effective and improved ordering procedures in real time   **(2 marks)**

9.2   An expert system describes

   A   A database built upon past knowledge and experience
   B   A powerful off the shelf software solution
   C   An on-line library of operating advice and handy hints
   D   An electronic version of working papers assembled by the Research and Development department
                                                                                         (2 marks)

9.3   'Corrective' refers to a type of systems maintenance performed to:

   A   Remedy software defects
   B   Allow executive level unstructured decision-making
   C   Adjust applications to user preferences
   D   Prevent future operation delays   **(2 marks)**

9.4   Data redundancy arises as a result of:

   A   Viruses and computer misuse
   B   Downsizing the organisation
   C   A lack of password controls
   D   Duplication of data held   **(2 marks)**

Each of the sub-questions numbered **9.5** to **9.7** below require a brief written response. Each sub-question is worth 4 marks. The response should be in note form and should not exceed 50 words.

The following scenario is related to sub-questions 9.5, 9.6 and 9.7.

Quickbuild is an organisation which hires out architects to the construction industry. The architects work on the clients' premises using a laptop because of a lack of office space at Quickbuild's headquarters. They can use whatever design software they prefer. However as a consequence of this none of the architects use software which is compatible. Therefore a team of architects must work in the same location to share ideas as files cannot be shared electronically.

To improve its services, Quickbuild intends to invest in a suite of compatible software products that all architects will use in their work. However, this will mean the workers having to switch over from their existing software to the new system. Senior management of Quickbuild are concerned that this will be unpopular with architects who are used to working with their own familiar software.

9.5   Explain how the new system will transform Quickbuild as an organisation.   **(4 marks)**

9.6   Explain the concept of the 'virtual team.   **(4 marks)**

9.7   Explain the reasons why an organisation such as Quickbuild might choose a direct approach to system changeover.   **(4 marks)**

                                                                                         (Total = 20 marks)

10 Objective test questions: Information systems 2 — 36 mins

10.1 Which approach to system changeover has the highest risk?

    A   Parallel
    B   Direct
    C   Pilot
    D   Phased   **(2 marks)**

10.2 Dial-back security protects an information system by:

    A   Disabling part of the telecoms technology to prevent unauthorised intrusions
    B   Scrambling and unscrambling data transmissions
    C   Requiring users to identify themselves before a connection to the system is provided
    D   Providing the user with a private key   **(2 marks)**

10.3 Which type of security risk involves overloading an Internet site with traffic?

    A   Worms
    B   Trojan horses
    C   Denial of service attacks
    D   Hacking   **(2 marks)**

10.4 Which type of information system outsourcing involves third parties managing and distributing services and solutions to clients over a wide area network?

    A   Multiple sourcing
    B   Incremental outsourcing
    C   Joint venture sourcing
    D   Application service provision   **(2 marks)**

> Each of the sub-questions numbered **10.5** to **10.7** below require a brief written response. Each sub-question is worth 4 marks. The response should be in note form and should not exceed 50 words.

The following scenario is related to sub-questions 10.5, 10.6 and 10.7.

Comseek is a manufacturing company which currently uses a number of unrelated software applications in each of its processes - design, procurement, inventory control, production, sales and accounts. It is now considering whether an enterprise-wide system is a suitable replacement.

10.5 Identify **four** roles the new information system may play in Comseek.   **(4 marks)**

10.6 Explain the features of an 'enterprise-wide' system.   **(4 marks)**

10.7 Describe the types of test that should be conducted before the new information system goes 'live'.

    (4 marks)

    (Total = 20 marks)

> If you struggled with the MCQ and OT questions in Q9 and Q10, go back to your BPP Study Text for Paper E1 and revise Chapters 3 and 4 before you tackle the longer questions on Information Systems.

11 S&C software project (OMIS 5/06 - amended) 54 mins

S & C is a medium sized firm that is experiencing rapid growth evidenced by increased turnover. It has been able to develop a range of new consultancy and specialist business advisory services that it offers to its growing customer base. To cope with these developments several organisation-wide initiatives have been launched over the past two years.

The existing financial systems are struggling to cope with these developments, but replacement software is due to be installed within the next six months. The new system was justified because it could reduce costs and subsequently improve productivity, although precise details have not been given. The application software does not fit existing business processes exactly. However, it has the clear advantage of giving S & C access to a state of the art system which is not yet available to its competitors.

A three-person project steering group has recommended that a phased approach to introduction should be used and has undertaken most of the project planning. A programme of events for implementing the system has been agreed but is not yet fully operational. This group has not met for a while because the designated project manager has been absent from work through illness.

You are Head of S & C's Central Support Unit. You also serve on the project steering group.

A partners' meeting is due to take place soon. The firm's senior partner has asked you to prepare a PowerPoint presentation to other partners on implementation issues. You understand that partners are conscious that system implementation represents a form of further organisational change. They are asking questions about the approach that will be taken to the introduction of the new system, likely changes to practices, critical areas for success, system testing, support after implementation, system effectiveness, etc.

Required

You are required to produce **outline notes** that will support your eventual PowerPoint presentation. These notes should:

(a) Explain the importance of ensuring the system is aligned with the firm's business strategy, including the options to overcome the fact that the software does not fit existing business processes exactly. **(5 marks)**

(b) Explain why a phased approach to introducing the system is, in this case, more suitable than a direct 'big bang' approach. **(5 marks)**

(c) Discuss the ways in which particular individuals and groups within S & C are important for implementation to succeed. **(5 marks)**

(d) Explain how users should be involved in the implementation phase of the project. **(5 marks)**

(e) Describe the training that should be given to targeted groups within S & C. **(5 marks)**

(f) Explain how the success or failure of the system could be evaluated. **(5 marks)**

Note. Your notes should not exceed one page per topic. **(Total = 30 marks)**

12 S1K (Specimen paper)   45 mins

The S1K group has grown from a single optician's shop in a provincial town into (what it describes as) a 'lifestyle retail group'. S1K's policy is to buy existing shops in fashionable city centre shopping malls which it believes are 'underperforming'. In addition to traditional services offered by opticians, S1K offers eye correction (laser) treatment, designer sunglasses, cosmetic tinted contact lenses and, for certain spectacle frames, a range of complementary jewellery.

S1K also plans to sell own-brand 'augmented' products and treatments such as eye creams and drops, make-up, etc. at premium prices from its premises. S1K is due to expand from thirty to thirty five geographically diverse shops in the south of the country within the next year.

The Board of S1K recognises the challenges ahead and has recently appointed a new Chief Executive who has a background in both retail operations and information solutions. He has just completed an initial review of systems and technology within S1K. His main findings are highlighted below.

- The opportunities for the use of information technology (IT) need to be grasped, particularly in the implementation and running of the information system network in support of management operations both in shops and in the main functional areas of S1K's headquarters.

- Systems are generally weak and the benefits of modern software applications lacking. The accuracy and completeness of information received by headquarters from shops needs to improve and there needs to be better coordination of activities. Through its acquisition policy S1K has 'inherited' a series of shops operating independent systems of varying sophistication and effectiveness. Several different systems are used and some are very inefficient. (For example, the equivalent of over 40% of a full time worker's time is spent manually analysing and searching for information in shops.)

- Internet possibilities are being missed and there is no virtual network.

- Common computerised stock records will also be required when new products and treatments are sold.

- Some shops still use manual systems, others use basic stand-alone computers, but none take full advantage of software capabilities and most only use basic software functions. The financial system is the only shared system.

- The existing financial system is struggling to cope with the rapid growth of the group. Replacement software is due to go ahead within the next six months. Although the software does not fit existing business processes exactly, it has the clear advantage of giving S1K access to an industry best practice system and is identical to that used by all its main competitors. As such, it is a good choice. The least problematic implementation approach is a phased approach, and a programme of events for implementing was drawn up by the previous project manager who has now left S1K. A replacement project manager from within S1K needs to be appointed to oversee the introduction of the project as a matter of priority.

Required

(a) Identify the ways in which information technology and information systems might improve S1K's operations. **(10 marks)**

(b) Discuss the Chief Executive's analysis of ways of overcoming potential problems in the implementation of the new financial system. **(10 marks)**

(c) Identify the main individuals and groups S1K's Human Resources Department should target first for training and whether training provision should be made in-house or not. **(5 marks)**

(Total = 25 marks)

13 New system   45 mins

A company which services all of its customers from one central warehouse has decided to computerise the inventory control, order processing and sales accounting procedures. It has also decided to close the central warehouse and establish five regional warehouses, each of which will be based on a central mainframe computer with on-line links to regional warehouses where data entry of customer orders and stock replenishment will take place. You are responsible planning the implementation of this system.

Required

(a) Describe four possible changeover strategies and recommend one for this situation. **(14 marks)**

(b) List five general issues that should be considered in the implementation of this system. **(5 marks)**

(c) Explain the three main types of software maintenance encountered in computer systems. **(6 marks)**

(Total = 25 marks)

14 System implementation   45 mins

A large organisation is intending to implement a new information system which will completely replace the outdated system which is currently in place.

The system will be designed and built by a third party under an outsourcing arrangement. However senior management are anxious about the implementation phase as they have had no experience of implementing systems in the past.

The company's main strength lies in its management of human resources. The organisation regularly communicates with its employees through group briefings and a company newsletter is produced each month containing current and future developments. Senior management are committed to providing employees with first class training and each employee is provided with counselling and a personal development plan.

The company also operates an industry leading reward package that aims to ensure the company's and employees' goals are the same.

The senior management are concerned that the new system will have a detrimental effect on the workforce's morale as it will fundamentally change they way employees work. As a consequence they are expecting some resistance from employees to the new system.

The company has asked you as a consultant to provide them with advice for the implementation phase of the project.

Required

(a) Briefly describe the following aspects of system implementation:

     (i) The role and conduct of user acceptance testing **(3 marks)**
     (ii) File conversion **(2 marks)**
     (iii) System changeover **(2 marks)**
     (iv) Review and maintenance **(6 marks)**

(b) Identify six general techniques the company could use to overcome resistance to this change and list two examples of each technique the company could use. **(12 marks)**

(Total = 25 marks)

15 K1S (OMIS 5/08 - amended)   45 mins

K1S is a fast growing chain of hair and beauty salons (shops) located throughout the prosperous north of the country. The company is due to expand from thirty to thirty five salons within the next year. K1S's policy is to buy existing salons in fashionable city centre shopping malls which it believes are 'underperforming' by offering too limited a range of treatments and charging too low a price. (All K1S's salons charge 'top' prices but provide excellent customer care. In addition to hairdressing services, K1S offers beauty treatments.) K1S also plans to sell own-brand products at premium prices from its premises. K1S's managing director (MD) sees training as critical to 'keeping our service sophisticated and professional, with a distinctive K1S style'. K1S now operates its own hairdressing training academy from purpose built premises.

The MD has, however, identified a number of areas which need to be addressed if K1S is to continue to prosper.

- Due to the expansion policy and lack of investment in IT, each salon has different degrees of computerisation. Some are fully computerised, others have no computers.

- A coherent information system is needed. This should be primarily based on the needs of the company as a whole but also mindful of the need to support salon management operations locally.

- The opportunities for the use of information technology need to be taken, particularly in the implementation and running of the information system network and in support of management operations.

- The threat posed by competitors who are copying K1S's approach.

You are part of the management consultancy team responsible for the report and have been asked to prepare notes on key themes for discussion with the MD.

Required

(a) Explain how information systems should be developed to serve K1S's management operations both centrally and within salons.   **(15 marks)**

(b) Discuss the factors that need to be considered when developing staff training associated with the installation of a new computer system for K1S.   **(10 marks)**

(Total = 25 marks)

OPERATIONS MANAGEMENT

Questions 16 to 23 cover Operations Management, the subject of Part C of the BPP Study Text for Paper E1.

16 Objective test questions: Operations management 1   36 mins

16.1 Which one of the following is the best indicator of 'quality'?

    A   Cost
    B   Price
    C   Fitness for purpose
    D   Number of complaints   **(2 marks)**

16.2 Which of the following measures customer, operational and financial aspects of quality?

    A   SERVQUAL
    B   Balanced scorecards
    C   Value for money audits
    D   Total quality management   **(2 marks)**

16.3 Gaining International Standards (ISO) in quality is mainly dependent upon:

    A   Effective processes for documentation and control
    B   A shared quality philosophy
    C   Commitment from middle managers
    D   Benchmarking customer related performance against competitors   **(2 marks)**

16.4 Optimised production technologies (OPT) is an operations management system which aims to:

    A   Improve distribution networks
    B   Improve supply sourcing alternatives
    C   Integrate operations and quality assurance
    D   Reduce production bottlenecks   **(2 marks)**

16.5 An ABC system refers to:

    A   A Japanese style problem solving device that is particularly helpful in inventory management
    B   An inventory management method that concentrates effort on the most important items
    C   Accuracy, brevity and clarity in the quality of system reporting
    D   A manual solution to managing inventory   **(2 marks)**

16.6 Kaizen is a quality improvement technique that involves:

    A   Continuous improvement by small incremental steps
    B   A complete revision of all organisational processes and structures
    C   Immediate, often radical 'right first time' changes to practice
    D   A problem solving fishbone technique to identify cause and effect   **(2 marks)**

Required

Each of the sub-questions numbered **16.7** and **16.8** below require a brief written response. Each sub-question is worth 4 marks. The response should be in note form and should not exceed 50 words.

The following scenario is related to sub-questions 16.7 and 16.8.

Forlan is a well established, family run organisation which has been in business for the past forty years. It purchases and assembles a range of electronic components from a large number of suppliers.

The Managing Director, who has run the company for the last twenty-five years, explained that using a large number of suppliers is necessary so that the company does not become too reliant on them. However in recent times the quality of the components supplied has been variable and delivery times unreliable.

In a recent industry shortage, Forlan failed to source a number of vital components. However, during this time the Managing Director found out that its suppliers continued to supply its competitors.

The Managing Director now believes that the organisation's supply chain is underperforming and that the company should follow a strategic approach to supply.

As a consultant to Forlan's Managing Director:

16.7   Identify the reasons why the company should form closer relationships with its suppliers.   **(4 marks)**

16.8   If the company follows a strategic approach to supply, describe the organisational factors ('spokes in a wheel') that need to be integrated, co-ordinated and developed.   **(4 marks)**

(Total = 20 marks)

---

17   Objective test questions: Operations management 2   36 mins

17.1   Sustainability in operations management is primarily concerned with

    A   Making charitable donations to environmental protection groups
    B   Sourcing raw materials from developing nations
    C   Improving the productivity of employees
    D   Efficient use of resources   **(2 marks)**

17.2   Which of the following is the main characteristic of a demand network?

    A   Products are pushed onto the market by the manufacturer
    B   Products are developed in response to market signals
    C   Businesses in the network operate relatively independently
    D   Interdependence of channel members is reduced   **(2 marks)**

17.3   A manufacturer concerned mainly with developing new product features is known as:

    A   Production orientated
    B   Product orientated
    C   Market orientated
    D   A learning organisation   **(2 marks)**

17.4   According to Porter's value chain, the final primary activity is referred to as:

    A   Marketing and sales
    B   Outbound logistics
    C   Procurement
    D   Service   **(2 marks)**

Required

Each of the sub-questions numbered **17.5** to **17.7** below require a brief written response. Each sub-question is worth 4 marks. The response should be in note form and should not exceed 50 words.

The following scenario is related to sub-questions 17.5 to 17.7.

Goldseek manufactures jewellery from gold and precious stones which it sells to jewellers in the world's most exclusive locations. Goldseek's products are sold for very high prices to extremely wealthy and demanding customers.

Recently a number of customers have reported poor workmanship to Goldseek's customer services department. A reoccurring problem seems to be precious stones missing from rings and earrings. As a consequence, the customer services department have been busy sending out replacement products, organising repairs and providing refunds.

The cause of the problem has been traced to a number of machines involved in the manufacturing process. Whilst they are not old, they have not been serviced for some time and often breakdown. These breakdowns have affected the production schedule and the company has missed a number of delivery dates.

Goldseek's board of directors are extremely concerned with these issues and have asked you as a quality consultant to provide them with information they can use to address the problem. In particular they have asked you to explain the types of failure cost and how introducing Total Productive Maintenance (TPM) may help reduce instances of quality failure.

17.5   List **four** types of internal failure cost that might arise for a manufacturing organisation such as Goldseek.

(4 marks)

17.6   Identify examples of Goldseek's external failure costs, and state their significance.   **(4 marks)**

17.7   Briefly describe how Total Productive Maintenance (TPM) might improve the quality of Goldseek's products.   **(4 marks)**

(Total = 20 marks)

If you struggled with the MCQ and OT questions in Q16 and Q17, go back to your BPP Study Text for Paper E1 and revise Chapters 5, 6 and 7 before you tackle the longer questions on Operations Management.

18   Capacity, supply and demand   54 mins

Required

(a)   Explain why a level capacity strategy is incompatible with an organisation adopting a just-in-time (JIT) philosophy.   **(5 marks)**

(b)   Explain the impact of demand strategies on an organisation's marketing practices.   **(5 marks)**

(c)   Explain the relationship between chase strategies and the flexible organisation.   **(5 marks)**

(d)   Identify the differences between service and manufacturing organisations in relation to capacity management.   **(5 marks)**

(e)   Explain how supply portfolios are of benefit to an organisation.   **(5 marks)**

(f)   By reference to an industry of your choice, describe the types of assistance information and communications technology could provide to those wanting to improve sales.   **(5 marks)**

Note. (a) to (d) should have particular regard to quality, capacity and other organisational issues.

(Total = 30 marks)

19   W company (5/10)   45 mins

W Company is a white goods manufacturer that has been particularly hard hit by the recent recession. Faced with a dramatic fall in orders and two years of losses, shareholder pressure has resulted in the early retirement of the Chief Executive and his replacement by JH, who has a track record of turning companies around. JH has, in the past, led different process design improvement initiatives including Business Process Re-engineering (BPR) and has used tools such as process maps (or charts).

In an initial review, JH finds that W's operations require urgent attention. A benchmarking exercise reveals that W's costs of production are much higher than those of its competitors. In addition, innovations in operations theory and techniques such as those in supply chain management and process design have not been seized. Clearly this needs addressing.

An added area of concern is the way that some line managers are reported to have behaved under the previous management regime. The misappropriation of funds by some line managers has come to light, as have a number of unethical practices and JH is concerned that such things should not occur in the future.

Required

(a)   Describe the developments in strategic supply chain management in recent years and explain how the adoption of the new approaches could assist W Company to improve its competitive performance.

(10 marks)

(b)   With reference to BPR and process maps (or charts), explain how process design could contribute to a more effective and efficient system of operations in W Company.   **(10 marks)**

(c)   Explain briefly how a code of ethics could help W Company to limit future incidents of unethical behaviour.   **(5 marks)**

(Total = 25 marks)

20 TQM and sourcing 45 mins

PicAPie employs a total quality management program and manufactures 12 different types of pie – from chicken and leek to vegetarian. The directors of PicAPie are proud of their products, and always attempt to maintain a high quality of input at a reasonable price.

Each pie has four main elements:

- Aluminium foil case
- Pastry shell made mainly from flour and water
- Meat and/or vegetable filling
- Thin plastic wrapping

The products are obtained as follows:

- The aluminium is obtained from a single supplier of metal related products. There are few suppliers in the industry resulting from a fall in demand for aluminium related products following increased use of plastics.

- The flour for the pastry shell is sourced from flour millers in four different countries – one source of supply is not feasible because harvests occur at different times and PicAPie cannot store sufficient flour from one harvest for a year's production.

- Obtaining meat and vegetables is difficult due to the large number of suppliers located in many different countries. Recently, PicAPie obtained significant cost savings by delegating sourcing of these items to a specialist third party.

- Plastic wrapping is obtained either directly from the manufacturer or via an Internet site specialising in selling surplus wrapping from government and other sources.

Required

(a) Explain what a supply portfolio is and the extent to which PicAPie is currently using one. **(3 marks)**

(b) Identify the sourcing strategies adopted by PicAPie and evaluate the effectiveness of those strategies for maintaining a constant and high quality supply of inputs. **(16 marks)**

(c) Recommend changes that PicAPie will need to make to improve its sourcing. **(6 marks)**

(Total = 25 marks)

21 YO and MX (OMIS 5/07 – amended)   45 mins

YO employs buyers, designers, machinists, tailors and sales people to produce and sell its coats, jackets, trousers, dresses and skirts. YO has a long standing relationship with MX which sells directly to the public from a chain of out of town stores. Over 80% of YO's sales are to MX whose approach has been to sell clothing in great volumes at lower prices than the high street stores. It expects its suppliers (including YO) to take account of new fashion designs and to manufacture its clothes at competitive prices.

MX is rethinking its strategy and wishes to move more 'upmarket' by introducing a better quality clothing range, which it believes its customers will be prepared to pay a little more for. Already YO has noticed that MX has started to be more demanding by sending back any batches it feels are in the slightest way unsuitable.

MX wants to work with fewer suppliers but develop a better relationship with each of them. MX wants to renegotiate its contract with YO (which expires soon in any case). MX is prepared to talk with YO about the need to improve the quality of its products and has indicated that if it receives the right assurances, it would be prepared to pay a slightly higher unit price per item. It also proposes to work more closely with YO's designers to maximise production of the type of clothing that it feels its customers want.

If these talks are unsuccessful, MX will use one of its other suppliers when the existing contract expires. YO is aware that MX has experimented by using a few trusted overseas suppliers who have managed to achieve both relatively low prices and superior quality through the adoption of total quality management (TQM) techniques.

Anxious to maintain its relationship with MX, YO recognises that it must change from its present focus on price to one that includes quality considerations.

Required

(a)   Evaluate the way in which MX is proposing to manage its suppliers as part of a value system. **(10 marks)**

(b)   Discuss the requirements for achieving total quality within YO. **(10 marks)**

(c)   Describe how YO's human resource practices must change in order to meet MX's new requirements.

(5 marks)

(Total = 25 marks)

22 Electro   45 mins

Electro manufactures an electrical product, the Viper, at its production facility in Modland. The factory facilities are modest, although they were state of the art around forty years ago. The Managing Director has decided that it is now appropriate for the organisation to 'move with the times' and upgrade its systems and processes. This decision was made because Electro's competitors all use modern facilities based on lean production methods and they have seen improvements in both the quality of their products and company profitability. An overview of the production process for the Viper follows.

The production process begins with the latest sales forecast. This sales forecast is updated weekly with expected sales for the forthcoming four week period. The organisation seeks to produce enough units to meet the amount of sales forecasted plus an additional 10% as it is company policy to avoid running out of inventory. The company has found that despite this it often either runs out of inventory or has to find alternative locations to store an excess of production.

To produce a unit of Viper requires several stages including production of a sub-assembly. This sub-assembly then passes through a number of processes before the final product emerges.

Throughout the production process, sub-assemblies are moved from one location in the factory to another. Very often, these processes are some distance apart and require the movement of machinery and production units around the plant.

Sub-assemblies which have been produced but cannot be processed until the machinery required for the next stage of production is available are stored as work-in-progress on the factory floor.

Much of the machinery used in production is old and often breaks down. Additionally, where a piece of machinery is used by two processes, there is a considerable delay between them as the machine is re-configured.

After the finished product is created, it is inspected for quality. Any products that are found to be defective are re-worked or scrapped. Around 9% of production has to be re-worked and 4% is scrapped.

The Managing Director is concerned that if Electro does not move away from its traditional views on quality and production methods, it will soon be forced out of business.

As a consultant, the Managing Director has requested you to provide some information on how the introduction of a lean production system could benefit the company.

Required

(a)   Identify three aspects to the traditional approach to quality management.   **(3 marks)**

(b)   Briefly explain four categories of quality costs and provide an example for each relevant to an electrical goods manufacturer such as Electro.   **(8 marks)**

(c)   Explain the concept of lean production and how it can improve Electro's manufacturing process.
                                                                                      (14 marks)

                                                                                  (Total = 25 marks)

23 DOH (OMIS 5/08 - amended)   45 mins

DOH is a long established family run firm which supplies parts for local motor car manufacturers. For the past thirty years DOH has exercised quality control over its manufacturing processes by employing one quality control (QC) inspector for every 40 workers. (QC inspectors sample completed batches and remove defective parts before they are dispatched.)

Recently, DOH was reluctantly forced to subcontract a batch of work to another firm so that it could meet new delivery deadlines. Fears by DOH's managing director that this subcontracted work might be of an inferior standard proved to be unfounded. In fact, no defects whatsoever were discovered in the subcontracted batch. At the same time DOH's main customer is unhappy with some of the batches it has received and is insisting that in future quality failures due to defective parts produced by DOH will incur strict penalty charges, including the cost of labour involved in removing the part from the vehicle under construction. The managing director is worried that unless DOH improves its quality standards, it might in future lose contracts with key customers.

At the next staff liaison committee, the managing director raises the issue of quality processes and a frank discussion follows. Apparently the workforce believes that 'mistakes happen' and 'we are all human after all'. Scrap and reworking costs are thought to be 'inevitable in our business'. It is also a generally held view that:

- Senior managers are 'out of touch' with the problems of maintaining quality standards whilst meeting production targets;

- The value of middle managers is not apparent;

- QC inspectors are not liked but are respected because they are hardworking and exercise their individual professional judgement diligently when deciding which parts to reject as unsuitable for despatch.

Worried by these developments, the managing director discusses DOH's quality problems with an advisor at the government funded regional trade and industry office. The advisor negotiates access for him to see first hand how other manufacturers are improving quality in similar industries so that lessons might be learned. The managing director is very impressed by:

- Teamwork within the workforce;

- An absence of middle managers and QC inspectors

- The way in which individual workers demand better quality and get senior manager support to achieve it.

The managing director organises a weekend hotel meeting for all senior managers, where he presents his analysis of the problems of quality within DOH. He makes it clear that he is looking beyond temporary 'quick fixes' to overcome the challenges DOH faces. After much discussion he formulates a plan for bringing about change through a programme he calls 'putting quality first'. The programme aims to drive up quality standards through training, improved teamwork and a review of roles within DOH, particularly quality control inspectors and middle managers. If successful, he believes the programme will bring lasting improvements and longer term, increased customer satisfaction and reduced costs. Senior managers support the programme but have warned that it needs to be both 'sold' to the workforce and carefully implemented.

Required

(a) Analyse the problems of quality that DOH is facing.   **(13 marks)**

(b) Discuss the way in which the problems of quality are being addressed by DOH.   **(12 marks)**

(Total = 25 marks)

MARKETING

Questions 24 to 31 cover Marketing, the subject of Part D of the BPP Study Text for Paper E1.

24 Objective test questions: Marketing 1   36 mins

24.1 Which one of the following statements best represents 'a marketing orientation'?

A   Support for the marketing department from top management
B   A large marketing budget
C   High profile advertising campaigns
D   A focus on customer needs   **(2 marks)**

24.2 PESTEL analysis can be used to analyse an organisation's environment. What does the 'P' stand for?

A   Political
B   Prices
C   People
D   Products   **(2 marks)**

24.3 Which of the following can be considered to be customers of a charity?
(i)   Beneficiaries
(ii)   Trustees
(iii) Regulators
(iv)   The government

A   (i), (ii) and (iii) only
B   (i) and (iii) only
C   (ii) and (iii) only
D   All of the above   **(2 marks)**

24.4 'Market shakeout' involves the weakest producers exiting a particular market and occurs in a period between

A   Growth through creativity and growth through direction
B   Introduction and market growth
C   Market growth and market maturity
D   Market maturity and decline   **(2 marks)**

Required

Each of the sub-questions numbered **24.5** to **24.7** below require a brief written response. Each sub-question is worth 4 marks. The response should be in note form and should not exceed 50 words.

24.5 Explain the concepts of viral and guerrilla marketing.   **(4 marks)**

24.6 Explain how experiential marketing differs from traditional marketing. **(4 marks)**

24.7 Explain the importance of a brand to an organisation.   **(4 marks)**

(Total = 20 marks)

25 Objective test questions: Marketing 2   36 mins

25.1 Undifferentiated market positioning involves the targeting of:

    A   A single market segment with a single marketing mix
    B   A single market segment ignoring the concept of the marketing mix
    C   An entire market with a different marketing mix for each segment
    D   An entire market with a single marketing mix   **(2 marks)**

25.2 The use of 'skim pricing' as a marketing technique will result in:

    A   Non-recovery of promotional costs
    B   Enticing new customers to buy a product or service
    C   High prices, normally at an early stage of the product lifecycle
    D   Low prices so denying competitors opportunities to gain market share   **(2 marks)**

25.3 Which method of market research would be most appropriate to use where the objective is to explore customers' unconscious attitudes and motives for behaviour?

    A   Focus groups
    B   Depth interviews
    C   Questionnaires
    D   Observation   **(2 marks)**

25.4 Why is the characteristic of a service known as 'perishability' significant in a marketing context?

    A   Because perishability makes it likely that refrigerated facilities will be required
    B   Because perishability increases ethical concerns
    C   Because perishability makes anticipating and responding to levels of demand crucial
    D   Because perishability means demand fluctuates wildly   **(2 marks)**

> *Required*
>
> Each of the sub-questions numbered **25.5** to **25.7** below require a brief written response. Each sub-question is worth 4 marks. The response should be in note form and should not exceed 50 words.

25.5 Explain what an organisation's promotion mix consists of.   **(4 marks)**

25.6 Explain the importance of internal marketing to an organisation's external marketing activities.   **(4 marks)**

25.7 MNA produces four products.

Jupiter - a product which has high market growth and high market share.

Mars – a product which has high market growth and low market share.

Pluto – a product which has low market share and low market growth.

Neptune – a product which has low market growth and high market share.

Classify each product according to the BCG matrix.   **(4 marks)**

     (Total = 20 marks)

> If you struggled with the MCQ and OT questions in Q24 and Q25, go back to your BPP Study Text for Paper E1 and revise Chapters 8, 9 and 10 before you tackle the longer questions on Marketing.

26 V (OMIS 5/05 - amended) | 54 mins

V is an innovative company run according to the principles of its entrepreneurial owner. V operates a package distribution service, a train service, and sells holidays, bridal outfits, clothing, mobile telephones, and soft drinks. V is well known for challenging the norm and 'giving customers quality products and services at affordable prices and doing it all with a sense of fun'. V spends little on advertising but has great brand awareness thanks to the 'visibility' of its inspirational owner.

V has just announced the launch of 'V-cosmetics' to exploit a gap in the market. The cosmetic range will be competitively priced against high street brands and have the distinctive V logo.

You work for a market analyst who is about to appear on a radio discussion of V's business interests. You have been asked to provide a clear, short briefing for the market analyst on the thinking behind V-cosmetics. Your research of the V-cosmetics range identifies innovative marketing proposals. V-cosmetics will not be on sale in shops, instead it will use two approaches to promotion and selling, namely:

- The use of 'cosmetic associates'. Individuals may apply to become an associate and, if accepted, will be required to buy a basic stock of every V-cosmetic product. The associate will then use these products as samples and 'testers'. After initial training, associates organise parties in the homes of friends and their friends where they take orders for products at a listed price. Associates receive commission based on sales.

- The Internet and mobile telephone technology will also be heavily used to offer V cosmetic products to the public.

Required

Prepare brief notes containing bullet points and no more than two to three sentences for each of the key points identified below. Do not exceed one page per question part.

(a) Explain how the proposed approach can be understood within the context of the marketing mix.

(5 marks)

(b) Explain the human resource implications of using 'cosmetic associates'. **(5 marks)**

(c) Explain the concept of direct marketing. **(5 marks)**

(d) Explain the advantages of the Internet as a marketing channel. **(5 marks)**

(e) Describe how V might use the Internet as part of its marketing approach. **(5 marks)**

(f) Identify the main ethical issues associated with the proposal to market V cosmetics. **(5 marks)**

(Total = 30 marks)

27   CW (Specimen paper)   45 mins

CW is an established charity based in the capital city of the developed country of Statesland. It raises funds locally to finance clean water and sustainable agricultural projects in some of the poorest areas of the world. CW relies heavily on the work of unpaid volunteers and prides itself on low operating overheads and directing a large proportion of its income to 'on the ground' projects. CW's sources of income involve donations from the public and the operation of charity shops in the north of the country selling unwanted clothes and household items. Recently however, a downturn in the economy, 'charity fatigue' and competition from other causes has made fund-raising more difficult. It is clear that CW needs to either reduce the level of projects it currently funds or increase income.

The Chief Executive of the charity has convinced her Board of Trustees that the charity needs to professionalise its operations, be more 'outward facing' and employ modern marketing practices. Consequently, an independent consultancy firm with expertise in this area has been engaged to advise the charity. Trustees are supportive of the Chief Executive but are worried that certain marketing practices, particularly promotional activities, might be seen as unethical and damage the good reputation of the charity.

In the first meeting between a partner of the consultancy firm and the Board of Trustees, a number of areas were covered including.

- A discussion of the application of the marketing mix to the charity

- Market research options for CW

A second meeting has been arranged. You work for the consultancy firm and have been asked to produce some briefing notes for the partner to help him with this second meeting

Required

(a)   Explain what aspects of marketing could be helpful to CW. (Do not include matters covered in the first meeting or segmentation and targeting.).   **(10 marks)**

(b)   Explain the processes and implications of market segmentation and targeting to CW.

                                                                                             (10 marks)

(c)   Identify two types of promotional activity and for each explain the ethical concerns that might arise for CW using them.   **(5 marks)**

                                                                                    (Total = 25 marks)

28 Marketing action plan (OMIS 11/05 – amended) 45 mins

SX is a growing company that has successfully used local radio advertising for the past few years to raise awareness of its brand. It supplies fresh 'quality' sandwiches, home baked snacks, the finest coffees and freshly squeezed fruit juices for sale at premium prices in petrol filling stations. Products are produced by traditional methods from very early morning by a team of employees at a central depot and are delivered throughout the day by a few casual workers in a fleet of vehicles.

SX has for the first time undertaken a full strategic marketing planning process. One weakness identified was that the number of deliveries required was increasing, while some of the drivers were becoming increasingly unreliable. The owner is worried that this may create an unfavourable image with customers and lead to delays in delivery.

A second weakness found was that the company's brand, whilst well known to petrol stations, is still relatively unknown to the general public. Subsequently sales are low as the public is unwilling to pay premium prices for a brand they do not know much about.

In terms of opportunities, the owner of SX is now aware that by using technology to a greater degree and identifying customer needs more fully, the firm can grow at an even greater rate. To this end it is proposed that time saving food preparation and packaging equipment be purchased. This will mean considerably fewer people involved in food preparation but the owner feels that some employees could be redeployed as drivers on a permanent basis. The role of driver would be redefined, and in addition to making deliveries, they would be expected to:

- Get direct feedback from customers

- Persuade petrol stations to take new product lines

- Provide intelligence on competitor's products and likely future demand

- Hopefully persuade other petrol stations and outlets (such as railway stations and newspaper shops) to stock SX products

The owner is keen to progress change, consequently:

- The Head of delivery and customer relationships has been tasked with developing new job and person details for the driver posts. These will then be discussed with existing food preparation staff.

- A marketing action plan will soon be prepared based on the strategic marketing plan, which will contain immediate marketing issues and actions required. Some detail is already available on people and price so the main areas to consider are product, place and promotion.

- The head of marketing is keen to increase awareness of SX's brand and has been asked to report on the benefits of branding to the owner.

Required

(a) Based on your understanding of the changes proposed by SX, identify the main issues that will be included in the marketing action plan and discuss the implications of these. Your response should consider issues of product, place and promotion only. **(10 marks)**

(b) Briefly explain five benefits that increased brand awareness would have for SX. **(5 marks)**

(c) The marketing action plan provided the following information relevant to pricing:

- Unit costs fall with increased output

- The local market is price sensitive

- SX is concerned that a competitor may enter the local market in the near future

Briefly explain any four price setting strategies and recommend one to the owner in light of the information available. **(10 marks)**

(Total = 25 marks)

29 Consumer purchasing   45 mins

The PCW Company sells motor cars from 5 different shops located in one country. Prospective purchasers visit a dealership where cars being sold can be viewed. Test drives, that is taking a car out on the road to see if the purchaser likes the car, are available from dealerships.

Mr P is considering purchasing a different, and possibly larger, motor car. The purchase decision has occurred because of the need to transport his children and their musical instruments to school and the need to take more luggage on family holidays. Mr P is the director of a successful engineering company located three kilometres from his house. He plays golf with his colleagues every Saturday although his golf clubs are normally stored at the place where he plays golf because they will not fit in his existing car.

Mr P is interested in purchasing a Yotoda car, although his children prefer Sissan. Mr P is also concerned that arriving at the golf club in a Sissan would not be 'the done thing'. He also wants to ensure that environmental damage is limited as far as possible by his transport choices.

Required

(a) Identify the stages of the decision making process Mr P will go through regarding the purchase of a motor car.
                                                                                  (5 marks)

(b) Identify and explain the social and other factors that will influence Mr P in making the purchase decision.
                                                                                 (10 marks)

(c) Explain and illustrate with examples the benefits that marketing can provide to business organisations, consumers and society.
                                                                                 (10 marks)

                                                                       (Total = 25 marks)

30 Marketing, segmentation and ethics (OMIS 11/06 - amended)   45 mins

CM's founder first began producing breakfast food from a start-up unit on a small industrial estate. Now CM is the market leader in Europe and Oceania. Once established in Europe, the company made the breakthrough into Oceania thanks to demand from ex-pats and contacts with a family member who happened to be a director of a supermarket chain in Australia. The company's founder is very 'hands on' and has made all the major strategic decisions to date based on intuition.

CM spends heavily on promoting most of its twenty products on television, normally before and after childrens' programmes with high viewing figures. Research conducted ten years ago shows that children love small gifts contained within packs and the association of certain of the products to cartoon characters. CM also manufactures its most popular lines and packages them as 'own brand' alternatives for some large supermarket chains. These sell more cheaply than CM branded products, are less costly to produce (they contain inexpensive packaging and no gifts) but sales remain low.

CM is now facing a more uncertain environment with increasing competition (from a North American firm), sales levels that seem to have peaked and the prospect of the founder retiring very soon. Management consultants advising CM have identified a need to develop a structured marketing strategic plan for the organisation and for greater involvement of other staff in future strategic decisions. As a further complication, CM has recently received some adverse publicity from an international health 'watchdog' body that claims that CM's products contain potentially harmful levels of both sugar and salt.

Required

(a) Evaluate CM's situation making specific mention of marketing and ethical issues.   **(10 marks)**

(b) Explain how CM might develop a marketing strategic plan.   **(10 marks)**

(c) Briefly explain five benefits of market segmentation to CM.   **(5 marks)**

                                                                       (Total = 25 marks)

31 4QX (OMIS 11/07 - amended)   45 mins

4QX is a large exclusive hotel set in an area of outstanding natural beauty. The hotel is a little remote due to the relatively poor public transport network. It is located ten miles away from the region's main centre Old Town (the castle ruins of which attract a few tourists during holiday periods). The hotel has attained a high national star rating and specialises in offering executive conference facilities. Unsurprisingly therefore, it caters mainly for corporate guests.

It is a requirement of the hotel rating system that 4QX has, amongst other things, sports and leisure facilities to an approved standard. In order to attain this standard it has, within the last two years, installed a sports and fitness centre ('the centre'), employing fully qualified staff to give instruction and assistance. (Facilities include a small indoor heated swimming pool, an extensively equipped gymnasium, a spa bath and a steam room.) Due to legislation, children under the age of 16 staying in the hotel cannot use the pool without adult supervision or the gymnasium without the supervision of a suitably qualified member of staff. The centre is costly to maintain and underused.

The hotel's manager is currently drawing up a business plan for the hotel and is reviewing all areas of operation. In discussions with sport and fitness centre staff, a proposal has emerged to offer the facility to carefully selected non-guests at certain times of the day in order to bring in some revenue. This could be in the form of annual membership fees (the manager's preferred idea) or a 'pay-as-you-go' charge. The discussions with staff confirm a number of facts:

- The local economy is extremely healthy. The local population is relatively affluent with high levels of disposable income.

- Professional groups are used to paying annual membership fees for the local theatre, a nearby golf club (the manager is also a member and has contacts there), and substantial fees for their children's activities (eg dance academies and junior football teams, etc.)

- Old Town has a public swimming pool that is dated but almost of Olympic standards. It is used mainly by school children in the day and by a swimming club in the evenings. Taking advantage of government tax incentives to help keep the population fit and healthy, a privately operated, female only, health and beauty facility has recently opened in Old Town. Beyond these facilities, little else in the way of sports and fitness provision exists in the region.

The manager explains that:

- The hotel is unlikely to upgrade the centre's facilities any further in the short term, despite the fact that new, more sophisticated fitness equipment is coming onto the market all the time.

- Any promotional budget to attract members would be limited.

- An estimate of additional revenue potential is needed to complete the business plan.

Required

(a)   Explain the importance of the centre understanding its external (or macro) environment and identify the most significant influences in that external environment that are relevant to the centre   **(15 marks)**

(b)   Explain how the centre's income potential can be estimated   **(10 marks)**

                                                                              (Total = 25 marks)

MANAGING HUMAN CAPITAL

Questions 32 to 38 cover Managing Human Capital, the subject of Part E of the BPP Study Text for Paper E1.

32 Objective test questions: Managing human capital 1   36 mins

32.1   F W Taylor's thinking on motivation in the workplace involved a belief that:

     A   Social groups and individuals as part of a culture should be key considerations
     B   Reward for effort and workplace efficiency should be key considerations
     C   Managers had two different sets of assumptions about their subordinates
     D   'Motivators' and 'hygiene factors' should be key considerations   **(2 marks)**

32.2   The so-called 'psychological contract' is a notion that is based on:

     A   Segmenting then accessing a market
     B   The buyer/supplier relationship
     C   A distinctive style of testing used in selection procedures
     D   The expectations the organisation and employee have of one another   **(2 marks)**

32.3   In terms of employment CIMA's ethical guidelines require members to:

     A   Act responsibly in the way that all other professionals do
     B   Act responsibly but in a way that satisfies organisational demands and pressures
     C   Act responsibly but in a way that satisfies the individual's own ethical code
     D   Act responsibly, honour any legal contract of employment and conform to employment legislation   **(2 marks)**

32.4   An assessment centre:

     A   Helps selection by assessing job candidates by using a comprehensive and interrelated series of techniques
     B   Is the training headquarters where job interviews take place
     C   Is a desk based process of reviewing job application forms for suitability
     D   Is the place where job applicants are subjected to psychological testing   **(2 marks)**

Required

Each of the sub-questions numbered **32.5** to **32.7** below require a brief written response. Each sub-question is worth 4 marks. The response should be in note form and should not exceed 50 words.

The following scenario is related to sub-questions 32.5 to 32.7.

DES Insurance is a company which provides specialist insurance for professional athletes who often need advice in tailoring insurance products to meet their needs. DES provides access to such insurance products through its call centre which is staffed by highly trained and knowledgeable employees.

The call centre is open twenty-four hours a day and staff work on shifts which are allocated to them each month. There is little flexibility in the system and shifts cannot be changed once they are allocated.

In recent months the company has experienced recruitment problems as fewer high quality potential employees are looking to DES for employment. Additionally, the company is finding it difficult to retain the staff that it does employ, many feel undervalued and do not enjoy working anti-social hours. Consequently, employee motivation is falling and staff turnover rates and absenteeism levels are rising – a recent survey found that employee job satisfaction is at an all time low.

The Managing Director of DES has heard that 'hygiene factors' and 'flexible working' are important factors that the company should consider when looking to reverse its employment problems and has come to you for advice.

32.5 Distinguish between recruitment and selection.   **(4 marks)**

32.6 Explain what a 'hygiene factor' is in relation to employment and provide an example. **(4 marks)**

32.7 Identify and explain the potential benefits of flexible working to DES and its employees. **(4 marks)**

(Total = 20 marks)

33 Objective test questions: Managing human capital 2   36 mins

33.1 The set of activities designed to familiarise a new employee with an organisation is called:

    A   Job analysis
    B   Induction
    C   Selection
    D   Manipulation and co-optation   **(2 marks)**

33.2 The main weakness of performance related pay is:

    A   There is no attempt to link profits with the pay structure of individuals
    B   If targets are not met then employees may become demotivated
    C   Employees rarely work harder for additional remuneration
    D   It is almost impossible to set appropriate performance targets for manual workers **(2 marks)**

33.3 An effective appraisal system involves:

    A   Assessing the personality of the appraisee
    B   A process initiated by the manager who needs an update from the appraisee
    C   Advising on the faults of the appraisee
    D   A participative, problem-solving process between the manager and appraisee **(2 marks)**

33.4 Charles Handy's vision of a 'shamrock' organisation suggests a workforce that comprises three different types of worker, namely:

    A   Strategic, operational and support
    B   Qualified, trainee and unskilled
    C   'White collar', 'blue collar' and e-worker
    D   Core, contractual and flexible labour   **(2 marks)**

Required

Each of the sub-questions numbered **33.5** to **33.7** below require a brief written response. Each sub-question is worth 4 marks. The response should be in note form and should not exceed 50 words.

33.5 Briefly state two advantages and two disadvantages of in-house training.   **(4 marks)**

33.6 Briefly explain the four main elements of the human resource cycle.   **(4 marks)**

33.7 Briefly explain three general purposes of appraisal and the overall purpose of appraisal. **(4 marks)**

(Total = 20 marks)

If you struggled with the MCQ and OT questions in Q32 and Q33, go back to your BPP Study Text for Paper E1 and revise Chapters 11 and 12 before you tackle the longer questions on Managing Human Capital.

34 Corporate upheaval (OMIS 11/08 – amended)   54 mins

ARi9 is an information systems solution company employing 250 staff. When staff are not at clients' premises they work from a corporate headquarters (HQ) in the country's capital city. The premises, which are owned by the company, are spacious and modern but have extremely limited car parking.

A senior staff meeting takes place every month. The agenda for last month's meeting included a number of significant issues. Unfortunately, the start of this meeting was delayed because of a public transport strike which led to gridlocked roads during rush hour. Those travelling by car found public parking spaces scarce, and parking charges high. When the meeting eventually started, a report by the Director of Human Resourcing identified a number of difficulties:

- ARi9 is losing talented staff when they take career breaks or maternity leave and never return.

- Competition amongst firms in the industry for talented individuals who live within a reasonable commuting distance is intense.

- Recruitment is becoming more difficult as local property prices are very expensive.

- ARi9 employs significantly fewer people with disabilities than the Government's suggested quota.

- Clients are making demands on staff outside normal working hours resulting in staff dissatisfaction and increasing claims for overtime payments.

- Staff productivity is declining, in part due to interruptions to work caused by the office environment (which is 'open plan' and has crowded workstations where conversations can be easily overheard).

At the same meeting, a review by the Finance Director of the company's cost structure showed the high cost of office space, which was contributing to reduced profitability. Someone joked that ARi9 is in the technology not the property business!

In the debate that followed, the option of relocating the HQ to somewhere outside the capital was suggested. The Chief Executive tasked both directors to collaborate and produce some 'radical solutions' for the future.

At this month's meeting their joint report outlined a number of ideas:

- ARi9 should sell its HQ and relocate to much smaller accommodation outside the capital. When they are not at clients' premises, staff would be expected to work mainly from home. On the occasions when they were required to be at the HQ, the new building should contain a flexible area where staff can 'hot desk'. There should also be some meeting rooms that could be booked in advance, if needed.

- In future, staff working from home would be expected to stay in touch with colleagues and clients through email, webcams and teleconferencing (so-called 'teleworking' or 'telecommuting'). Full on-the-job training will be given to all staff who will use these applications.

- New equipment purchased for staff would be financed from anticipated improved productivity gains.

The report concluded with the claims that the proposals were 'win/win/win'. The company would produce significant HR and financial gains, society would benefit environmentally through reduced travel, and the employees would be given greater autonomy to structure their own working arrangements.

Required

(a) Identify the advantages and disadvantages of on-the-job training.   **(5 marks)**

(b) Explain the likely benefits of the proposals to the company.   **(5 marks)**

(c) Explain the likely costs of the proposals to the company.   **(5 marks)**

(d) Explain the benefits of the proposals from the employees' perspective.   **(5 marks)**

(e) Explain the problems of the proposals from the employees' perspective.   **(5 marks)**

(f) Explain Maslow's motivation theory in the context of the potential impact of the move to teleworking by ARi9.   **(5 marks)**

(Total = 30 marks)

35 HR division and strategy (OMIS 11/05 – amended)   45 mins

NS is a large insurance company. The company is structured into four Divisions and supported by a small headquarters that includes the personnel function (recently renamed the Human Resources (HR) Division).

The post of Head of HR is vacant following the retirement of the long serving post holder, and the HR strategy is in urgent need of review and revision.

NS has recently announced a new corporate initiative of continuous improvement through the empowerment of its workforce. The Chief Executive explained: 'we value our people as our most prized asset. We will encourage them to think, challenge and innovate. Only through empowering them in this way can we achieve continuous improvement. Staff will no longer be expected just to obey orders, from now on they will make and implement decisions. We want to develop clear performance objectives and be more customer focused.'

Your line manager is one of the four Divisional directors and will soon form part of a panel that will interview candidates for the vacant role of HR director. She is particularly keen to ensure that the successful candidate would be able to shape the HR Division to the needs of the organisation. She is aware of your CIMA studies and has asked for your help in preparing for the interview.

Required

Produce outline notes for your Divisional director which discuss the main points you would expect candidates to highlight in response to the following two areas she intends to explore with candidates at the interview, specifically:

(a)   The likely role that the HR Division will perform in the light of the changing nature of the organisation; and   **(13 marks)**

(b)   The aspects of the HR strategy that will change significantly, given the nature of recent developments within NS.   **(12 marks)**

(Total = 25 marks)

36 Human resource plan and activities (OMIS Pilot Paper – amended)   45 mins

A year ago, the owner-manager of a taxi service also moved into a new business area of fitting tyres. This came about as a result of the experience of using unbranded tyres on the fleet of ten taxis. Based on several years of use, the owner-manager found that the unbranded tyres lasted almost as long as the branded tyres, but had the advantage of being obtainable at half the price. The set-up costs of the tyre-fitting business were relatively modest and the owner-manager initially fitted the tyres himself. Demand picked up quickly, however, and he was forced to employ an experienced fitter. A few months later, demand accelerated again and he has just advertised for another fitter but, unfortunately, without success.

The tyre-fitting business has produced additional challenges and the owner-manager is finding it increasingly difficult to manage both the taxi service and the new business where he seems to be spending more and more of his time. He already employs one receptionist/taxi controller, but has realised that he now needs another.

As if this were not enough, he is in the middle of extending his operations still further. Customers who buy tyres frequently request that he check the wheel alignment on their car following the fitting of new tyres. He has started to provide this service, but when done manually it is a slow process, so he has invested heavily in a new piece of electronic equipment. This new technology will speed the alignment operation considerably, but neither he nor his tyre-fitter can operate the equipment. The owner feels that tyre fitters should be able to operate the equipment, and an additional member of staff is not required just to operate it.

To add to all these problems, two of his taxi drivers have resigned unexpectedly. Past patterns suggest that of the ten drivers, normally one or two leave each year, generally in the summer months, though now it is winter.

Given all these staffing difficulties, the owner-manager has made use of a relative who happens to have some HR expertise. She has advised the owner-manager on recruitment and selection, training and development. The relative also suggests that the business needs a well thought out human resource plan.

Required

(a)   Explain the main elements of a human resource plan for the business.   **(8 marks)**

(b)   Discuss the important human resource activities to which attention should be paid in order to obtain the maximum contribution from the workforce.   **(7 marks)**

(c)   Discuss how organisations can review and improve their recruitment policy and practice.   **(10 marks)**

(Total = 25 marks)

Important. For requirement (a), exclude those areas upon which the relative has already provided advice to the owner-manager (recruitment and selection, training and development).

---

37 Training and development (OMIS 5/07 - amended)   45 mins

ZnZ is a large government funded body that employs several hundred staff performing a wide variety of roles. ZnZ is proud of its commitment to people development and is well known for providing equal opportunities for all its employees. ZnZ employs people regardless of race, religion, gender, sexual orientation or physical disability. The organisation invests heavily in training and development and employs a number of trainees who are studying for their professional examinations. It is left to each professionally qualified member of staff to identify their own training needs and then submit requests for support to their department.

ZnZ's human resource plan is currently being reviewed. As part of this process two significant recommendations have emerged from groups and committees considering future human resource issues.

Recommendation one (*From the HR planning group*)

The group has recommended that to improve the flexibility of ZnZ's workforce, a more systematic approach to the training and development of qualified staff should be adopted.

Recommendation two (*From the Diversity Committee*)

The Committee has recommended that every person who is part of a minority or disadvantaged group should have an individual career coach. Under such a scheme, individuals from these groups would be paired with an experienced colleague on a higher grade who would act as their personal individual career coach. The Committee has issued the following guidelines:

- The scheme will not be associated with the appraisal process.

- Coaches should be approachable, suitably experienced and appropriately trained.

- Coaches will not be the individual's own line manager.

- Regular meetings should take place between the two individuals where they should be able to confidentially discuss any concerns and areas for self-development. Inevitably individuals will wish to discuss career related issues and they should receive appropriate advice from their career coach.

You work for the Director of Human Resourcing who is very sympathetic to the recommendation of the Diversity Committee in particular. (So much so that she feels that the scheme should include all trainees and those middle managers that have been identified as having promotion potential.) She has asked you to investigate both recommendations and brief the management team appropriately.

Required

(a)   Explain the concept workforce flexibility and how training and development improves the flexibility of ZnZ's workforce.   **(5 marks)**

(b)   Briefly explain the difference between training and development and identify four benefits of training and development to ZnZ's employees.   **(5 marks)**

(c)   Explain how the human resources department and Znz's management can successfully implement the career coach scheme.   **(5 marks)**

(d)   Explain the stages involved in the development of ZnZ's systematic approach to the training and development of professionally qualified staff.   **(10 marks)**

(Total = 25 marks)

38 Motivation and reward (OMIS 5/06 – amended) 45 mins

CQ4 is a leading European industrial gas production company. CQ4's directors are each responsible for a geographical region containing several small strategic business units (SBUs). SBU managers report in monthly review meetings in great detail to their directors. CQ4 is showing signs of declining profitability and a new chief executive has been appointed and wishes to address the situation. She has complete freedom to identify organisational problems, solutions and strategies.

At their annual conference she tells SBU managers that they hold the key to improved company performance. She has a vision of CQ4 achieving longer-term strategic goals of increases in profitability, risk taking and innovation. Under the slogan 'support not report' directors will in future support and provide assistance to their managers to a greater degree, and the frequency and detail of reporting by managers will be reduced.

She announces two new initiatives 'to address the lost years when managers were prevented from delivering truly excellent CQ4 performance':

- Revision of the existing performance appraisal system. Bonuses paid on turnover will be replaced by performance related pay for achievement of individual 'performance target contracts'. Individual SBU managers will sign contracts to deliver these targets. Performance will now be reviewed at yearly rather than monthly meetings with directors. The remuneration and reward package will be adjusted appropriately with the current emphasis on increasing turnover shifting to profitability and innovation.

- A structural review to focus resources and efforts of SBUs on improving net profit. Part of the restructuring will involve SBUs no longer providing their own 'enabling' services such as finance, information technology, and health and safety. These 'distractions from doing the real job' will in future be organised centrally. SBUs will be given far greater responsibility, autonomy and influence over their own profitability.

She tells managers that she is stripping away the things that stop them doing their job properly. In return they must manage their SBU in the way they see most appropriate. They will be better rewarded and 'star achievers' will be fast tracked to senior positions. SBU managers are informed that the HR department has already been tasked with redesigning the remuneration and reward package.

Informal discussions amongst managers afterwards confirm that the new chief executive's message has been well received. Comments such as 'work might be more enjoyable without central interference' and 'for the first time I can do my job properly' were overheard.

Required

(a) Explain in general terms how performance appraisal systems may be ineffective and identify how the appraisal system at CQ4 could be improved (other than those identified by the new chief executive)

(10 marks)

(b) Explain the thinking behind the two initiatives announced by the new chief executive using Herzberg's motivation-hygiene (dual factor) theory as a framework. **(10 marks)**

(c) Identify five factors that should be taken into account by the HR department when redesigning the remuneration and reward package for SBU managers. **(5 marks)**

(Total = 25 marks)

MIXED SECTION A MULTIPLE CHOICE QUESTIONS

Questions 39 to 45 are Section A questions covering the whole syllabus. None of the questions are related to a scenario.

39 Multiple choice questions: General 1 (5/10)   36 mins

39.1 Electronic Executive Information Systems (EIS) and Expert Systems (ES) are examples of

    A   Customer relationship management software
    B   Database management systems
    C   Computer networking
    D   Decision based software   **(2 marks)**

39.2 Technology which encourages user contributions and interactivity is known as

    A   Web 2.0
    B   Business 2 Consumer (B2C)
    C   E-commerce
    D   Teleworking   **(2 marks)**

39.3 Dispersed and virtual teams are normally a result of

    A   An economic downturn
    B   Developments in technology and information systems
    C   Poor staff morale and motivation within the workforce
    D   Ineffective human resourcing practices   **(2 marks)**

39.4 Integrated solutions in product design and control of machinery are based on

    A   A shared customer focused outlook
    B   A JIT philosophy
    C   CAD and CAM technologies
    D   Decision support systems   **(2 marks)**

39.5 A main outcome of electronic data interchange (EDI) is

    A   User independence
    B   To save paperwork by using structured electronically transmitted data
    C   Home working
    D   Improved internal communication   **(2 marks)**

39.6 A manufacturer concerned mainly with production efficiencies and reducing unit costs is known as

    A   Product oriented
    B   Production oriented
    C   Operationally strategic
    D   A learning organisation   **(2 marks)**

39.7 The influence an organisation will normally have over its macro environment will be

    A   Limited or non existent
    B   High
    C   Extremely high
    D   Continual   **(2 marks)**

39.8 Non-political, not-for-profit, cause-orientated organisations drawn from more than one country are known as

   A   Strategic business units
   B   Non-governmental organisations (NGOs)
   C   Conglomerates
   D   Globalised networks   **(2 marks)**

39.9 Merit goods are commodities that

   A   Comply with stringent international quality standards
   B   Society believes individuals should have for their wellbeing
   C   Are produced using expensive and highly valued ingredients
   D   Are earned through belonging to company loyalty schemes   **(2 marks)**

39.10 The cognitive paradigm theory explains consumer behaviour through

   A   Product branding
   B   Rational problem solving and decision making
   C   Past experience and levels of satisfaction
   D   Inertia or a lack of time   **(2 marks)**

                                                                        (Total = 20 marks)

40 Multiple choice questions: General 2 (Specimen paper)   36 mins

40.1 A deliberate addition of new, stimulating requirements to a person's job normally carried out by someone more senior is called

    A   Job enrichment

    B   Job enlargement

    C   Responsibility 'creep'

    D   Multi-skilling   **(2 marks)**

40.2 Employers wishing to attract and retain talented employees by bringing together pay and non pay elements and emphasising a positive organisational culture are said to operate a

    A   Benefit scoping strategy

    B   Total reward package

    C   Talent strategy package

    D   A consolidated remuneration package   **(2 marks)**

40.3 Which of the following does NOT represent a 'spoke' in Cousins' strategic supply wheel?

    A   Performance measures

    B   Organisational structure

    C   Organisational culture

    D   Cost/benefit analysis   **(2 marks)**

40.4 Customers' direct participation in the delivery process is a feature of

    A   Cellular production

    B   The value chain

    C   The service industry

    D   Lean product manufacture   **(2 marks)**

40.5 An operations management programme involving a series of long term continuous development practices is referred to as

    A   Queuing theorry

    B   A sustainability programme

    C   Optimised production technologies improvement

    D   Stakeholder engagement strategy   **(2 marks)**

40.6 The acronym/phrase/term 'BRIC' is normally associated with

    A   A Japanese quality development technique

    B   A stock control method

    C   Supplier development through buying, relating, investing and collaborating

    D   The emerging combined economies of Brazil, Russia, India and China   **(2 marks)**

40.7 Organisations engaged in off-shoring

    A   Have some operations carried out in a different country

    B   Diversify their operations

    C   Brand themselves as 'global'

    D   Maximise competitive advantage by being based in a particular country   **(2 marks)**

40.8 Which of an organisation's competences should NOT be outsourced?

    A   Allied competences

    B   Core competences

    C   Complementary competences

    D   Residual competences   **(2 marks)**

40.9 A formal definition of a level of service to be provided is usually found in

    A   Documented quality assurance arrangements

    B   A marketing plan

    C   A corporate strategy

    D   A service level agreement   **(2 marks)**

40.10 A country's earnings from investment abroad is included in its

    A   Gross Domestic Product

    B   Gross National Product

    C   Relative Trade Balance Index

    D   Quality of Life Index   **(2 marks)**

    (Total = 20 marks)

41 Multiple choice questions: General 3   36 mins

41.1 Which of the BRIC economies is the largest?

    A   Brazil
    B   Russia
    C   India
    D   China   **(2 marks)**

41.2 Herzberg's contribution to understanding people in the workforce included

    A   Personality testing
    B   Explaining factors associated with job satisfaction as 'motivators'
    C   Problem-solving processes that encourage team spirit and cooperation
    D   An integrated framework involving appraisal, training and motivation   **(2 marks)**

41.3 The unwritten expectations that the organisation and the individual have of each other is referred to as

    A   A valence
    B   Work/life balance
    C   The psychological contract
    D   Expectation management   **(2 marks)**

41.4 A duplication of data held by an organisation is called

    A   Data synthesis
    B   Data redundancy
    C   Data integrity
    D   Data archiving   **(2 marks)**

41.5 Aptitude testing is most commonly used in

    A   Staff appraisal processes
    B   Exit interviews
    C   Staff selection
    D   Market research and testing   **(2 marks)**

41.6 Direct mailing, branding activities and public relations campaigns are all examples of

    A   Market process
    B   Product placement
    C   Promotion
    D   Market research   **(2 marks)**

41.7 Economies of scale and manufacturing experience might help a firm to compete successfully by

    A   Pricing its products more cheaply than its competitors
    B   Introducing value adding features to its products
    C   Better understanding buyer behaviour
    D   Offering a broader product range   **(2 marks)**

41.8 To be of use for marketing research purposes a segmentation variable must define a market segment that has three characteristics. What are they?

    A   Measurability, stability, accessibility
    B   Stability, substantiality, measurability
    C   Substantiality, measurability, accessibility
    D   Stability, accessibility, substantiality   **(2 marks)**

41.9 Selling at a low price with the intention of damaging weaker competitors is referred to as

    A   Price skimming
    B   Opportunistic pricing
    C   Penetration pricing
    D   Predatory pricing   **(2 marks)**

41.10 The product life cycle is depicted on a chart or diagram as a line against the variables of

    A   Cash flow and market share
    B   Number of customers and sales value
    C   Sales volume and time
    D   Relative market share and market growth rate   **(2 marks)**

    (Total = 20 marks)

42 Multiple choice questions: General 4 — 36 mins

42.1 Kurt Lewin's ideas on change are based on the view that change is:

A   Capable of being planned
B   Emergent
C   Inevitable and uncontrollable
D   Transformational   (2 marks)

42.2 The US, Canada and Mexico are the three members of which trade organisation?

A   EFTA
B   AFTA
C   NAFTA
D   APEC   (2 marks)

42.3 Charging a very low price on one item in order to generate customer loyalty and increased sales of other items is called:

A   Market penetration
B   Loss leader pricing
C   Product penetration
D   Skim pricing   (2 marks)

42.4 In the expectancy theory of motivation 'valence' refers to:

A   A belief that an outcome will satisfy organisational tasks
B   A person's own preference for achieving a particular outcome
C   A belief that the outcome will be shared by others equally
D   An understanding of the probability of an event happening   (2 marks)

42.5 In the context of information systems, a widget is:

A   A web 2.0 application
B   A component of a customer relationship management system
C   An expert system
D   An element of a management information system   (2 marks)

42.6 The TQMEX model is a framework that integrates processes associated with:

A   Total quality management and ISO accreditation
B   Supply chain management
C   Both operations and quality management
D   Organisational development   (2 marks)

42.7 Approval of documentation, procedures manuals and work instructions is associated with:

A   Registration under the standards required for quality certification
B   Total quality management (TQM)
C   Lean production methods
D   Job evaluation   (2 marks)

42.8 Rodger's seven-point plan refers to:

A   Quality targets for world class operations
B   Implementation guidelines for introducing new hardware
C   The likely headings to be found as part of a person specification
D   Lean production processes   (2 marks)

42.9   Activities aimed at attracting a number of suitable candidates interested in joining an organisation are called:

A   Human relationship marketing
B   Recruitment
C   Selection
D   Human capital harvesting   (2 marks)

42.10 The expectations that the individual and the organisation have of one another is referred to as:

A   A hygiene factor
B   A psychological contract
C   Dual theory motivation
D   A person specification   (2 marks)

(Total = 20 marks)

43 Multiple choice questions: General 5 — 36 mins

43.1 An approach of producing goods or purchasing inventory only when required is known as:

    A   Just-in-time
    B   Ad hoc
    C   Level capacity strategy
    D   Plan-do-check-act (PDCA) quality   (2 marks)

43.2 Intelligence, aptitudes and disposition are often factors identified in:

    A   A job description
    B   Appraisal targets
    C   A person specification
    D   360 degree documentation   (2 marks)

43.3 The evaluation of candidates for a job using a comprehensive and interrelated series of selection techniques is known as:

    A   Psychometric testing
    B   Developing a balanced scorecard
    C   Job evaluation
    D   An assessment centre   (2 marks)

43.4 Shareholders are an example of which type of stakeholder?

    A   Connected
    B   Internal
    C   External
    D   Coalition   (2 marks)

43.5 The concept of 'reliability' of staff selection techniques means:

    A   Effective testing of a candidate's desire for the job and natural abilities
    B   Overcoming poor performance in the interview due to nervousness
    C   The techniques produce consistent results if repeated
    D   Choosing the most reliable candidate every time   (2 marks)

43.6 In purchasing, the 'Reck and Long' positioning tool is by nature:

    A   Strategic
    B   Independent
    C   Supportive
    D   Passive   (2 marks)

43.7 The technique PDCA represents:

    A   A programme development control activity used in information management
    B   A framework for bringing about continuous improvement in quality management
    C   A software inventory system used in warehouse management
    D   People, developments, controls and appraisal in strategic human resourcing   (2 marks)

43.8 System testing before software production is known as:

    A   On-line testing
    B   Off-line testing
    C   Logic testing
    D   User acceptance testing   (2 marks)

43.9 The 5-S model refers to

A Internal analysis involving structure, sub-structure, systems, sub-systems and strategy
B Internal analysis involving style, shared values, skills, staffing and 'soft' information
C Operations management practices of structurise, systematise, sanitise, standardise and self-discipline
D The Japanese six-sigma model adapted to Western practice (2 marks)

43.10 Corrective work, the cost of scrap and materials lost are:

A Examples of internal failure costs
B Examples of external failure costs
C Examples of appraisal costs
D Examples of preventative costs (2 marks)

(Total = 20 marks)

44   Multiple choice questions: General 6   36 mins

44.1 Which one of the following statements represents the ultimate aim of Total Quality Management (TQM)?

- A   Eliminate the costs of poor quality
- B   Eliminate all quality-related costs
- C   Reduce costs of poor quality
- D   Reduce the workforce   **(2 marks)**

44.2 Which one of the following statements relating to Quality Management is true?

- A   Internal failure due to poor quality has no effect on delivery time
- B   Reducing internal failure reduces losses of capacity
- C   As the quality level of a process increases, appraisal costs will go up due to increased testing effort
- D   The cheapest way to improve quality is to increase post-production inspection   **(2 marks)**

44.3 Marketing strategy will normally:

- A   Provide priorities for the overall corporate strategy
- B   Drive the productive capacity of the company
- C   Meet the objectives of the company in terms of price and product features
- D   Be consistent with other organisational business planning processes   **(2 marks)**

44.4 Improvements to a system aimed at extending its facilities is an example of:

- A   Perfective maintenance
- B   Adaptive maintenance
- C   User maintenance
- D   Corrective maintenance   **(2 marks)**

44.5 Which one of the following is the factor that Taylor believed would be most effective in motivating workers?

- A   Remuneration levels
- B   Job security
- C   Good working conditions
- D   Minimal supervision   **(2 marks)**

44.6 Which of the following is sometimes used to refer to the process of 'continuous improvement'?

- A   Kaizen
- B   Six Sigma
- C   Lean principles
- D   Kanban   **(2 marks)**

44.7 To reduce inflation a government may decide to:

- A   Raise interest rates
- B   Reduce interest rates
- C   Weaken the national currency
- D   Strengthen the national currency   **(2 marks)**

44.8 Which one of the following options represents possible supply sourcing strategies?

- A   Internal, external and combined
- B   Local, regional, national and international
- C   On-line, off-line, domestic and overseas
- D   Single, multiple, parallel and delegated   **(2 marks)**

44.9 Who developed the concept of 'social man'?

    A   Mullins

    B   Lawrence and Lorsch

    C   Weber

    D   Schein   **(2 marks)**

44.10 Which one of the following statements best represents the principle of 'integrity' as explained in CIMA's Ethical Guidelines?

    A   Professional accountants must not tell lies

    B   Professional accountants must not be party to anything which is deceptive or misleading

    C   Professional accountants cannot be expected to resign over a matter of principle

    D   Integrity is almost as important as technical competence   **(2 marks)**

(Total = 20 marks)

45 Multiple choice questions: General 7   36 mins

45.1 For firms wishing to build market share in a market new to them, 'penetration pricing' involves pricing

A   High enough to convey an impression of quality
B   Low enough to challenge buyer loyalties
C   Low enough on a few items to attract customers to a wider product range
D   To cover fixed costs only   **(2 marks)**

45.2 A system that simulates the problem solving techniques of human experts is known as:

A   An expert system
B   A knowledge transfer programme.
C   A smart system
D   A management information system   **(2 marks)**

45.3 Attainments, general intelligence, circumstances and special aptitudes are part of Roger's seven-point plan for person requirements. What are the remaining points?

A   Expectations, attitudes and flexibility
B   Experience, past progression and characteristics
C   Qualities, responsibility taken and life experience
D   Physical make-up, interests and disposition   **(2 marks)**

45.4 Motivation theories that assume that behaviour is caused by, and directed towards, the satisfaction of personal needs are referred to as:

A   'Carrot and stick' theories
B   Content theories
C   Process theories
D   Satisfaction theories   **(2 marks)**

45.5 Porter's value system reflects the value created through the relationship of:

A   Suppliers, manufacturers, distribution channels and customers' value chains
B   Customers and sales staff
C   Production and sales departments
D   Economy, efficiency and effectiveness in the use of resources   **(2 marks)**

45.6 Inventory management using a method that concentrates effort on the most expensive items is called:

A   PDCA
B   JIT
C   Five S
D   ABC   **(2 marks)**

45.7 A duplication of an organisation's data in two or more files is called:

A   An integrated data set
B   Second life
C   Data redundancy
D   Entropy   **(2 marks)**

45.8 A company that concentrates on product features it instinctively believes to be 'right' is referred to as:

A   A learning organisation
B   Production orientated
C   Product orientated
D   Early stage entrepreneurial   **(2 marks)**

45.9 'Teleworkers' is a term applied to staff using communication technology and working:

    A   In an unstructured way

    B   In the telecommunications industry

    C   Off-site, for example from home

    D   In a call centre   **(2 marks)**

45.10 The induction process refers to:

    A   A test used as part of employee selection

    B   An understanding of expectations between the individual and the organisation

    C   Ways of familiarising new employees to the organisation

    D   Felings of complacency or dissatisfaction caused by a reward system   **(2 marks)**

(Total = 20 marks)

46   Various topics 1 (5/10)   54 mins

Required

(a)   An organisation has decided to outsource its IS function. Explain the main issues it needs to address.

(5 marks)

(b)   Describe the ways in which IS and IT might help an organisation's human resource function perform its role effectively.   **(5 marks)**

(c)   Explain how a manufacturer's promotional activity might vary depending upon the sort of distribution channel that operates.   **(5 marks)**

(d)   Construct a basic marketing mix for an online company selling branded sportswear.   **(5 marks)**

(e)   Describe the range of internal possibilities that exist for an organisation wishing to fill a job vacancy.

(5 marks)

(f)   Discuss what an organisation could do to motivate its workforce without offering financial incentives.

(5 marks)

(Total = 30 marks)

47 Various topics 2 (Specimen paper) 54 mins

Required

(a) Explain the benefits a collaborative process of Human Resource planning might bring to an organisation.

(5 marks)

(b) Explain what types of costs are associated with internal failure costs and the significance of these for an organisation with a reputation for quality. **(5 marks)**

(c) Describe the features and benefits of SERVQUAL to organisations where it might be relevant. **(5 marks)**

(d) Identify the key issues for a manufacturing organisation considering adopting Six Sigma philosophy.

(5 marks)

(e) Explain why a business with shareholders might take into account the interests of a wider group of stakeholders when considering a policy decision. **(5 marks)**

(f) Identify the nature and effects of risks for an organisation considering doing business in a country that has a government and political system that it is unfamiliar with. **(5 marks)**

(Total = 30 marks)

48 Various topics 3   54 mins

Required

(a)   Describe the benefits an information system centred around a database should bring to an organisation.
                                                                                        (5 marks)

(b)   Explain the benefits of effective management information systems and executive information systems.
                                                                                        (5 marks)

(c)   Explain the issues organisations should consider if switching from business-to-business trading (B2B) to business-to-consumer trading (B2C).   **(5 marks)**

(d)   Explain how the effectiveness of staff training events can be assessed.   **(5 marks)**

(e)   Identify the advantages to an organisation of using specialist providers as well as employees in delivering a training programme.   **(5 marks)**

(f)   Describe the ways in which organisations might encourage the development of the use of quality circles.
                                                                                        (5 marks)

                                                                                (Total = 30 marks)

49 Tracey plc 54 mins

Tracey plc manufactures and sells garden equipment via mail order. The Board of Tracey plc is about to consider investing in a new computer system for the marketing department, which will include an updated marketing database and broadband Internet access.

The existing database was implemented 10 years ago, and due to lack of training and knowledge, only the marketing manager can currently use the programme. This database only provides a list of marketing contacts which can be printed using key fields of name or geographical region.

As a result of the implementation, the marketing department staff will be reduced from 26 to 21 employees – the 5 middle managers will be made redundant. The rationale behind this move is that all staff in the marketing department will be able to use the new computer system, freeing up time for the marketing manager to actually manage staff rather than process all requests through the computer.

The new marketing database will hold information about customers and potential customers, clearly identifying:

- Name and address
- Company products information requested on
- Promotion method that the customer used to contact the company
- Product enhancements requested
- Amount of sales made
- Date of last sale/amendment of contact details
- Narrative of discussions with the customer

The marketing database is only one of the initiatives currently being followed with Tracey plc; many other databases and computer systems are being upgraded. This means that a data controller will have to be recruited with key responsibilities for managing data across the whole of the company. This person will need to negotiate with all departmental managers to ensure that databases conform to Tracey plc standards and that access is provided for appropriate personnel.

The Board of Tracey plc want to know more about the proposed change, with specific reference to how that change will be managed and the benefits of the new database. As the management accountant in the company, you have been asked to make a presentation to the Board on the change.

Required

Prepare briefing notes for the management accountant's meeting with the Board of Tracey plc covering the topics below. Your briefing notes should take no more than one page for each topic.

(a) Recommend a formal procedure, with brief explanation of the key stages, that can be followed to change from the old to the new database system. **(5 marks)**

(b) Explain the 4 P's of the marketing mix, showing how the new database provides additional information on these factors. **(5 marks)**

(c) Describe the new marketing information that can be obtained from the database. **(5 marks)**

(d) Evaluate the extent to which marketing information can be used to determine production strategy. **(5 marks)**

(e) Explain the effect of the new database on the organisational structure and culture of the marketing department. **(5 marks)**

(f) Provide job competences for the new data controller. **(5 marks)**

(Total = 30 marks)

50 Zodiac plc   54 mins

Zodiac plc manufactures 'outerwear' clothing (eg coats, boots, fleeces etc) from about 250 different inputs. Clothing is sold by mail order direct to the customer. When orders are received, they are entered into a customer ordering system, which is based on generally available software. On order fulfilment, details are transferred electronically to the receivables ledger system.

The re-order and production systems are based on ensuring that sufficient stock is always available to manufacture the required clothing. This means that the production controller normally orders large quantities of stock to try and avoid stockouts. However, the system which is based on the controller 'guessing' how much stock is required, does not always work. This means that 'emergency' orders have to be processed taking up valuable time of the controller.

Manufacturing systems include the use of CAD/CAM, particularly in the cutting of cloth ready for manufacture into coats etc. However, this is a stand alone system using standard software; there are no links to any other computer systems in Zodiac.

Quality of the production system is currently measured under the headings *customer*, *internal operations*, *innovation* and *learning* and *financial*.

The board of Zodiac are currently considering whether to implement a Materials Requirements Planning (MRP) system. This will be used to control materials requirements (by having links to production and order databases) including automatically issuing orders to suppliers based on materials usage. Some orders will be sent via Electronic Data Interchange (EDI) with other suppliers having direct access to the MRP via an Extranet to see precisely what stock is required in Zodiac.

Given Zodiac's lack of experience with MRP systems, the board are considering whether or not to outsource the setup and maintenance of this system.

Following the implementation of the MRP, the production controller will continue to be in charge of production, although without the responsibility for ordering stock. He will continue to report to the senior management accountant and be responsible for the overall quality of goods being produced.

Required

(a) Evaluate the feasibility of the Materials Requirement Planning (MRP) system in Zodiac under appropriate headings.   **(5 marks)**

(b) Explain the benefits of implementing a MRP system for Zodiac plc.   **(5 marks)**

(c) List and explain the reason for a series of questions that can be used by the board of Zodiac to assist in making the decision on whether or not to outsource the new MRP system.   **(5 marks)**

(d) List the performance measures that can be used to check the quality of production under the headings currently used by Zodiac. Note changes that can be expected in these measures with the implementation of the MRP system.   **(5 marks)**

(e) Explain the term market segmentation and discuss whether segmenting the clothes market would be beneficial to Zodiac.   **(5 marks)**

(f) Outline the steps of an appropriate appraisal system for the production controller.   **(5 marks)**

Note. Your answer should not exceed one page per question part.   **(Total = 30 marks)**

51 Hubbles (OMIS - Pilot Paper) 54 mins

Hubbles, a national high-street clothing retailer has recently appointed a new Chief Executive. The company is well established and relatively financially secure. It has a reputation for stability and traditional, quality clothing at an affordable price. Lately, however, it has suffered from intense competition leading to a loss of market share and an erosion of customer loyalty.

Hubbles has all the major business functions provided by 'in house' departments, including finance, human resources, purchasing, strategy and marketing. The Strategy and Marketing Department has identified a need for a comprehensive review of the company's effectiveness. In response, the new Chief Executive has commissioned a review by management consultants.

Their initial findings include the following:.

- Hubbles has never moved from being sales-oriented to being marketing-oriented and this is why it has lost touch with its customers;

- Hubbles now needs to get closer to its customers and operate a more effective marketing mix;

- Additional investment in its purchasing department can add significantly to improving Hubbles' competitive position.

The Chief Executive feels that a presentation of interim findings to senior managers would be helpful at this point. You are a member of the management consultancy team and have been asked to draft a slide presentation of some of the key points. The Chief Executive has identified six such points.

Required

Prepare a slide outline, and brief accompanying notes of two to three sentences, for each of the Chief Executive's key points identified below. Do not exceed one page per question part.

(a) Describe the difference between a company that concentrates on 'selling' its products and one that has adopted a marketing approach. **(5 marks)**

(b) Explain how Hubbles might develop itself into an organisation that is driven by customer needs. **(5 marks)**

(c) Explain what is meant by the 'marketing mix' (include the 4 traditional elements and 'people' as the fifth part of the mix). **(5 marks)**

(d) Identify examples of ways in which the management of Hubbles could make use of the marketing mix to help regain its competitive position. **(5 marks)**

(e) Describe the main areas in which Hubbles' Human Resources Department might reasonably contribute to assist the Purchasing Department. **(5 marks)**

(f) Explain how an efficient Purchasing Department might contribute to effective organisational performance. **(5 marks)**

(Total = 30 marks)

52 OK4u (OMIS 11/08 – amended)   54 mins

OK4u is a national leisure and sports chain selling specialist equipment and clothing for 'every sport'. A relatively young organisation, all OK4u's growth has been internally generated and has been led by its entrepreneurial founder and Chief Executive Officer (CEO) who is known for his creativity and person centred approach. Store managers are given discretion to display items in imaginative ways and use promotions to generate sales locally. All store managers report directly to the CEO who tries to oversee all aspects of the organisation's functioning without the help of a management team.

In its advertising, OK4u makes a feature of the creative way in which it is reducing non- recyclable packaging. It also claims to follow ethical policies. It has a few trusted long term suppliers of sports equipment and clothing. All suppliers are personally known to OK4u's CEO, and some are close friends. Good logistics mean that valuable floor area is not taken up by excessive in-shop storage. Known for good design, broad appeal and no 'stock outs', OK4u has established itself over the past five years as one of the country's favourite high street brands. Unfortunately, all that changed last year.

A year ago, OK4u expanded its product range by introducing fashion clothing into its stores. This was manufactured by a number of new suppliers. Initially sales were disappointing, until OK4u decided to discount prices. Thanks to tightly negotiated contracts, OK4u was able to pass the costs of the campaign on to its many new suppliers. As sales improved, these same suppliers were pressurised by threats of financial penalties into meeting late orders to tight deadlines.

Six months ago, a national newspaper ran a story under the front page headline 'The Shame of Sweatshop OK4u'. The article claimed that the chain was using workers from third world countries and paying them a fraction of the selling price. Further, it had discovered cases of children as young as eight years old working long hours. This was television news for two days and sales fell by 40% within a week. The CEO's investigation of the newspaper's claims found that:

- The incidents related to a few of the new fashion range items.

- None of the workers featured in the story were OK4u employees. The fault lay with its new clothing suppliers, some of whom OK4u knew little about.

- In some cases, these new clothing suppliers had sub-contracted work in order to keep costs low and meet delivery deadlines. In doing this, they had exploited vulnerable workers.

OK4u immediately withdrew its new fashion range and issued a public apology. In it, it explained that the fault had been with its suppliers and that it would be more careful in developing new supplier relationships in future. Although sales have recovered over the past six months, they are nowhere near their previous levels. The brand was also voted one of the most poorly regarded in a recent independent survey. The events have also affected morale and staff turnover has increased.

Last week, OK4u's CEO reviewed the situation and acknowledged a need to combat the negative public perception. He sent a personal letter to all employees in which he explained that OK4u intended restoring confidence with the public that OK4u is still following ethical policies. He explained that 'the key to becoming one of the country's favourite high street brands again is to deliver excellent customer satisfaction. This can only be achieved through a superb combination of marketing, HRM and operations'.

Required

For (a) – (f), do not exceed one page per question part.

(a) Explain OK4u's ethical and management failings associated with its expansion into selling fashion clothing. **(5 marks)**

(b) Describe appropriate measures OK4u might take in order to restore public confidence that it is following ethical policies. **(5 marks)**

(c) Explain how marketing, HRM and operations in OK4u could deliver 'excellent customer satisfaction'. **(5 marks)**

(d) Evaluate OK4u's strategic relationship with the two sets of suppliers – those supplying sports equipment and clothing and those who supplied fashion clothing. **(5 marks)**

(e) Explain the past year for OK4u using the basic marketing mix variables as a framework. **(5 marks)**

(f) OK4u is considering introducing a performance appraisal system to improve employee performance. Explain the purpose and objectives of such a system. **(5 marks)**

(Total = 30 marks)

ANSWERS

1 Objective test questions: Global business environment

1.1   B   Public sector organisations aim to use their resources efficiently.

1.2   A   Import tariffs and import quotas support import–substitution. Currency devaluations and industry subsidies are used to develop an emerging nation's industry as part of a strategy of export-led industrialisation.

1.3   C   The EU is an example of a common market, (it developed out of a customs union – the EEC). Transition economies are former Soviet Union states which are moving away from a communist system towards that of a free market.

1.4   A   According to monetarist theory, increasing the money supply will increase prices.

1.5   **Economic nationalism** is a nation's view that it should protect its own economy and industries.

      Economic liberalisation involves nations moving away from economic nationalism towards working with others in a group to benefit all member economies and industries.

1.6   **Emerland's government** can influence a number of factors that may create competitive advantages for the nation and encourage foreign investment.

      The **three main areas** that Emerland's **government can influence** are:

- The macroeconomic environment
- Legal and market regulation
- Corporate governance and social responsibility

1.7   **Emerland's government** could introduce:

      Legislation. A law could be introduced that requires monopolies to be broken down into individual businesses.

      Regulation. Market regulation could be introduced which is enforceable by a regulator. For example, mergers would have to be approved by the regulator which acts in the interests of competition.

2 Various global business environment topics

> **Text reference.** Chapters 1, 2 and 3.
>
> **Top tips.** In section B questions, read each requirement carefully and answer it directly. Try to make five concise but explained points to pick up five marks for each part.

(a) Porter's factor conditions relate to those factors used as inputs in the production of goods and services. These factors include human resources, physical resources, knowledge, capital and infrastructure.

Porter distinguished between basic and advanced factors.

Basic factors are natural resources, climate, semiskilled and unskilled labour. They are inherent within a nation, or can be created with minimal investment. They cannot be sustained as a source of national competitive advantage, since they are widely available. For example, the wages of unskilled workers in industrial countries are undermined by even lower wages elsewhere.

Advanced factors are associated with a well-developed scientific and technological infrastructure and include modern digital communications networks, highly educated people (eg computer scientists), university research laboratories and so on. They are necessary to achieve high order competitive advantages such as differentiated products and proprietary production technology.

An abundance of factors is not enough. It is the efficiency with which they are deployed that will create a competitive advantage for a nation.

Porter also stated that generalised factors, such as transport infrastructure are not significant in establishing competitive advantage as specialised factors. Specialised factors are relevant to a limited range of industries, such as knowledge bases in particular fields and logistic systems developed for particular goods or raw materials. Such factors are integral to innovation and very difficult to move to other countries.

(b) One argument in favour of free trade is that conflict is less likely between countries that trade and communicate with each other, but this is unlikely to be a crucial factor in deciding to adopt free trade.

Free trade facilitates specialisation by countries in the production of the goods and services they are best suited to producing. However this could lead to a nation becoming dependent upon a single product. This is particularly seen to be the case with some oil exporting countries in the Middle East.

Free trade also enables countries to develop and invest in resources leading to more efficient production. It is argued that it can also create inefficiencies, particularly as a result of increased consumer expectation, such as long distance transport costs for food products to satisfy demand when the product is out of season in a particular country.

Free trade should encourage entrepreneurship and economic growth, but this may be limited to areas in which a competitive advantage exists. It is also argued that free trade can prevent the development of new industries and that some form of protection may be required for these types of industries.

Free trade encourages all countries to export, but less developed countries will become dependent on more developed countries for certain products, particularly technologically advanced products.

Some people argue that it leads to better quality goods and a better quality of life although it has also been argued that free trade undermines local cultures especially with many countries becoming increasingly Americanised.

(c) The information technology function is outsourced by many organisations, but before making the decision to outsource or not, the following factors should be considered.

An important issue to consider as part of outsourcing is the potential for competitive advantage. The lower the potential for competitive advantage, the more suitable an activity is for outsourcing. In some organisations, information technology, often combined with branding, is a source of comparative advantage (for example Google, Amazon, Facebook). In other organisations IT is used to help efficiency, but isn't core to what the organisation does.

If IT is considered to be a residual competence of the organisation, ie it is not core to the organisation or essential to a core competence, then it will be suitable for outsourcing. If the organisation relies on IT in an area that creates a competitive advantage then it is less likely to be suitable for outsourcing.

Whether outsourcing IT will impact the organisation's ability to deliver its goods or services to market will also need to be considered. Increasingly though organisations are utilising IT to help deliver its goods or services and to provide customer service. Some relatively self contained IT services, for example payroll processing, may still be suitable for outsourcing.

If cost uncertainty is an issue, then outsourcing can be used to remove this. Costs are set in the contract where services are specified in advance for a fixed price.

If the current level of IT expertise is low within the organisation, then a specialist company will increase the level of expertise.

It is also important that the outsourcing company provides a service that matches the needs of the organisation. It should be possible to negotiate a Service Level Agreement that achieves this.

(d)   Macroeconomic factors can affect the balance of payments as follows.

Availability, price and quality of goods produced by local producers

If local producers are able to supply their home market with high-quality, competitively priced goods, then overseas producers will find it difficult to export to that market.

Inflation

Where a nation's inflation rate is higher than its competitors, producers in that country will face higher costs which will cause the price of their products to rise. This will make them less competitive and demand for their products is likely to fall.

Exchange rates

If a nation's currency weakens against those which export to it, then the goods it imports become more expensive. These imported goods will therefore be less competitive.

Trade agreements

Trade agreements affect the volume of imports and exports between nations. Nations are more likely to be able to export competitively to nations they are on an 'even playing field' with.

Taxes, tariffs and trade measures

Taxes and tariffs increase the price of imports, making them less attractive to buy. Governments may attempt to help home producers with subsidies or import quotas, although free trade agreements mean this may be difficult (or lead to tit-for-tat retaliation).

The business cycle

Nations looking for export-led growth require sufficient demand in overseas markets for their products. This is more likely to occur when overseas countries are experiencing a period of growth.

(e)   Deregulation measures may affect a manufacturing industry in the following ways.

There will be improved incentives for internal/cost efficiency. Greater competition means the most efficient manufacturers should be the most successful.

Allocative efficiency should also improve. This is because competition keeps prices closer to marginal cost, and organisations therefore produce closer to the socially optimal output level.

In some industries, liberalisation of regulations could have certain disadvantages. There may be a loss of economies of scale. If increased competition means that each manufacturer produces less output on a smaller scale, then the unit costs will be higher.

Deregulation can also lead to lower quality of products. The need to reduce costs may lead manufacturers to reduce quality or eliminate unprofitable but socially valuable services.

Regulation may be required within an industry in order to protect competition. It may be necessary to implement a regulatory regime to protect competition where inherent forces have a tendency to eliminate it. This would typically be in an industry with high barriers to entry which would otherwise be controlled by a few large suppliers.

(f)   Developing economies face different challenges to corporate social responsibility (CSR) than developed nations.

Key drivers for CSR in developing economies include:

Culture

Many developing nations already have in their culture a tradition of ethics and community. Often this has come about through religion. As businesses are part of a nation's culture it is natural for such traditions to be followed.

Politics

Political reform and the introduction of democracy is common in developing countries as this is often the spark which drives economic development. Countries undergoing development often follow examples of good practice, such as CSR, in developed nations.

Socio-economic priorities

Developing countries often face a conflict of priorities. For example, reducing pollution may be desirable to preserve the environment, but cleaner production methods may be more expensive and hinder economic progress.

Governance gaps

CSR can be used as a form of governance to 'plug the gaps' that result from poor government services. For example, organisations can be used to provide healthcare or education where the government cannot afford to.

Market access

As developed nations have high public pressure for CSR, companies in developing nations must follow the same principles if they are to sell in the same market.

Multinational companies

Multinational companies strive for consistency across all their international subsidiaries and production units. Where these are located in developing countries, they will adopt the same policies as those in developed countries. Countries (or companies) that do not adopt CSR are less likely to receive investment (or orders) from multinational companies..

3 McBride Gibbon

(a)   MG's **shareholders** clearly want the company to cut costs and increase profits so that they receive a better return on their investment. This is conflicts with a number of other stakeholder viewpoints.

Customers

Many customers purchase MG's products because they are ethically made and the company is socially responsible. Cutting costs might result in lower ethical standards and less socially responsible behaviour. Therefore products may no longer fulfil the needs of the customer and the company might even stop recalling defective products if it does not have to legally.

Suppliers

MG's current suppliers are selected because they conform to its ethical requirements. Cutting costs may mean they have to supply the same product at a lower cost or face losing business to a company with lower standards.

Banks

Banks are usually in favour of cost cutting measures to increase profitability. However, if this involves relocating operations to a country which is unstable, this may put the company at significant risk – affecting its ability to repay loans or overdrafts.

Employees

MG's employees currently enjoy excellent working conditions. This is one area which could be dramatically affected by cost cutting measures. If the business remains in Blueland, employees may have to put up with poorer working conditions. However, employees may lose their jobs if manufacturing relocates overseas.

Community

MG supports community based activities. This is another area which could be reduced or stopped altogether in a cost cutting exercise since it represents expenditure that the company does not have to make. If the company relocates overseas then existing projects may stop.

(b)   **Social responsibility in developing nations**

The following are drivers of social responsibility in developing nations.

Culture

Many developing nations already have in their culture a tradition of ethics and community. As businesses are part of a nation's culture it is natural for such traditions to be followed.

Politics

Political reform and the introduction of democracy is common in developing countries as this is often the spark which drives economic development. Countries undergoing development often look for examples of good practice in developed nations to make their development a success.

Governance gaps

Social responsibility can be used as a form of governance to 'plug the gaps' that result from poor government services. For example, organisations can be used to provide healthcare or education where the government cannot afford to.

Market access

Developing nations must follow the same socially responsible principles if they are to sell in the same market as developed nations.

Multinational companies

Multinational companies strive for consistency across all their foreign subsidiaries and production units. Where these are located in developing countries, they will adopt the same policies as those in developed countries.

(c) **Political risk**

Political risk is the risk of an organisation incurring losses due to non-market factors within a particular country. It is also related to financial factors, such as currency controls and the economy, and stability factors, such as rioting and civil war.

Political risks of Redland

The following are identified political risks of Redland:

Political

The military government recently overthrew a democratically elected parliament. Therefore the country is still likely to be unstable and subject to future political upheaval. For example, there may be pressure for the military government to be replaced.

Economic

Redland has high inflation which means that the cost of raw materials and labour will be rapidly rising. The fluctuating exchange rate will mean that businesses will not be able to forecast costs and revenues with any degree of certainty.

Social

There is likely to be a high degree of civil unrest, partly due to the recent change in government and partly due to the high levels of unemployment. Civil war may be a distinct possibility.

Technological

Redland is an undeveloped country and therefore it may not be technologically advanced enough to support a multi-national company's manufacturing operations.

(d) **Transnational vertical integration**

Transnational vertical integration is the process of locating production facilities in countries where production costs are low and then moving completed goods around the world for sale.

Outsourcing

Outsourcing involves an organisation sub-contracting business activities to third party providers. These providers can be in the same country as the main business, but increasingly foreign outsource providers are used.

MG

MG could outsource aspects of its business such as design or manufacture and move parts or completed products around the world to where they are needed. For example, a toy may be designed in Country A, its components manufactured in Country B and assembled in Country C.

Offshoring

Offshoring involves an organisation relocating its operations from one country to another. The whole business does not have to be moved, just the parts which would benefit the most from the conditions in the new location.

MG

MG could move its manufacturing operations to a country such as Redland where costs are low. The business would probably keep its design function in Blueland if the technological demands of the design process are high. Completed products would be sent back to Blueland where they are sold.

(e)   **Corporate culture**

Corporate culture refers to the common set of values that an organisation and its employees embody. It can be referred to as 'the way things are done around here'.

Cultural constraints on organisations which operate globally

Farmer and Richman identify four categories of constraint:

Educational constraints

The level of literacy and the availability of secondary education, vocational training and higher education in the countries an organisation operates will affect the quality of employees. Poor educational facilities will inevitably result in poor management.

Sociological constraints

These are social factors that will affect relations within the organisation. For example, some countries have a tradition of antagonism between trade unions and management. Therefore in such countries, an organisation will have to be careful when management deals with trade unions.

Legal and political constraints

Some countries have higher levels of legislation and regulation than others. For example in some countries it is easier to reduce headcount than others. Such rules restrict how organisations can operate.

Economic constraints

Countries have different economic variables. For example, some countries have high inflation and some have favourable exchange rates. Others may have restrictions on the availability of credit. These factors will affect demand for products within the country and the possibility of an organisation expanding its operations.

(f)   **Risk management**

If MG relocates its manufacturing operations to Redland it could take the following steps to minimise the probability and impact of risk.

Abandon or postpone the relocation

MG could postpone the relocation until the political uncertainty is reduced and the country is more stable. If this is not expected for some time then it may consider abandoning the project altogether.

Corporate political activity

MG could open negotiations with Redland's government in order to gain assurance that the project will be safe if there is civil unrest. The government may be persuaded to offer large tax breaks or other investment incentives that would minimise any losses to MG if the company has to cease its operations.

Monitor the environment

If the project goes ahead, the company should continually monitor the political environment to ensure it can react without delay should it appear that the operation is in danger.

Prepare contingency plans

The company should have detailed contingency plans prepared that it can turn to quickly if the need arises. As well as steps to safeguard its investment, MG should also source alternative methods of production (for example outsourcing if necessary) so that any disruption is minimised.

Insurance

MG should ensure that it has suitable political risk insurance in place to provide some financial protection if operations cease.

4 G banking group

Text reference. Chapters 1, 11 and 12.

Top tips. Think about why the BRIC economies are so attractive to multinational businesses, their population represents both a huge resource and a huge potential market. Do not confuse 'outsourcing' (using a vendor company to provide services) with 'offshoring' (moving operations overseas). The workers in India are employed by the G Banking Group, not a third party.

The examiner has emphasised the importance of 'writing enough'. Remember to make your point, explain it and relate it to the scenario.

Easy marks. Identify the BRIC countries. The advantages and disadvantages of offshoring should be familiar material.

Marking scheme

		Marks
(a)	Up to 2 marks for each relevant, fully explained point	10
(b)	Up to 2 marks for each relevant explained advantage, maximum 5 marks	
	Up to 2 marks for each relevant explained problem, maximum 5 marks	10
(c)	1 mark for redundancy and 1 - 2 marks for each relevant explained point	5
		25

Our answer shows what we consider the most appropriate points to make. Other relevant points that answer the question would earn marks. However, irrelevant points that do not answer the question would not earn marks.

(a)

Brazil, Russia, India and China have all experienced rapid economic growth in recent years. They are becoming increasingly important in the world economy, both individually and even more so collectively. They are representative of a shift in economic power that's likely to accelerate in future years, and are collectively referred to as the BRIC economies.

Factors involved in the emergence of the BRIC economies

Large pool of labour and consumers. The BRIC economies represent a huge market, which makes them attractive to multinational businesses wishing to both reduce production costs and sell more of their goods. As the purchasing power of the population as a whole increases they will provide even larger potential markets for both domestic and multinational producers.

The emergence of a relatively wealthy middle class. The BRIC countries have experienced the emergence of a relatively wealthy middle-class living in urban areas and fuelling economic growth through consumer spending.

Relatively low wage rates. The relatively low wage rates in the BRIC economies has made them very attractive to multinational businesses looking to relocate and reduce costs. China in particular has a huge pool of relatively cheap labour and manufacturing skills.

Increasingly educated population. There are now sufficient numbers of well educated locals to set up well managed, efficient production facilities in the BRIC countries.

Natural resources. The developing world economy needs the resources that the BRIC countries can provide. Brazil and Russia have extensive raw materials such as agriculture, iron ore and oil.

Globalisation has helped fuel the growth of the BRIC economies. Globalisation refers to the growing interdependence of countries worldwide through increased trade, increased capital flows and the rapid diffusion of technology.

Particular features of globalisation that have benefited the BRIC economies (and other economies) include:

- The ability of individuals and organisations to enter into transactions with individuals and organisations based in other countries

- Increased influence and power of multinational enterprises and increased mobility of skilled people

- The rise of globally linked and dependent financial markets, with easier access to capital

- The trend to increased similarity in consumer tastes around the world fuelled by increased trade and the global media

- Reduced transaction costs through developments in communications, transport and technology

- The rise of emerging and newly industrialised nations with governments more willing to embrace free markets and remove internal restrictions to doing business overseas

It is now common for components for a product to be manufactured in a number of different countries. China is sometimes referred to as 'the workshop of the world'.

(b)

Offshoring

Offshoring is the relocation of some part of an organisation's activities to another country. Developments in technology have made offshoring feasible in many situations, such as back office support for banking operations.

Offshoring has grown significantly in recent years. India is one popular offshoring country, many UK banks and other companies now have service centres based in India.

Offshoring offers a **number of advantages** to the G Banking Group.

1. **Lower overall cost**. Labour and other costs (eg premises) will be lower in India than in country D.

2. **Able to afford a more qualified workforce**. Call centre positions in India are often filled by better qualified individuals than would be the case in country D.

3. **Investment by host government**. Infrastructure (for example communication) in emerging economies has often been heavily invested in by the host governments, in order to attract inward investment.

4. **Economies of scale / centralised operations**. The back office operations will now be able to concentrate its back office operation in India, where it already employs 3,000 people. Economies of scale are likely to result. Long-term moves such as this also encourage strategic planning.

5. **Allows specialisation**. Offshoring back office operations to India will allow the G Banking group to concentrate on the more complex side of its banking operations and grow its international business by allowing other staff to focus on specialised areas of operation. This is necessary in a global economy where competition is increasing

On the other side of the discussion, managing operations based in another country will involve a **number of challenges for the G Banking Group**:

1. **Risks associated with currency exchange rates**. As an experienced banking group, this should be manageable. Exchange rates will always be liable to fluctuate and this may erode some of the cost savings.

2. **Language barriers and cultural differences**. This may not be such a significant hurdle to overcome for G Group as they already have a large presence in India. There may be some resistance by customers based in country D, due to perceived problems dealing with call centres based overseas.

3. **Technical challenges**. Staff in India will need to be properly trained to ensure that service levels in the offshored function do not suffer. Some functions may be retained at the call centres in country D, so that customer service and satisfaction levels remain high.

4. **Exercising control from a distance**. Offshoring can lead to a loss of control, particularly over quality.

5. **Dealing with different time zones.** This is a challenge that a multinational company should be able to meet reasonably comfortably, although employees may find themselves inconvenienced occasionally (for example the timing of telephone conference calls). Globalised business operates 24 hours a day and the G Group would be no exception to this.

(c)

Role of the Human Resources Division

The 500 employees of The G Group that aren't redeployed following the offshoring will be dismissed through reason of redundancy.

The Human Resources Division should have policies governing redundancy and ensure these are followed.

The HR Division's role should include setting policies that cover areas such as:

- Selection for redundancy – the criteria for selection must be clear and must be communicated as clearly as possible

- Pre-redundancy consultation and clear communication of where and when redundancies are to occur to enable staff to plan their futures

- Help with developing a CV and clear guidelines covering time off to attend interviews

- Clear guidelines on redundancy payments, with clear communication of packages and negotiation where appropriate

- Assistance with re-development of skills, re-training to learn new skills for a new career, or re-location of redundant employees

- Careers advice, counselling and post-redundancy support

Redundancy is likely to be an unpleasant experience. The HR Division must ensure affected staff are handled with care and sensitivity.

HR should also play a part ensuring remaining employees remain motivated, and morale is as high as can be expected in the circumstances.

5 F Food

(a)

Objectives

Initially it will be necessary to examine the objectives of F Food. If they are seeking to expand sales volume by expanding into Asia, but only looking for a small market share and concentrating on the home market of North America, the issues are not as important as if they are seeking to operate as a truly global organisation.

Organisational and local culture

The **culture** of F Food needs to be assessed so that it does not conflict with local cultures within Asia. Similar to the way McDonalds operates in parts of Asia, the choice of food may have to be **altered in particular locations** to match religious or cultural requirements.

Similarly, by failing **to allow for diversity** or to understand the local culture, planners based in North America could make mistakes when drawing up marketing campaigns in Asia.

Ronen and Shenkar identified four key characteristics of national culture, which are all important to consider when expanding operations overseas.

The four characteristics are: the **importance placed on work goals**, the role of **job satisfaction**, the impact of **organisational and managerial factors** and the impact of **work roles and interpersonal relationships**.

F Food will need to ensure that the roles they offer at least **match the characteristics at different locations**. In some locations where job satisfaction is not considered as important, F Food may wish to ensure their employees do have higher job satisfaction anyway (Corporate Social Responsibility).

Managers need to be flexible enough to adapt to cultural differences and be able to ride what Ronen and Shenkar referred to as 'the waves of culture'.

Management structure

The management structure of the Asian operations needs to be considered. A variety of factors influence management methods in an international setting. These factors pull in different directions and it may be that compromise is necessary.

The **geographical distance** between North America and Asia will cause some issues.

Central control, based in North America, may be the most appropriate structure as F Food's experience in international operations is low. Centralisation is seen as promoting **efficiency** and prevents duplication of effort between regions. For example, the Asian operations may have to accept supervision of its quality assurance or financial reporting functions from North America. For this to be successful though, consideration must be given to **time differences** and it may be necessary to have staff available in North America during normal working hours within the Asian locations.

The need for a **quick response to local opportunities and threats** may mean that there needs to be a significant measure of **decentralisation**. National, political and cultural sensitivities may reinforce this need for a level of local management, but a shortage of local talent may limit the scope.

Another issue could be poor **information systems and communications**. However, the rapidly falling costs of telecommunications through the use of Voice over Internet Protocol (VoIP) and the spread of e-mail and video-conferencing facilities mean this is less likely to be a problem than it would have been in the past.

Holding meetings can also become difficult and expensive when a company expands internationally. Air **travel and hotel costs** can be significant if many people are travelling from overseas. **Video-conferencing** is an alternative to face-to-face meetings which would give a considerable cost saving.

(b)

The bonus scheme and the dominance of the CEO both present corporate governance concerns to F Food.

Bonus scheme

The existing bonus scheme gives an incentive for individuals to manipulate short-term results in order to achieve a certain level of bonus. To mitigate this risk, there should be a review of results by an independent body.

A separate risk arising from this bonus scheme is that it encourages short-term thinking. Decisions are likely to be taken that improve results in the short-term, to earn the bonus, but these decisions may not be in the long-term interests of F Food. This is an example of goal incongruence. Changing the bonus scheme to incorporate longer term measures may help to eradicate this.

Dominant CEO

The dominance of a company by one individual is a cause for concern as this has been a feature in several high profile corporate governance failures in the past. The CEO may be operating in his own interests rather than those of F Food. The presence of non-executive directors on the board is felt to be an important safeguard against domination by a single individual due to their independence from the company.

The dominance of the CEO may indicate other issues with the board such as a lack of meetings or a failure to oversee the activities of F Food. The board should meet regularly in order to be able to effectively run the company.

Audit committee

Another area where F Food may want to improve is its audit committee. The role of the audit committee is to oversee the work of the internal audit function and to challenge the external auditors to ensure that their audit procedures are appropriate and rigorous. It is important that there are enough individuals on the committee with sufficient technical knowledge or expertise in auditing.

Remuneration policy

Director remuneration should be sufficient to attract, retain and motivate directors of the quality required, but should not be more than is necessary (as this wastes company resources). A significant proportion of executive directors' remuneration should be linked to individual performance. An appropriate policy encourages behaviour that benefits the director (proportionately) and improves the long-term health of the company.

(c)

Factors favouring expatriate staff

Poor educational opportunities in the market may require the import of skilled managers. Expatriates have been needed in many western business operations operating overseas because they understand the importance of profit.

Some senior managers believe that a business run by expatriates is easier to control than one run by local staff.

Expatriates might be able to communicate with the corporate centre better than local staff.
The expatriate may know more about the organisation overall, which is especially important as they are representing the organisation in a new territory.

It may be hard for locals to assimilate into the corporate culture of F Food, which might lead to communication problems.

Factors favouring the use of local staff

Local staff are cheaper than expatriate staff due to the saved relocation costs and other expenses such as subsidised housing and school fees.

The expatriate may fail to adjust or immerse themselves into the local culture (eg by associating only with other expatriates). This is likely to lead to poor management effectiveness, especially since the business is likely to require personal contact.

Local staff have greater local knowledge of how business is conducted. A substantial training programme might be needed to educate expatriate staff about the local culture. This may need to include language and cultural training and cover local social and business customs and norms..

Other relevant factors to consider

A glass ceiling might exist in some companies. Local managers may not make it to board level due to favouritism to western members of management.

Local management will have greater local knowledge but may not have an understanding of the wider corporate picture. However, this is true of many management staff at the operational level whether local or expatriate.

6 HU3

Text reference. Chapter 1.

Top tips. PEST analysis and Porter's diamond provide ready-made structures for your answer.

Marking scheme

		Marks
(a)	Up to 2 marks for each environmental factor referenced to the scenario	12
(b)	Up to 2 marks for explaining 'competitive advantage'	2
	Up to 2 marks for each strategy referenced to the scenario, maximum 11 marks	<u>11</u>
		13
		<u>25</u>

Our answer shows what we consider the most appropriate points to make. Other relevant points that answer the question would earn marks. However, irrelevant points that do not answer the question would not earn marks.

(a) **Environmental Factors**

HU3 should consider the following environmental factors when deciding whether or not to expand into Highland.

Political

The government of Highland is keen to attract investment from foreign companies as it provides grants and an attractive tax regime. Overall, the political environment is favourable.

Economic

The economy of Highland seems stable as inflation, interest rates and exchange rates have not changed much in the last few years. This means that HU3's market in the country should be fairly safe as demand will be constant and credit continually available.

Social

Highland's culture is much the same as HU3 is used to and therefore it should not find any problems with fitting into society. However, there may be a language barrier to overcome. In tough economic times, people from Lowland who move to Highland for employment may face social pressures.

Technological

Highland is more technologically advanced than HU3. This means it will have to employ experts to help it make the most of the available technology and invest substantially in training its current staff in that technology.

Ecological

Many areas of Highland are protected from further development and this will impact on where HU3 can locate its facilities. Ideally it would locate near other similar industries to make the most of the benefits that industry clusters provide, but this might not be possible.

Legal

Highland law offers more protection to employees than Lowland. This will mean HU3's managers have to treat Highland employees more carefully than those in other parts of the organisation. HR staff would particularly benefit from training in Highland employment law.

(b) **Competitive advantage**

Competitive advantage involves a country or business organisation being better placed than its rivals to compete in the business market. For example, a country which has vast natural resources has a competitive advantage over one which has limited natural resources. A company that uses technology that its rivals do not have access to is another example.

HU3 and competitive advantage

HU3 wishes to enter Highland's market, but the quality of its products are too low for it to compete. The following strategies may help improve its competitive position.

Compete in the most challenging market

If HU3 can compete successfully in a market where quality is vital, it should have gone through a quality improvement process that will allow it to do well elsewhere. So, if HU3 puts in place the requirements to do well in Highland, it will be well placed to move into other markets.

Spread out research and development activities

HU3 could locate its own research and development activities in Highland's established research zone. This will enable it to tap into the knowledge and experience available in that area relating to product quality.

Invest in human resources

HU3's employees are the source of its creativity and strength. Investing in their training and development may help the company become more creative and stronger that its rivals in Highland.

Collaborate with Highland companies

Collaboration will help HU3 enter the competitive market place and learn some successful techniques from Highland companies. A joint venture may be worth considering.

Supply Highland companies

Highland companies have higher standards of quality than HU3 is used to. By raising its standards to meet them, the quality of its products will improve. These strong relationships could then be utilised to expand further into Highland and elsewhere.

Source components from Highland companies

If HU3 sources its own components from Highland companies then the overall standard of quality of its own products will increase. Strong, mutually beneficial relationships with suppliers will help raise standards at HU3.

7 Gus

Text reference. Chapter 1.

Top tips. Part (a) is a straightforward test of 'book knowledge', but you need to relate your recommendation to the scenario. In part (b), all the points you make must be related to the scenario.

Note – in part (b) only six points are required, others are given to demonstrate alternative solutions.

Easy marks. Stating four types of business organisation in part (a).

(a) **Types of business organisation**

The following types of business organisation may be appropriate to Gus.

Sole trader

Gus could continue to develop and take his product to market on his own without formally setting up a business organisation. If he does so he will become what is known as a sole trader. An advantage of this approach is there is less paperwork and no need to file accounts at companies house. A disadvantage of this is that he will have unlimited personal liability for any debts he incurs.

Partnership

Gus could go into business with one or more other individuals, maybe those with more business experience than him who can look after the more commercial aspects of operating a business organisation. This would create a partnership. No formal procedures are necessary to do this, although a clear partnership agreement is advisable. Like a sole trader, Gus (and the other partners) would have unlimited personal liability for business debts.

Private limited company

Gus could formally set up a legal entity (known as a private limited company) to take over the business. He would provide the company with investment in return for shares and the company would own the business' assets and liabilities. This would provide Gus with the protection of limited liability should the business have financial difficulties. The maximum amount Gus could lose would be restricted to the nominal value of his shareholding.

Public limited company

This type of company is identical to a private limited company although it is permitted to solicit investment from the general public – a private limited company cannot. If a large amount of investment is required and this is unable to be raised from other sources, Gus could form a public limited company.

Recommendation

Given Gus's desire for limited liability he should set up a company. As it will be a new entity, and one which might not be successful, it is unlikely that members of the public would wish to invest in it. Also, Gus has access to the funds he needs. Therefore a private limited company is most appropriate.

(b) **The use of expatriate staff**

Gus should consider the following **issues** when deciding to use **expatriate staff** to manage the production facility.

Education

As identified in the scenario, local employees may lack the necessary education to run the operation. This problem can be overcome by using staff from the organisation's home country. Longer-term, local staff may be able to be trained to perform management roles.

Control

Gus may find it easier to control managers from the country he now lives in as they are likely to have a similar business background and approach.

Communication

Language and educational constraints might mean that expatriates are better able than locals to communicate with Gus's corporate centre. This might not be such a problem for Gus if he can speak the language of his native country, but could be an issue for other corporate staff.

Cost

Expatriates will demand greater remuneration than local staff because they have a higher standard of living to maintain and will see their salary relative to what they could earn in their home country. There will also be additional costs such as housing and school fees to pay. Given that it is an ethically sound choice of Gus to locate the factory overseas (creating employment in a developing country), he may see the additional cost of ex-pat management as necessary to facilitate this.

Culture shock

Expatriates may fail to adjust to the culture where they are to be based. This may lead to poor management effectiveness, especially as the business requires them to deal with local staff employed on low-level tasks.

Training

Before expatriates relocate, a substantial training programme is likely to be needed. This may just include basic facts about the country, language training, and some briefings about cultural differences. However, more detailed immersion training involving language, culture and simulation of social and business experiences may be required.

Corporate culture

Expatriates may assimilate into the corporate culture better than locals as they understand the way the organisation operates. Longer term, it may be beneficial to incorporate some local attitudes and values into the corporate culture.

Local knowledge

Even if ex-pats are trained in 'local ways', local staff will have better local knowledge and grasp of the local language. This may mean local management would be better placed to manage local staff. In the long term, a lack of local management may lead to resentment and a possible backlash.

Note: Only six issues required

8 FutureGreen

> **Text reference**. Chapter 2.
>
> **Top tips**. *Caroll and Buchholtz's* theory applies to part (a) although you might have come up with some different responsibilities yourself. Part (b) could be answered by applying general knowledge of corporate governance to the scenario.
>
> **Easy marks**. Defining corporate social responsibility and corporate governance.

Marking scheme

		Marks	
(a)	Up to 2 marks for explaining 'corporate social responsibility'	2	
	1 mark for stating a relevant theory and two marks for each type of responsibility referenced to the scenario	9	
			11
(b)	Up to 2 marks for explaining 'corporate governance'	2	
	Up to 2 marks for each benefit referenced to the scenario	12	
			14
			25

Our answer shows what we consider the most appropriate points to make. Other relevant points that answer the question would earn marks. However, irrelevant points that do not answer the question would not earn marks.

(a) **Corporate social responsibility**

The term corporate social responsibility is used to describe the range of obligations that an organisation has towards its external stakeholders, including the society and communities in which it operates. For example an organisation may feel it should employee local people or operate in an environmentally friendly way such as FutureGreen.

Types of social responsibility

Caroll and *Buchholtz* argued that there are four types of corporate social responsibility and they can be applied to FutureGreen as follows:

Economic responsibilities

Companies have economic responsibilities to employees wanting fair employment rewards and conditions, and customers seeking good-quality products at a fair price. With the prospect of future expansion and floatation, additional economic responsibilities such as getting the maximum return on investment and providing a good return to the new shareholders will be created.

Legal responsibilities

FutureGreen is bound to follow the laws of the country in which it operates, for example, laws concerning the health and safety of employees or the production of its products.

Ethical responsibilities

These are responsibilities that require FutureGreen to act in a fair and just way even if the law does not compel it to do so. These may include paying its employees above the minimum wage or exceeding minimum standards on pollution during the production process. As well as being ethical, this is likely to be a business necessity for FutureGreen to retain brand credibility.

Philanthropic responsibilities

These responsibilities are desired rather than being required of FutureGreen. Examples of philanthropic responsibilities include charitable donations, contributions to local communities and providing employees with chances to improve their own lives.

(b)   **Corporate governance**

Corporate governance is the system by which companies and other entities are directed and controlled. It therefore consists of the processes and procedures put in place by an organisation's senior management which control how the business operates.

Benefits of developing corporate governance

Benefits to FutureGreen of developing a corporate governance policy include:

Risk reduction

The ultimate risk FutureGreen faces is of it making such large losses that the business is forced to close down. A corporate governance policy which focuses on internal controls, reducing the risk of an environmental mishap (which could destroy the brand) and fraud reduction measures can help minimise this risk.

Aligning directors' performance objectives with that of the business

The prospect of the company's financial success can be improved by taking action to align directors' interests with the company's strategic objectives. This because it encourages directors to act in the business' best interests.

Performance

A good corporate governance policy makes it clear who is to be accountable for what. This will help improve the performance of FutureGreen since individual accountability of the organisation's senior management is unclear.

External support

With business expansion in mind and a potentially large group of new shareholders to cater for, it is important that FutureGreen gains support amongst its external stakeholders.

An effective corporate governance policy helps maintain or improve perceptions of the organisation held by external stakeholders. This may help the company raise further finance in future and improve relations with, for example, customers and employees.

Stock Exchange Combined Code

The Stock Exchange Combined Code sets out standards of best practice in relation to corporate governance. UK companies are not legally required to follow it, although quoted companies must explain any departures from it in a note to their financial statements.

If FutureGreen develops a corporate governance policy that is based on the Stock Exchange Combined Code, as well as accruing the benefits described above, it will not have to make further changes following Stock Exchange quotation.

Attracting investors

Early adoption of the Combined Code's principles may help attract investors. They will see that the business already follows good corporate governance policies even though it is currently not required to do so. This indicates strong management and a potentially safer investment.

9 Objective test questions: Information systems 1

9.1   B   An intranet provides a storage and distribution point for information accessible to staff.

9.2   A   An expert system could be described as a database built on knowledge and experience.

9.3   A   Corrective maintenance is carried out to correct residual faults. Options B and C are enhancements (perfective maintenance). D takes account of anticipated changes in the processing environment (adaptive).

9.4   D   Data redundancy occurs when data is duplicated.

9.5   The **new system** will:

Change the way architects work

- Compatible software allows workers to share ideas electronically.

Change the way the company's services are provided

- As the architects can share ideas electronically, they no longer need to work together at the client's premises.

9.6   **Virtual teams** are interconnected groups of people who may not be present in the same office or organisation but who:

- Share information and tasks
- Make joint decisions
- Fulfil the collaborative function of a team.

9.7   A **direct approach** may be preferred because:

- There is **complete confidence** in the new system
- To **overcome a reluctance** to 'let the old system go'
- It is **cheaper** and **more convenient** than running two systems
- The change may be **implemented before staff are able to object**

10   Objective test questions: Information systems 2

10.1   B   As the direct approach involves the old system ceasing operation completely at a given time, this approach is the most risky.

10.2   C   Dial-back security requires users to identify themselves before the system dials them back on their authorised number before allowing access.

10.3   C   Denial of service attacks attempt to disable an Internet site by overloading it with traffic.

10.4   D   Application Service Providers are third parties who manage and distribute services and solutions to clients over a wide area network.

10.5   **Four roles** that the new system may play in Comseek are:

- **Planning** future operations

- **Recording** transactions

- **Performance measurement** (comparing actual results against plans)

- To help senior management **make decisions**

10.6   **Enterprise-wide systems** are designed to co-ordinate all business functions, resources and information. Under an enterprise-wide system each business area is provided with a system that fulfils its needs, however each module shares a common database that is the basis of all the information within the organisation.

10.7   **Testing** should include:

- **User acceptance testing** – to establish whether user acceptance criteria is met

- **Realistic tests** – realistic data and environment

- **Contrived tests** – how the system copes with unusual and unexpected events

- **Volume tests** – ensure the system can cope with the expected number of transactions, and more

11   S&C software project

(a)   **Alignment with business strategy**

The system is likely to be a source of competitive advantage for the firm because the cost savings and subsequent productivity gains will not be available to its competitors. To make the most of the advantage, it must be aligned with the firm's overall business strategy.

Fitting the software and business processes

S & C has two choices if the software does not fit its business processes.

1.   **Customise** the **software** to the match the process.

2.   **Change** the **processes** to match the software.

Customise the software

The benefit of this option is that there will be less disruption within the firm as the business processes remain unchanged. However, there could be a large financial cost if external experts have to be brought in or if the changes are complex. There is also a risk that new programming introduces glitches into the system.

Change the processes

This option saves the cost of additional programming and the risk of introducing glitches. However, changing business processes could have a negative impact on the morale and efficiency of the staff as it would represent a major change in the way they work.

(b)   **Direct approach**

Under a direct approach, on one particular day the old system is switched off and the new one switched on. There is no overlap or period of dual running of both systems.

Phased approach

A phased approach involves selecting a complete section of the system for direct changeover.

The phased approach is more suitable than a direct approach as it **controls the risk** involved when switching over to a new system – this is particularly important as S & C will be introducing a brand new system that no one else has used.

The firm would implement the new system in **discrete stages** – corresponding to the current system they replace.

This would have the following advantages:

*   **Risk is reduced** as glitches will be limited to the new subsystem only.

*   **Staff will adapt** to change more easily as it occurs over a longer period in small chunks.

*   It allows **time for feedback** from staff involved in earlier phases to be considered when rolling out later ones. For example, small glitches or user-friendliness.

*   There is **less disruption** so the benefits of the changes can be felt more quickly.

(c)   The following roles within S & C are important for the implementation to succeed.

Partners

Their support in terms of visible behaviour and making sufficient resources available is crucial.

Project manager (change agent)

It is their organisation and drive that will keep the project on track and focussed. This will ensure business performance is not affected by the change. A regular presence is required to ensure this.

If the current manager cannot keep regular attendance they should be replaced.

Steering group

The group should be available to support staff in the weeks immediately prior and subsequent to the implementation. They also have a key role to play in winning over staff who resist it.

HR department

HR should ensure staff receive suitable training and support during the implementation. Where system success depends on targets being met a reward system should be put in place. It should also develop policies to deal with staff who resist the change.

Staff

It is their acceptance of the system that will decide if it is a success. It is important that they communicate ideas and suggestions as this will help them feel that the system is theirs.

Managers

They have a key role to ensure information regarding the change is communicated in a clear, timely manner to the staff. This will help minimise any disruption to the business.

(d)   **User involvement** in system implementation is essential to obtain user acceptance. Specific examples of activities users should be involved in include:

Testing

Developers should ask a group of users to test the system to check that it works as it should and actually meet their needs.

Training

The implementation phase is usually towards the end of the development. Users should start their training on the new system so they are prepared for the changeover.

File conversion and transfer

Data within the old system will need to be transferred to the new system. Users should be involved in the transfer as their knowledge will help ensure data is interpreted correctly.

Quality circles and discussions

Forums that include users should be set up to discuss the overall quality of the system and how it could be improved.

Championing change

Users who can see the benefits of the new system should become involved in winning over other users who may resist the change.

(e)   There are three distinct groups within S & C who have different training needs.

Partners

Partners will not be using the system on a day-to-day basis, however, they should have a good basic understanding of it so they understand how the work they review was assembled. Such training could be provided by an executive presentation. Some additional, hands-on training may be required covering how reports and 'snapshots' performance are obtained.

Managers

Managers should receive training to enable them to understand the software involved in areas they are responsible for. In particular, security features that prevent unauthorised access or loss or damage to data.

Users

Users need to be trained in the day-to-day features and processes that the system provides. This would include data-entry and report writing amongst others.

Methods of training can include:

- In-house demonstrations

- On-line learning

- Computer based training using dummy data

(f)   A number of methods can be used to evaluate the success or failure of the system.

Cost-benefit review

Following the completion of the project a cost-benefit review can begin. This analyses the actual costs incurred in developing and implementing the system with the actual benefits the system provides. Benefits can be difficult to quantify so the firm may have to make use of estimates. This review will help determine whether the system is a financial success or failure.

Performance reviews

Performance reviews consider whether the system is performing as expected and may cover issues such as:

- **System efficiency** – is the system operating quickly enough, does it slow down when processing large volumes of data?

- **Security** – is the system secure, have there been many breaches?

- **Error rates** – does data in the system contain errors? If there are then there may be problems in data collection and file conversion.

- **Output** – does the system produce its output on a timely basis, is it being used as expected, does it go to the right people?

Post-implementation review

This establishes whether or not the system's objectives and targeted performance criteria have been met. It compares the system's actual and predicted performance. The contents of this and the other reviews are used in a formal post-implementation review report to judge the system's success or failure.

12 S1K

Text reference. Chapters 3, 4 and 12.

Top tips. Part (a) gives you scope to include any aspect of information technology and information systems. Ensure you explain how the uses of IT/IS you identify will improve SK's operations. Be concise though, don't waste precious time with waffle. In part (b), avoid providing a general discussion of the points highlighted by the Chief Executive. Instead, focus on potential implementation problems (as stated in the requirement). Ensure you cover both aspects of part (c) - identifying the main individuals and explaining whether their training should be in-house or not.

Easy marks. You are told in the scenario that 'Internet possibilities are being missed' - development of an effective website provides easy marks in part (a). Commenting on the need to appoint a project manager and discussing whether the proposed phased implementation approach is appropriate provides some easy marks in part (b). In part (c), the new project manager and all shop staff are two obvious candidates for training.

Marking scheme

		Marks
(a)	Two marks for each relevant, explained use of IS/IT at S1K	10
(b)	Two marks for each relevant, explained point related to the Chief Executive's analysis	10
(c)	Up to two marks for each individual/group and training method (total max 5 marks)	5
		25

Our answer shows what we consider the most appropriate points to make. Other relevant points that answer the question would earn marks. However, irrelevant points that do not answer the question would not earn marks.

(a)   Five ways in which either information technology (IT) or information systems (that these days tend to utilise IT) could be used to improve S1K's operations are identified below.

Establish a well designed website

SK1 could invest in a website to provide information to customers, enhance the brand, offer online booking for optical appointments and sell own-brand products. It would be essential that the site was integrated with back-office systems, to ensure the booking process went smoothly.

The site should include e-commerce and also be a key marketing tool.

Establish a Wide Area Network (WAN)

By linking computers at shops together, a WAN would facilitate improved communication and collaboration between shops.

The WAN would enable data and information to be shared quickly and effectively, and would also provide a platform for the implementation of organisation-wide systems.

Implement a new integrated sales, stock and financial system

There are currently a series of shops operating independent computer-based systems and some shops using manual systems. A common stock and point of sale system, integrated into the proposed new financial system, would save time analysing and searching for information in shops and enable quicker and more accurate production of financial information.

Integration between systems is important to reduce the need for keying data, as this is expensive and likely to introduce data inconsistencies and errors.

Introduce consistent, simplified operational procedures

The new sales system referred to above should include an EFTPOS system. This would enable staff to process sales more efficiently, improving customer service. It would also mean less time spent on accounting and administration tasks, as the calculation of sales figures and the updating of stock would be largely automated.

All shops should use the same system, allowing procedures to be standardised – bringing an additional benefit of staff being able to work at more than one shop.

Implement an Executive Information System (EIS)

An EIS sitting 'on-top' of the new integrated sales, stock and financial system would enable the new Chief Executive and other senior managers to produce tailored high-level information to support strategic decisions.

The software should facilitate the monitoring of Key Performance Indicators (KPIs) linked to Critical Success Factors (CSFs).

(b)   The key points from the Chief Executive's analysis of potential implementation problems are discussed below.

No project manager in place

There was a project manager in place who was responsible for the implementation of the new financial system, but that person has left and not yet been replaced.

The Chief Executive recognises the need to appoint a new project manager as soon as possible. He also believes the project manager should come from within S1K, rather than appointing an external person.

Appointing from within SK1 would ensure the new project manager was familiar with the organisation and the processes surrounding the existing finance system.

However, project management requires specific skills - there may not be a suitable individual within SK1 for the role. A specialist project manager appointed from outside SK1 should have the required skills and experience of similar implementations and may also bring a fresh perspective to the situation.

The proposed software does not fit existing business processes

The Chief Executive recognises that the new software does not fit existing business processes exactly, but he still believes it to be 'a good choice'. This belief is based on the fact that competitors use the software and that it is recognised as 'an industry best practice system'.

However, software and systems should facilitate efficient working practices and business processes. Changing processes to fit a particular type of software could actually introduce inefficiencies. This requires further investigation. On the other hand, it could be that due to its rapid growth S1K operates in an inconsistent and inefficient way, so a change in processes could be beneficial.

A possible complication in any review of the choice of software is that S1K may already be committed contractually to take the proposed software.

The implementation approach to adopt

The Chief Executive states that the previous project manager recommended a phased approach to implementation and drew up a timetable for implementation under this approach. The Chief Executive agrees that a phased approach is the best option as it would be the 'least problematic' for S1K.

A phased or modular changeover involves changing part of the system first, for example the receivables ledger, then changing other parts of the system over in stages. A phased approach could also take the form of implementing the whole new finance system in a particular location (such as a shop) at a time.

The phased approach is less risky than a direct approach as the area of change or upheaval is restricted. It allows for problems to be identified and corrected in a relatively restricted environment, before the system is introduced organisation-wide.

The phased approach is a good option for SK1 both as a risk management technique and to reduce the impact on staff already under pressure from takeovers and the change of Chief Executive.

(c)   The main individuals and groups S1K's Human Resources Department should target initially for training are:

The new project manager

Assuming the new project manager comes from within SK1, he or she will require training in project management skills.

Training should be provided by a specialist and the recipient should be free from the distractions of day-to-day work. Therefore, this should be held off-site.

S1K senior management

Successful implementation of IT projects requires support from the top of the organisation. SK1 senior management must understand the role of the new system and be seen to support the project.

Senior managers may require training to fully understand (and then be able to explain to staff) the benefits the system will bring. This training would probably best be provided in-house, to senior managers as a group, with the new project manager present. It should be provided by a combination of the software supplier and the new project manager, ideally with some input from the Chief Executive (given his background).

Head office finance staff

Head office finance staff will use the new system to consolidate shop results into organisation-wide financial statements. Depending upon how operations are structured, they may also provide a centralised accounts function (eg payables and receivables).

Even though this is an off-the-shelf package, the supplier should offer training options (for example a consultant) either as part of the contract or for an additional fee. As the software is widely used, private training courses may be available. An external trainer delivering training in-house may be the most appropriate option, followed up with 'on-the-job' training.

Shop staff

Staff operating in shops will need training to ensure they can process transactions efficiently, maintaining standards of customer service.

Training should cover operating procedures, data entry requirements, payment processing, system commands and security aspects (eg passwords).

This would best be achieved through a combination of an initial out of hours face-to-face session, and then on the-job training through the use of internal 'system champions' who have been trained by the software vendor in advance of other users. Online help, printed manuals and a telephone helpline should also be provided.

13 New system

Marking scheme

		Marks	
(a)	Up to 3 marks for each strategy referenced to the scenario	12	
	Up to 2 marks for justified recommendation	2	
			14
(b)	1 mark per relevant issue	5	
(c)	Up to 2 marks per correctly described type of maintenance	6	
			25

Our answer shows what we consider the most appropriate points to make. Other relevant points that answer the question would earn marks. However, irrelevant points that do not answer the question would not earn marks.

(a) The following **changeover strategies** are possible.

Direct changeover

This involves the total replacement of the old system by the new one at a particular point in time. The main advantage is that it is probably the cheapest strategy to use. Also, any confusion caused by the concurrent operation of two systems is minimised. However, a crucial disadvantage is that it places too much reliance on system testing, as there may be unforeseen problems which only emerge after implementation. Additionally, all staff must be trained at the same time, which may cause a certain amount of disruption.

Parallel running

Such a strategy involves running both systems at the same time for a certain period. This has the advantage that the results of the new system can be checked against the results of the old. Also, should the new system break down, then the old one can be run until the problem is sorted out. A disadvantage is that the extra time involved is considerable. This method may not be suitable for situations where not only has the system changed, but also the organisational structure in which it operates.

Pilot operation

In this case, the entire system is run in one location, or part of the system is run in all locations, so that any bugs can come to light before wholesale implementation. Once these difficulties have been ironed out, then each of the other locations can be changed over to the new system immediately.

Phased or staged implementation

This is a strategy which sets out a detailed timetable, so that each location is changed over separately. This has the advantage that short term disruption is minimised, in comparison to a direct changeover. Also, the change-over is easier to manage by systems professionals and management. Within phased implementation, individual locations may be switched over by parallel running or direct changeover as appropriate.

Recommendation

The appropriateness of any particular strategy depends on the context. In this case a crucial factor is that both the computer systems and the company's entire method of distribution are changing. Parallel running is not really possible, given that the two situations are so different. The same could be said both for a pilot operation and a strategy based on a phased implementation. **Direct changeover** is the only viable option.

(b) Whatever **implementation strategy** is adopted, the following issues will be crucial to its success:

- **System testing** before changeover.

- **File conversion**, with old files reconciled to new.

- Full staff **training**.

- Organisation of **backup** and **standby facilities**.

- Effective **project management**, to ensure smooth implementation.

(c) There are **three** main reasons for software maintenance.

- To **correct** errors or 'bugs' (corrective maintenance)

- To **meet changes** in internal operating procedures or external regulations (adaptive maintenance)

- To **make improvements** to the software (perfective maintenance)

Corrective maintenance

Testing procedures should identify most potential faults prior to installation. However, faults may not become apparent until certain combinations of conditions occur or if processing volumes exceed what was tested. Correction of these faults is known as corrective maintenance.

Adaptive maintenance

Adaptive maintenance is used to allow the system to respond to change whether within the organisation or the external environment.

External regulation often leads to mandatory changes in software, which can be quite extensive. A typical example is the change to various tax rates after the annual budget statement in the UK.

Perfective maintenance

Users may request enhancements to software which is not producing errors, but which could be made more user-friendly or improved in some other way. This may involve, for example, redesigning menu screens or switching to graphical user interfaces. This is known as perfective maintenance.

14 System implementation

Text reference. Chapter 4.

Top tips. There are many points you can make in both parts of the question. Therefore cover as many as you can but remember you won't need to go into too much detail. Use the question requirement and the mark allocation to establish the level of detail required.

Easy marks. *Kotter and Schlesinger's* theory is perfect to answer part (b) with. Stating six techniques will probably get you half marks.

(a)   **Role of user acceptance testing**

The role of user acceptance testing is to establish how well the system meets user needs and to identify any problems with the system in a realistic environment.

User acceptance testing is vital as a system may look great on paper and perform well when tested by analysts and programmers, but prove inefficient when used by users in the required operating environment.

User acceptance testing is concerned with the system performing as users expect (eg output/results are correct) and also with ease of use (usability).

Conduct of testing

Users could identify errors of logic, or identify relatively small changes (eg screen layout) that would enhance the user friendliness of the system. Testing should ultimately conclude with user sign-off – users accepting the system.

File conversion

This involves ensuring data to be held in the new system is in a suitable format. This process is likely to involve the conversion of data held in both existing computer and manual files.

System changeover

This involves the transfer from using the old system to the new one. The method of changeover is a key consideration (eg direct, parallel, phased or pilot). The most appropriate method will depend upon the individual circumstances (eg the trade-off between cost and risk).

Review and maintenance

After a suitable time following implementation, the process of system development should be reviewed. The review should look at a wide range of systems functions and characteristics.

Metrics may be used as part of this process. Systems evaluation may also use indirect methods such as monitoring the number of calls to a help desk.

During the review, an evaluation of the system is carried out to see whether the targeted performance criteria have been met and to carry out a review of costs and benefits.

The review should culminate in the production of a report and recommendations.

(b)   Kotter and Schlesinger (1979) identify six techniques to reduce resistance to change:

(i)   **Education and communication**

- Small group briefings
- Newsletters
- Management development
- Training

(ii)   **Participation and involvement**
- Small groups
- Delegates and representatives

(iii)   **Facilitation and support**

- One-on-one counselling
- Personal development
- Provision of organisational resources

(iv)   **Negotiation and agreement**

- Provision of rewards
- Collective bargaining

(v)   **Manipulation and co-optation**

- Influence staff that are positively disposed
- Buy-off informal leaders
- Provide biased information

(vi)   **Explicit and implicit coercion**

- Threaten staff with penalties
- Create sense of fear
- Victimise individuals to send a positive message to the rest

Note. Only two examples for each technique were required.

15 K1S

Marking scheme

		Marks
(a)	1 mark per valid point referenced to the scenario	15
(b)	Up to 2 marks per factor referenced to the scenario	10
		25

Our answer shows what we consider the most appropriate points to make. Other relevant points that answer the question would earn marks. However, irrelevant points that do not answer the question would not earn marks.

Outline Notes: Developing K1S's Information systems

To: Managing director

From: Management Consultant

Date: November 20X8

(a)   The following step-by-step approach is recommended to develop K1S's information system.

Identify the problem

The starting point should be the initial suggestion that 'things could be done better'. There should be a study and analysis of the organisation's information requirements.

Feasibility study

Following a review of the existing system, a range of possible alternative solutions should be identified. The costs and benefits of each solution should be considered. A decision should be made as to which is the most feasible (from a technical, operational, economic and social point of view).

Planning

A project team should be put together to plan the project. A leader with suitable experience and skills should be selected. A steering committee may be formed. An implementation plan should be developed and clear objectives and completion dates should be specified.

System investigation and analysis

K1S's existing system should be investigated and documented to assess existing problems and future requirements. This process examines why current methods are used, what alternatives might achieve the same, or better, results, and what performance criteria are required from the new system.

System design and development

Once the exact needs of the system are established the new system may be designed. Off-the-shelf packages may need to be amended to meet K1S's needs or bespoke software may need to be written from scratch using external developers.

System implementation

This stage involves program testing, file conversion, acquisition and installation of hardware and 'going live'. Due to the lack of an existing coherent system, problems caused by incomplete or inaccurate data will need to be addressed. There is a high risk to the business caused by changeover problems, therefore a period of parallel running is recommended.

Staff training and motivation

Staff who are to operate the system should receive training and the system's benefits should be 'sold' to them. This is to ensure the system operates as expected and contains accurate information. Staff who are not interested in the new system are unlikely to operate it effectively.

(b)   A number of factors associated with **staff training** on a new computer system are relevant to K1S:

Time available

K1S is a busy organisation, therefore staff may not have much time available for training. The main consideration is that customers should not be affected in any way. To keep the salons open, staff should be trained a few at a time. The system should not go live until all staff who need training have received it.

User skill levels

Staff have different skill levels due to the varying degrees of computerisation in each salon location. Some have not used a computer; others have but do not posses a full range of skills. Training must therefore take into account different abilities.

Who is trained on what?

The two considerations above may lead K1S to consider the fact that not all members of staff need to be trained on all systems. For example, an experienced stylist may need training on the booking system, but not on the accounts system. Training should only be given to those who are likely to use a given system.

Method

A number of options are available for training, from classroom-based courses to CD-ROMS and DVDs. The most suitable method should be selected taking into account suitability, feasibility and the budget.

Budget

The various training methods will vary in cost. K1S should take this into account but must also consider the effectiveness of the method. It would be false economy to choose a cheap training method if it is ineffective and causes customer dissatisfaction.

16 Objective test questions: Operations management 1

16.1 C   Quality refers to fitness for purpose, which means how suitable a product or service is for its intended use.

16.2 B   The balanced scorecard approach to quality measurement focuses on customer, operational and financial perspectives.

16.3 A   To gain ISO accreditation an organisation is required to submit documentation to show that their processes meet ISO requirements. The other options are not necessarily required.

16.4 D   Optimised production technologies focus on the removal of production bottlenecks.

16.5 B   In this paper, you have studied ABC as an inventory management method that concentrates effort on the most important items.

16.6 A   Kaizen seeks to improve quality by small, incremental steps. It does not seek radical changes (options B and C) and is not a problem solving technique (option D).

16.7
- To obtain the **best possible purchase prices** – bulk buying contracts
- To **improve quality in the future** – quality standards can be agreed
- To ensure **continuity of supply** during periods of limited availability
- To **tie the supplier to the organisation** - reducing the supply options of competitors

16.8
- **Organisational structure**: How supply interacts with other functions
- **Relationship portfolio**: How many suppliers? 'Partnership' or price-driven?
- **Cost-benefit**: Is the chosen supply strategy the most cost-effective?
- **Skills and competencies**: Do staff have the skills required to integrate?
- **Performance measures**: To monitor and control the strategy

17   Objective test questions: Operations management 2

17.1 D   Sustainability in operations management is primarily concerned with efficient use of resources.

17.2 B   In a demand network, products are developed in response to market signals (demand).

17.3 B   A manufacturer who focuses on developing new product features is product orientated.

17.4 D   Primary activities are those across the base of the value chain – the supporting or secondary activities being shown above these. The last primary activity is supporting products sold, that is service, so D is correct.

17.5 **Internal failure costs** are identified before the item reaches the customer.

- Cost of materials scrapped due to poor inventory control
- Cost of materials lost during production
- Cost of output rejected during inspection
- Cost of re-working faulty output
- Cost of reviewing product specifications
- Losses due to selling faulty output cheaply

Note. Only four examples were required.

17.6 **External failure costs** are identified after the item reaches the customer.

- Delivery of faulty products and replacements
- Operating a customer services section
- Repair or replacement
- Refunds

Significance

- Loss of 'quality' reputation
- Loss of future custom
- Damaged staff morale
- Bad PR

17.7 **Total Productive Maintenance (TPM)** reduces breakdowns and helps ensure production consistency. This will help Goldseek ensure uniform output and reduce waste. It therefore lowers the cost of quality. TPM also improves the accuracy of production schedules and therefore facilitates on-time order delivery – an important aspect of customer service quality.

18 Capacity, supply and demand

Text reference. Chapters 3, 5, 6 and 7

Top tips. Don't forget to use headers and short paragraphs to make your answer readable. Part (f) gives you the opportunity to be creative and use your imagination. You could have used any industry as an example, we used the car industry.

Easy marks. Where possible define the terms you are required to explain.

(a) **Inventory**

A **level capacity strategy** involves building up an inventory buffer to enable orders to be met from held inventory when demand exceeds capacity.

A **Just In Time (JIT)** approach involves producing goods (eg cars) when they are needed – eliminating the need to hold inventory.

The **build up of inventory** required under a level capacity strategy contradicts the no inventory approach required under JIT. Therefore, the two approaches are **incompatible**.

Under **JIT**, **production** is **driven** by **immediate demand**. The capacity management approach consistent with JIT is a **chase strategy** – which involves adjusting production levels to match demand. This would allow nil (or minimal) inventory, as required under JIT.

(b) **Demand**

Demand management strategies attempt to **influence demand** to reduce fluctuations to levels above or below capacity. One of the ways demand may be managed is through marketing. Therefore demand strategies influence marketing practices.

If **demand** is below capacity, marketing initiatives such as price incentives and advertising campaigns may be used to increase demand.

If **demand exceeds capacity**, it may be decided to reduce some marketing activity (eg advertising) and/or to promote orders in a future period rather than those requiring delivery in the short term (eg order next year's new model now).

Marketing may also be used to try and **distribute demand evenly** throughout the year, for example though seasonal offers and other incentives to increase demand in less busy periods (eg interest free finance).

(c) **Chase vs flexible**

Chase strategies involve adjusting activity levels in response to fluctuations in demand. The ability to significantly change production levels quickly and efficiently (while maintaining quality levels) requires a high level of organisational **flexibility.**

The need to react quickly to an ever changing environment has led to organisations adopting **flexible structures** such as project based teams and virtual or networked firms.

In many industries, **world class manufacturing techniques** are used to provide flexibility. Computer Aided Design, Computer Aided Manufacturing and JIT can all be used to achieve this.

Concepts such as **'economies of scope'** are important in this context, as they provide the flexibility required to change what is being produced in relation to relative changes in demand.

(d) **Services vs manufacture**

Service organisations differ from manufacturing organisations when considering capacity management in the following ways.

Production and consumption occur at the same time

Inventories of services can't be built up in quieter times, which makes the balancing of capacity and demand more difficult.

Greater interaction

The customer plays an active role in the delivery process. Customer service quality is integral to the customer experience.

Output is different each time

Each customer service interaction is different in some way eg different conversation, attitude etc. Achieving a consistently high level of output is more challenging.

Generally greater reliance on staff

Service delivery depends on the people delivering the service. The 'mood' of staff on the front line shouldn't adversely impact upon the customer experience.

Intangible output

This makes measuring the quality level of output more difficult as there is no physical product to inspect. Obtaining feedback of customer satisfaction is important.

(e)   ### Supply portfolios

An organisation creates a supply portfolio by purchasing raw materials and components from a number of suppliers rather than just one. The suppliers are chosen for their individual attributes which enable the buyer to maximise the benefits each offers.

Benefits of supply portfolios

Quality

Suppliers provide products of varying quality. Buyers can use variances in quality to produce 'premium' or 'economy' ranges of their own products.

Cost

Suppliers charge different prices for their products. Buyers can turn to cheaper suppliers to reduce their costs of production if necessary.

Supply

Suppliers are of different sizes and produce different levels of output. Buyers can therefore match order sizes to appropriately sized suppliers. For example, a small supplier that can only produce a few products a day would be unable to meet the requirements of a large order. However, they would be able to supply a small order that a larger organisation, which may set minimum order quantities, turns down.

Expertise

Suppliers offer varying levels of expertise and may, for example, be able to advise the buyer which components would be best for their product. Building relations with a number of suppliers therefore helps the buyer to make more informed buying decisions.

(f)   ### Assistance from information and communications technology

The following types of **information and communications technology** could be used by people/organisations trying to improve demand for cars.

Advertising on websites

The car manufacturer could use pop ups on sites used by their target market eg the Automobile Association.

'Buy now'

Individual car dealers may offer a 'buy now' facility on their website. However the value of the transaction and need to sign contracts/purchase agreements means some face to face contact will still be required.

User registration

The use of user registration on websites could be used to help identify and track potential customers. The website could also include promotional material and virtual vehicle tours and virtual test drives to encourage purchase.

Database

A database could be used to manage relationships with potential and existing customers (repeat purchase is very important – particularly with fleet sales).

Mobile phone or 'M' marketing

This may be used to target young, IT literate potential customers (eg if mobile telephone numbers were collected during website registration). 'Text back now to arrange a test drive of the NEW Series 3' or similar messages may be appropriate.

Email

This could be used in a similar way to the text message approach described above.

Search engine optimisation

Websites should be configured to produce high rankings on search engines such as Google, for example for users searching for 'new car London'. Paid-for listings can also be used.

19 W company

Text reference. Chapters 5, 6, 11

Top tips. Supply chain management has changed dramatically in recent times, and reference is often made to supply chain 'networks'. Clearly apply your knowledge of this, and BPR, to W's circumstances

Easy marks. You could have referred to Cousins' strategic supply wheel in your answer. For part (b) provide a definition of BPR, explain what process maps are, and show how the two work together.

Marking scheme

		Marks
(a)	Up to 2 marks for each relevant, explained point	10
(b)	Up to 2 marks for each relevant, explained point	10
(c)	Up to 2 marks for each relevant point explained point, maximum 5 marks	5
		25

Our answer shows what we consider the most appropriate points to make. Other relevant points that answer the question would earn marks. However, irrelevant points that do not answer the question would not earn marks.

(a)

Developments in strategic supply chain management

Supply chain management is concerned with the flow of goods and services through the organisation with the aim of making the firm more competitive.

Supply chain management is now viewed as **a strategic function** that impacts significantly on organisational performance. It involves organisations working more closely with suppliers, establishing a **mutually beneficial long-term relationship**.

Cousin's Strategic Supply Wheel provides a useful framework when considering how an organisation deals with relationships relevant to overall strategy and supply strategy. Cousin's research showed that the more **collaborative** the relationship between the organisation and its key suppliers the greater the degree of strategic alignment required.

Increasingly, organisations are recognising the need for and benefits of establishing close links with companies in the supply chain. Market and competitive demands are compressing lead times and businesses are **reducing inventories** and excess capacity. **Links between businesses in the supply chain are becoming tighter**. Shorter lead times and integrated IT systems are typical.

Improving W Company's competitive performance

Management of the supply chain and supply network is now seen as a potential source of **competitive advantage**.

By adopting a more strategic approach to supply chain management, W Company can improve its competitive performance through:

- Greater **coordination** across the global supply network. This will allow W to develop relationships with suppliers worldwide.
- **Partnering with other companies** in the supply network (organisational integration). Reliability, trust and collaboration is highly important. W may even consider reducing the number of suppliers it uses, so deeper relationships can be developed with a select few (perhaps selected using cost-benefit analysis).
- Being able to meet **demanding customer service and product performance standards**. Innovation in consumer goods is required if products are to remain attractive to consumers.
- If necessary, restructuring the organisation to better facilitate closer supplier relationships and control processes.

W Company could establish a **supply chain network**. This is an interconnecting group of organisations which relate to each other through linkages between the different processes and activities involved in producing products/services.

Organisations now often **outsource non-core activities**, such as the distribution. W may be able to benefit from adopting this trend. The benchmarking exercise undertaken by JH may have indicated that W's competitors are already doing so, and that W needs to catch up.

Efficiencies can also be attained by **applying technology** to dealings with suppliers, using electronic data interchange (EDI) – this 'paperless' communication is more efficient in terms of administration, and is quicker and cheaper than traditional ordering methods.

(b)

Process design

Process design involves analysing and seeking to understand the activities or processes that enable an organisation to function. The aim is to ensure that these activities or processes are designed so as to be as effective and efficient as possible. Process design can be applied to the development of new processes or (as with W Company) it can be applied to improve existing processes.

Two tools often used in the context of process design are Business process reengineering (BPR) and process maps.

The use of BPR

Business process reengineering (BPR) is the fundamental rethinking and radical redesign of business processes to achieve dramatic improvements in performance, such as cost, quality, service and speed.

W could use BPR to redesign its processes with the aim of working more efficiently (and bringing costs down). W should implement BPR systematically, following these key stages:

- Planning - understand what needs to be done to improve performance in line with company goals and customer needs
- Learning - examine existing processes and how they enable the company to currently function
- Redesign - if necessary, or eliminate if they cannot be made effective and efficient
- Implementation - of new processes

Hammer and Champy identify four themes of BPR that can be applied to W Company.

- Process reorientation. The focus should be on resources and tasks - can the way these interact be redesigned?
- Creative use of IT. For example could W Company use CAD and or CAM?
- Ambition. Don't be restricted, think widely. For example, could W adapt processes to enable it to sell direct to consumers?
- Challenge and break rules. Old rules may not apply to new processes. For example is a flatter organisation structure required?

BPR could also play a part to help bring about improvements in supply chain management.

BPR can be a costly process, so the benefits need to outweigh the cost of implementation and the ongoing cost of operating and working under the new processes.

The use of process maps

One way of analysing and representing processes is with the use of process maps. Process mapping aims to identify and represent the steps involved in a process, in visual form.

The use of process maps will help W Company design effective and efficient operations by:

- Describing the flow of materials, information and documents – what is happening, and why?
- Showing how W Company takes components (inputs) and transforms them into white goods (outputs)
- Displaying the tasks contained within the process
- Help establish how efficient the process is and identify any waste
- The map will demonstrate the relationships between the process steps

Changing systems and working methods (for example, via BPR) without understanding the underlying processes can lead to costly mistakes. It can also create conditions that make it difficult for staff to work effectively. Moreover, if W does not understand a process, it will not be able to improve it.

Process mapping will enable W to clearly define and understand current processes. It will help identify likely problem areas such as bottlenecks, delays or waste.

The knowledge that process mapping provides will help W Company to develop solutions and plan new, improved processes. It will help identify responsibilities and key stages in the supply chain.

(c)

An organisational code of ethics is intended to be a guide for employees on what constitutes acceptable behaviour. For example, the code may provide guidelines relating to the acceptance of gifts from clients.

At W Company, there has been illegal behaviour (misappropriation of funds) as well as unethical practices. Unethical practices may not necessarily be illegal, but would be considered by most people to be wrong. For example using child labour in developing countries may not be illegal, but many developed world consumers feel it is wrong and avoid purchasing goods manufactured this way.

A code of ethics could help reduce unethical behaviour at W company in a number of ways.

1. **Reduce the potential for ambiguity**. Ethical dilemmas are often ambiguous or open to interpretation. A clear code would reduce the potential for ambiguity.

2. **Establish a consensus**. The code should be developed through a consultation process involving management and employees. This will enable a consensus of what is acceptable behaviour to emerge.

3. **Procedure to report breach**. The code should include the procedures to follow to report a breach of the code. The increased likelihood of a 'whistleblower' report should deter some individuals from acting unethically.

4. **Clear consequence for a breach**. The code should include clear consequences for unethical behaviour. For illegal behaviour such as misappropriation of funds, the consequence should be dismissal.

5. **Training**. To ensure the code is understood and is effective training covering what the code means may be necessary. Management and employees must understand what is expected of them.

20 TQM and sourcing

> **Text reference.** Chapter 5.
>
> **Top tips.** You cannot attempt Part (c) until you have completed Part (b). Manage your time carefully, leaving enough to do yourself justice in the final part.
>
> **Easy marks.** Explaining supply portfolios in Part (a).

Marking scheme

		Marks
(a)	Up to 2 marks for explaining 'supply portfolio'	2
	1 mark for stating its relevance to PicAPie	1
		3
(b)	1 mark for correctly identifying each strategy from the scenario	4
	3 marks for evaluating each strategy	12
		16
(c)	2 marks per recommendation referenced to the scenario	6
		25

Our answer shows what we consider the most appropriate points to make. Other relevant points that answer the question would earn marks. However, irrelevant points that do not answer the question would not earn marks.

(a)   **Supply portfolios**

Organisations often source their raw materials from a **number of suppliers** for various strategic reasons. For example certain suppliers may produce a better **quality** of product, others may be cheaper on **price**, and suppliers may also be selected from a number of countries to **guard against the risk** of supplies from one country being affected by circumstances such as bad weather.

The particular **mix of suppliers** that an organisation uses is usually optimised so that it maximises the benefits they offer and minimises any risks involved in supply. This mix is known as a **supply portfolio**.

PicAPie uses a **number of suppliers** for **flour**, **meat and vegetables** and **plastic wrapping** so it can be said to operate a supply portfolio for these products. The **aluminium foil** is sourced from **one supplier** so the organisation does not operate a supply portfolio for this item.

(b)   **Single sourcing**

Aluminium foil is obtained from a single supplier – a sourcing strategy termed '**single sourcing**'.

The **advantages** of this strategy include:

- It is easy to develop and maintain a relationship with a single supplier – which is especially beneficial when the purchasing company relies on that supplier.

- A supplier quality assurance program can be implemented easily to help guarantee the quality of products – again mainly because there is only one supplier.

- Economies of scale may be obtained from volume discounts.

However, the **disadvantages** of this strategy are:

- PicAPie is dependent on the supplier – providing significant supplier power. Issues such as quality assurance may not be addressed quickly because the supplier is aware that there are few alternative sources of supply.

- PicAPie is vulnerable to any disruption in supply.

Multiple-sourcing

The **pastry shell flour** is obtained from a number of suppliers – a strategy known as **multiple-sourcing**.

The **advantages** of this strategy include:

- The ability to switch suppliers should one fail to provide the flour. Having suppliers in different countries is potentially helpful in this respect as poor harvests in one country may not occur in another.

- Competition may help to decrease price.

Disadvantages include:

- It may be difficult to implement a quality assurance program due to the time needed to establish it with different suppliers.

- Suppliers may display less commitment to PicAPie depending on the amount of flour purchased making supply more difficult to guarantee.

Delegated sourcing

A third party is given the responsibility for obtaining **meat and vegetables** – this is termed **delegated sourcing**.

The **advantages** of this method include:

- It provides more time for PicAPie to concentrate on pie manufacture rather than obtaining inputs. Internal quality control may therefore be improved.

- The third party is responsible for quality control checks on input – again freeing up more time in PicAPie. Where quality control issues arise, PicAPie can again ask the third party to resolve them rather than spending time itself.

- Supply may be easier to guarantee as the specialist company will have contacts with many companies.

Disadvantages include:

- Quality control may be more difficult to maintain if the third party does not see this as a priority.

- There will be some loss of confidentiality regarding the products that PicAPie uses, although if there are no 'special ingredients' then this may not be an issue.

Given the diverse sources of supply, PicAPie are probably correct using this strategy.

Parallel sourcing

The **plastic film** is obtained from two different sources utilising two different supply systems, this is termed **parallel sourcing**.

The **advantages** of this method include:

- Supply failure from one source will not necessarily halt pie production because the alternative source of supply should be available.

- There may be some price competition between suppliers.

Disadvantages include:

- PicAPie must take time to administer and control two different systems.

- Quality may be difficult to maintain, and as with multiple sourcing, it will take time to establish supplier quality assurance programmes. Given that some stock is surplus to requirements from other sources, quality control programmes may not be possible anyway.

(c)   **Recommendations**

PicAPie should make three key changes.

Look for a backup foil supplier

Given that there are few suppliers in the industry this strategy may be appropriate. However, there is no guarantee that the current supplier will not go out of business so the directors of PicAPie could look for alternative sources of supply to guard against this risk.

Introduce quality control for flour suppliers

PicAPie appears to have covered the risk of supply well by having multiple sources of supply. The issue of quality remains and PicAPie could implement some quality standards that suppliers must adhere to in order to keep on supplying flour.

Plastic film sourcing required addressing

The weakness in the supply strategy appears to be obtaining film from the Internet site – in that quality control is difficult to monitor. Changing to single sourcing with a supplier quality assurance programme would be an alternative strategy to remove this risk.

21 YO and MX

> **Text reference.** Chapters 5, 6, 11 and 12.
>
> **Top tips.** Don't spend too long on any one part of this question. As all parts are worth the same marks, treat them equally, giving them the same amount of attention.
>
> Strong answers to Part (a) will set the evaluation in the context of the relevant theory – in this case Porter's value chain. In Part (b) ensure you explain some background principles of TQM. In Part (c) think of ways to motivate employees and then expand on them. A selection of relevant points will earn you a pass in this part.
>
> **Easy marks.** Defining a value system in Part (a).

(a) **Value system**

A value system links the value chains of individual companies together. In terms of Porter, each company has a value chain including inbound logistics, production and outbound logistics. The outbound logistics of one company becomes the inbound logistics of another company.

In the scenario, YO provides clothes to MX so the outbound logistic system of YO is therefore linked to the inbound logistic systems of MX. Similarly, YO receives inputs from its own suppliers linking inbound logistics back to those suppliers.

Value chain management

Management of this supplier value chain between companies is essential to create and maintain competitive advantage. If YO fails to supply the correct goods, or supplies the correct goods late, then MX's sales will be affected. It is in the best interests of all companies in the supplier value chain to ensure products pass along the chain in a timely fashion and appropriate quality is maintained.

Current strategy

MX's current strategy regarding suppliers has been multiple sourcing – this means that the same inputs are obtained from a number of different suppliers. This decreases individual supplier power, as MX can choose which supplier to purchase from. However, YO is heavily dependent on MX – 80% of YO's sales being made to MX. This means MX has additional power over YO – YO cannot afford to lose MX as a customer. MX's policy of paying minimum prices and returning goods not up to specification is therefore not surprising.

New management

MX is now considering limiting the number of suppliers, improving the quality of inputs and paying more per garment purchased. This change indicates that MX wants to be more actively involved in the supply chain and improve product quality for the benefit of both MX and YO. MX is sacrificing some supplier power (few suppliers to purchase from) for a better supplier relationship. This strategy should help to provide more competitive advantage for YO/MX's products.

(b) **YO's current position**

Currently, YO has focused on producing clothes at a relatively low price, because its major customer, MX, has the strategy of selling large volumes at low prices. However, MX is now moving 'upmarket' which means that the company is attempting to sell goods of a higher quality at a higher price. This has the effect that MX expects a higher quality of inputs and is now rejecting inputs which are below this new quality standard.

New quality requirements

From YO's point-of-view, production at high quality but low price is difficult. Provision of a higher quality output implies that the customer is prepared to pay for this quality, and it does not appear that MX is prepared to raise prices at present. YO therefore needs to raise quality for the same price. One method that some of MX's suppliers have used to do this is Total Quality Management (TQM), which is a technique that YO can consider using.

Quality system

YO will need to implement a three stage system to **monitor** the quality of clothes produced.

1. **Inspection** of the final product to detect quality errors

2. **Set quality standards** and assess performance against those standards

3. **Extend quality management** to all areas of the company, not just focus on production. For example, ensuring that design quality is maintained/improved.

Factors for the successful use of TQM include:

Quality culture

A culture of quality is required involving all staff from senior management to production workers. Commitment will be obtained because MX is YO's major customer, so all management levels will be committed to success of TQM.

Empowerment/training

All employees are encouraged to avoid mistakes (rather than detecting them), and are empowered to improve quality where they can. This also means that YO will provide training for employees in how to implement and use TQM techniques.

Continuous improvement

Improving quality is seen as an ongoing process, not a one-off change. Policies such as quality circles and communication of quality objectives will be required to ensure the ongoing success of TQM.

(c)   The changes YO must implement can be considered as follows.

Human Resource practices

YO will be changing the focus of production from cost to quality. This means that HR practices must focus on quality improvement, not cost minimisation. Specific changes that can be expected include:

- **Staff training** on how to improve the quality of products, including TQM techniques.

- **Remuneration packages** to focus on the achievement of quality, not quantity, of output. Many clothes manufacturers pay production staff on a piece-rate. YO needs to consider focusing some element of remuneration on attaining quality standards.

- Attempting to **retain workers** who can attain the quality standards necessary within YO. Provision of benefits such as more holidays or wage increases each year will assist this objective.

- **Recruitment of staff** who are already familiar with the concepts of TQM. This will limit training time (and cost) for YO.

- **Staff appraisals** to be linked to TQM targets to show the importance of these measures in YO.

22 Electro

Marking scheme

		Marks
(a)	1 mark per valid point in explanation of the traditional approach to quality	3
(b)	1 mark for explaining each category of cost	4
	1 mark per relevant example	4
		8
(c)	Up to 2 marks for explaining 'lean production	2
	Up to 2 marks per relevant improvement referenced to the scenario	12
		14
		25

Our answer shows what we consider the most appropriate points to make. Other relevant points that answer the question would earn marks. However, irrelevant points that do not answer the question would not earn marks.

(a)   **Traditional approach to quality**

Inspection was the main traditional approach to quality. It is based on the following aspects.

- There is an optimal level of quality effort that minimises total quality costs.

- There is a point beyond which spending more on quality yields a benefit that is less than the additional cost incurred.

- Diminishing returns therefore set in beyond the optimal quality level.

(b)   **Categories of quality costs**

The four categories of quality costs are outlined below.

Prevention costs

These are costs that are incurred to prevent defects before the production process is complete.

An example relevant to an electrical goods manufacturer would be the cost of staff time spent double checking machine settings before commencing a production run.

Appraisal costs

These are costs associated with establishing whether quality has been achieved.

At an electrical goods manufacturing plant, an example of an appraisal cost would be the detailed inspection of a number of components from every batch produced.

Internal failure costs

These are costs incurred fixing a sub-standard product before the product or service is delivered.

An example at an electrical goods manufacturer would be the reworking of a batch of components found to have been produced using slightly incorrect machine settings (assuming the problem was discovered on inspection before delivery to the customer).

External failure costs

These are costs incurred fixing a sub-standard product after the product or service has been delivered.

An example relevant to an electrical goods manufacturing operation would be paying for a sub-standard batch of components to be transported back from the customers' premises, and the cost of producing a replacement batch.

(c) **Lean production**

Lean production is a philosophy of production that aims to minimise the amount of resources (including time) used in all activities of an enterprise. It involves identifying and eliminating all non-value-adding activities.

Lean production at Electro

Lean production can lead to many improvements at a manufacturing plant, however the most relevant to Electro are:

Integrated single piece continuous workflow

Electro's current factory floor plan is disjointed with equipment and sub-assemblies being moved from one location to another. If a continuous work flow around the factory is created (ie where one process finishes the next begins) time and other resources which are currently being wasted will be saved.

Quick changeovers of machines and equipment

Under a lean system, equipment and machines are changed or turned around quickly to save time. This means there are no delays during each manufacturing process and the system becomes much smoother. This would be a great improvement on Electro's current system where there is considerable downtime during each process. However, it is likely to require investment in new equipment.

Just in time (JIT) processing

A key element of any lean system is JIT processing. Under this system, a sub-assembly which moves to a production operation, is processed immediately, and moves immediately to the next operation. This does not occur in Electro's current system as sub-assemblies are created before they are needed. This wastes factory floor space.

Minimal inventories at each stage of the production process

Electro's current system creates inventory at each production stage as a result of them being created before they are needed. Lean systems do not tolerate inventory and therefore sub-assembly production is driven by the next process. Following such a system will save Electro wasting valuable floor space through using it to store units of production.

Production based on orders rather than forecasts

Under lean systems, production is driven by customer demand. It is this demand which 'pulls' each sub-assembly through the production process. Under Electro's current system, production is driven by sales forecasts rather than actual demand. This has created the problems of over or under production which the company has experienced. These problems will be reduced or eliminated if the organisation switches to a lean system.

Defect prevention rather than inspection and rework by building quality into the process

The aim of lean systems is to build quality into the product rather than to detect poor quality through inspection as Electro is currently does. By building quality into each process, sub-standard output will be reduced or eliminated, reducing the organisation's overall 'cost of quality'.

23 DOH

(a)   DOH is facing a number of quality problems.

Loss of business

A lack of quality in the products it sells may result in DOH losing future contracts to competitors who can produce goods with zero or few defects. The sub-contractor that DOH used has demonstrated that other organisations produce the same products but with better quality.

Penalty charges

A major customer has introduced penalty charges that DOH must pay if it supplies defective goods. Depending on the level of defects, DOH may suffer from reduced profitability on this contract, affecting its financial performance.

Workforce attitude

DOH's workforce believes that defects are inevitable. This is likely to create a self-fulfilling prophecy where defects will happen. DOH will find it very difficult to reduce the incidence of defects whilst this attitude prevails.

High costs of quality

DOH has high costs of quality. Such costs include, scrap, re-working, the salaries of the quality control inspectors and the penalty charges. These costs could be reduced if the organisation minimises the number of defective products.

Quality control rather than quality assurance

DOH's production systems do not appear to create quality, the emphasis seems to be on controlling it.

Quality control is performed at the wrong stage in production. If the workers took responsibility for ensuring quality whilst the products were being made then the costs of quality would be substantially reduced or eliminated.

Systems that create quality are fundamentally better at reducing defects than those which attempt to control it and are known as quality assurance.

Inspectors

No matter how hard the quality control inspectors work they cannot check every product and therefore there is still a risk that defective products will be sold. In the current climate this risk is unacceptable, adding to the argument that quality should be built in, not inspected in.

No across the board commitment

Quality needs to be a priority in all areas of DOH. This includes the product design stage, the sourcing of materials, the machinery used in the production process, staff training and how operations are performed generally.

(b)   DOH's managing director has taken a number of steps to address the organisation's quality problems.

Acceptance of the problem

The MD has accepted that quality is a problem within the organisation and has taken steps to find a solution. If the company does not accept that a problem exists it cannot move forward. However, he needs to ensure the workforce of DOH also see his view.

Taking advice

The MD sought advice from the local government trade and industry office and has learned from other manufacturing organisations about how they deal with the issue of quality. The MD needs to go further and take advice from those employed within DOH. The middle managers, quality inspectors and the workers in general may all have ideas of how to improve things but have not been given the opportunity to let him know.

Making quality a strategic issue

By involving senior managers in his vision of improving quality the MD has made it a strategic issue, whereas before it was just an operational issue for the quality inspectors. The fact that he is not looking for a quick fix indicates how seriously the issue is being taken.

Producing a clear plan

A clear plan for change has been put forward called 'putting quality first'. This sets out the objectives and communicates the aim of the programme. This is an important step – people know now what the change aims to achieve.

Detailing how the objectives will be achieved

The MD has identified that quality will be improved by training, teamwork and a review of certain roles within the organisation. In particular, the need for middle managers is questionable and the role of the quality inspectors is in doubt if the workforce builds quality into their work.

Getting senior management support

Senior managers support the plan and this is vital for it to succeed. However, it must be 'sold' to the workforce and correctly implemented for it to be successful. Job losses and shifting responsibility for quality to the workforce may be subjected to initial resistance.

24 Objective test questions: Marketing 1

24.1 D A marketing orientation involves structuring an organisation's activities around the needs of the customer.

24.2 A In terms of a PESTEL analysis, 'P' standards for political.

24.3 A The government is not considered to be a customer of a charity. Beneficiaries, supporters, regulators and stakeholders (including trustees) are.

24.4 C A shakeout would occur between market growth and market maturity (shaking some of the weaker 'players' out of the market).

24.5 **Viral marketing** involves the use of pre-existing social networks to spread brand awareness using video clips and 'Flash games' etc.

Guerrilla marketing is unconventional and involves taking people by surprise and 'creating a buzz' in unexpected places. Publicity stunts are an example.

24.6 **Experiential marketing** involves creating an emotional connection between a person and a brand, product or idea. The person then makes a conscious decision that they want to make a purchase.

This differs from the **traditional marketing** approach where a product or service is directly 'sold' to the customer.

24.7 A **brand** is a name, term, sign, symbol or design intended to identify the product of a seller and to differentiate it from those of competitors. It is important because it is a key element of marketing and corporate strategy - it generates revenue and therefore has a financial value.

25   Objective test questions: Marketing 2

25.1   D   Undifferentiated marketing involves producing a single product and getting as many customers as possible to buy it. There is no market segmentation.

25.2   C   Skim pricing, otherwise known as market skimming, involves setting an initially high price for a product to take advantage of buyers who are prepared to pay it.

25.3   B   The aim of depth interviews is to explore customers' unconscious attitudes and motives for behaviour.

25.4   C   Perishability refers to the fact that services cannot be stored – for example an appointment at a hair salon. This makes anticipating and responding to levels of demand crucial.

25.5   An organisation's **promotion mix** consists of the blend of promotional tools that is considered appropriate for a given marketing campaign. For example, advertising, sponsorship, branding and direct marketing. However the process is very much an art and an experienced marketer will very often make the choice intuitively.

25.6   **Internal marketing** involves informing, training and motivating employees to support the organisation's external marketing activities. It aids employee understanding of how their tasks, and how they perform them, create and deliver customer value. Therefore, the success or failure of an organisation's external marketing efforts can be influenced by its internal marketing.

25.7   Using the **BCG matrix**, MNA's products can be classified as:

Jupiter – Star

Mars – Question mark

Pluto – Dog

Neptune – Cash cow.

26 V

> **Text reference**. Chapters 8, 9, 10, 11, 12.
>
> **Top tips**. Although this question focuses on marketing you are also required to discuss HR implications. You should always be prepared for questions such as this that cover a range of syllabus areas.
>
> **Easy marks.** You could probably answer Parts (d) and (e) without textbook knowledge providing you use the Internet regularly.

(a)   The **traditional marketing mix** includes **Product**, **Price**, **Promotion** and **Place**. Each of these factors play an important part in the overall offering to customers. V's proposed approach can be understood in this context.

Product

V's products are good quality, fun products with a strong brand. It is important the cosmetics offered are consistent with the established reputation of the brand.

Price

Pricing is competitive, but not the cheapest (ie affordable to most). An important decision is whether the 'list price' will include padding to enable agents to offer discounting. Website sales may be offered at a lower price – although this may make party purchases less attractive to customers.

Promotion

V will rely on word of mouth, public relations (such as the radio interview mentioned in the scenario) and the strength of the brand.

Place

V's distribution strategy is to use one level marketing (the cosmetic associates) and some web sales. This relies upon the skill of associates and user acceptance of e-commerce. V also needs efficient transportation options (eg partner a courier business) to ensure order fulfilment.

The 'fifth P', **people**, is relevant to the distribution strategy explained above. Further 'people issues' are covered in part (b).

(b)   **V has built a strong brand**. The **reputation** of V must be protected. Allowing cosmetic associates (who aren't employees) to use the V name/reputation carries considerable risk of damaging the brand.

The **human resource implications** of this include:

Agent selection

Ensuring cosmetic associates (ie agents) have the skills and attitude required is essential. Selection criteria should include a sense of fun, honesty, business awareness and trustworthiness. Formal selection procedures including an interview and reference checking by V HR staff are an important control.

Training

Training of cosmetic associates must be thorough and comprehensive. It should include how to arrange parties, how to ensure they provide a fun customer experience, sales techniques and product knowledge. Specific training will also be required for those dealing with orders/queries submitted via the website or SMS (text).

Remuneration

Cosmetic agents remuneration must be structured in a way that provides motivation/incentive, but without resulting in strong-arm sales techniques. Commission may also be linked to pricing – for example associates may be given the flexibility to sell at a lower price by reducing their commission.

Monitoring and control

On-going monitoring and control of associates is important to enable any potential problems to be identified before too much damage is done. Customer satisfaction surveys/questionnaires could be useful – as could the use of employed 'area supervisors' who visit or speak to associates and customers.

(c) **Direct marketing** is a concept that involves the producer of a product interacting directly with the end customer or consumer. The approach can be summed up as 'cutting out the middle-man'.

Channel

This is sometimes referred to as a 'zero level channel', as there are zero levels between supplier and the end customer.

Internet

The Internet has enabled more businesses to utilise direct marketing. For example, an airline such as British Airways may sell tickets direct to the public via its own website (selling flights via a general travel website isn't 'pure' direct marketing as this involves an intermediary – even if that intermediary happens to be based on the web).

Marketing mix

Using direct marketing has **implications for the marketing mix** – for example promotion can target web users. Order fulfilment (ie actually delivering the product) is key.

(d) **Advantages** of the **Internet** as a marketing channel include the following:

- **Communication** is **quick** allowing rapid response to customer orders/queries

- The **range of tasks** able to be performed eg promotion, display products, e-commerce

- Enables **quick price** and **feature comparison** for customers

- Can **lower costs** through reduced need for physical outlets

- Provides an **opportunity for global reach** even for very small organisations

- **Facilitates information collection** and **developing customer databases** for future promotions

- **Customer convenience** as it may be accessed from home or work at any time

(e) V could use **Internet** in the following ways.

E-commerce

A website with an e-commerce capability would enable orders to be submitted and paid for on-line (using credit and debit cards). Efficient order fulfilment is vital.

Product information

The website could also be used to provide detailed product information to customers, for example the ingredients of different cosmetic products (particularly relevant to those with allergies) provide cosmetic advice and related discussion groups.

Corporate information

General information about V as a group and about V cosmetics could also be communicated in this way – helping to cultivate the idea of a 'fun' organisation.

Promotion

The site could be used for promotion using web banners and could include links to 'partners' sites and a search facility (eg access to Google from within V's site).

Target marketing

Micro-site capability for specific target audiences or cosmetic needs could be established.

(f)   **Ethics** is concerned with **right and wrong** – acting **responsibly** and with a sense of **fairness**. The main ethical issues associated with Vs proposal are:

- **Will the cosmetics be tested on animals** – and if so will associates and customers be informed?

- **Where and how will the products be produced**? Will this involve factories in developing countries – what about employment conditions, worker remuneration, waste disposal?

- **Are associates treated fairly**? What mark-up is V making?

- **Is it acceptable to target customers through mobile phones**? This could be seen as intrusive and an abuse of personal information.

- **Is party selling ethical**? V should consider the blurring of business and pleasure and the use of alcohol at the parties. Are people pressured into attending and then made to feel they should 'join in' and buy?

27 CW

Text reference. Chapters 8, 9 and 10.

Top tips. You are told your answer to part (a) must not cover the application of the marketing mix and market research options (as these were covered in the first meeting). There are many possible aspects of marketing you could include, for example adopting a marketing orientation, the use of branding, relationship marketing and the use of experiential marketing.

Part (b) requires you to draw upon your knowledge of market segmentation and apply it to CW. Ensure you cover both aspects of part (c) - identifying the promotional activities and explaining possible ethical concerns.

Easy marks. Don't throw marks away in part (a) by covering aspects you were told to avoid! Explaining what segmentation is, and the processes involved, would earn a couple of easy marks in part (b). Identifying two types of promotional activity will earn marks in part (c).

Marking scheme

		Marks
(a)	Up to 2 marks for each relevant, explained aspect of marketing, related to CW	10
(b)	Up to 2 marks for each relevant, explained process or implication of segmentation /targeting related to CW	10
(c)	Half a mark for each promotional activity identified	1
	Up to 2 marks for each explained ethical concern for each activity	4
		5
		25

Our answer shows what we consider the most appropriate points to make. Other relevant points that answer the question would earn marks. However, irrelevant points that do not answer the question would not earn marks.

(a)

Five aspects of marketing that could be helpful to CW are explained below.

Adopt a marketing orientation

Adopting a marketing orientation involves identifying customer needs and then ensuring these needs are satisfied. CW has a number of different stakeholder groups that could be considered customers. The needs of donors, volunteers and of people who will benefit from the charity's work must all be identified and met. By satisfying the needs of these groups, CW is likely to achieve its overall objectives.

Partnering with commercial organisations ('cause marketing')

CW could attempt to form a close relationship with a number of businesses. Suitable organisations should be identified and approached with the aim of co-operating and collaborating on the running of fundraising events, and perhaps the running of the charity. The business organisation benefits through being seen as a good corporate citizen (Corporate Social Responsibility).

Branding

CW could use branding to help it stand out from other charities by establishing a distinctive identity that communicates its core values. A distinctive logo incorporating clean water and/or healthy crops, with a suitable strapline, would help keep CW in the forefront of people's minds. As water is such a basic commodity, CW could emphasise that every donation really does make a difference, giving donors and volunteers a reason to choose CW over other charities.

SWOT analysis

The general strategic technique of SWOT analysis could be utilised by CW. The SWOT exercise should reveal internal strengths and external opportunities that marketing activities should focus on. New income streams may be identified, and ideas generated from considering the actions of competitors.

Work more closely with key individual donors ('relationship marketing')

CW could identify donors who donate significant sums and/or donate regularly and seek to develop this relationship further (investment in CW's IT systems would be required to facilitate this). A group could be established, for example 'Friends of CW' who are consulted and communicated with, increasing their involvement with CW - with the ultimate aim of increasing revenue both directly from these individuals and indirectly from the insights they provide.

(b)

The process of market segmentation

Market segmentation recognises that every market consists of groups of potential buyers (or in this case donors) with different needs and different buying (or donating) behaviour.

The process of market segmentation subdivides the market into distinct groups, each group made of homogenous members who react in a similar way to marketing activity (to a distinct marketing mix). Therefore, a different marketing approach (mix) can be devised for each market segment.

The process of segmentation for CW would involve identifying groups of donors who react to marketing activity in different ways.

The implications of market segmentation for CW

The implications of market segmentation and targeting for CW are firstly that it needs to analyse the total potential market for charitable support in Statesland and identify specific groups within this, and secondly that CW needs to decide upon an appropriate marketing mix to target each group.

Factors that CW should consider as criteria for segmentation include:

- Individual or organisation
- Gender
- Age
- Occupation and income
- Lifestyle
- Geographical location

The process of targeting

Targeting would involve CW deciding which market segments to aim its marketing efforts towards. The process requires measuring and comparing the potential of segments, and considering how CW could reach each segment.

When selecting which segments should be targeted, questions CW needs to ask include:

- Can the segment be measured?
- Is the segment big enough?
- Is the segment stable?
- Do segments respond differently?
- Can the segment be reached cost effectively?

The implications of targeting for CW

External sources such as national statistics may help establish levels of charitable giving and provide an indication to the potential of a segment.

When devising an appropriate marketing mix the traditional 4Ps (product, promotion, place and price) and the three 'extra Ps' (people, process and physical evidence) should all be considered.

To target specific market segments CW's marketing activities will need to be more sophisticated, rather than simply using undifferentiated marketing (targeting the whole market with one marketing mix). It's likely that CW will decide to follow a differentiated (targeting several segments with distinctive mixes unique to each) approach rather than restricting itself to a single market segment with a single mix (concentrated approach).

(c)

Two types of promotional activity CW may consider using are **television advertising** and **viral marketing**.

Television advertising

Television advertising would involve producing an audio-visual commercial and purchasing broadcasting slots to air this on selected television channels.

Possible ethical concerns of television advertising

Television advertising is expensive and could be seen as inappropriate and wasteful for a charity that prides itself on low overheads. Donors may resent a proportion of their donation paying for advertising. Television advertisements often also tend to play on people's emotions to encourage them to donate, which some may see as unethical.

Using viral marketing as a promotion tool

Viral marketing involves the use of social networks to further marketing objectives. CW could set up a page on Facebook and Twitter, with links to a site such as Justgiving that allow donors to donate online. Video clips could be used to show the good work being done by CW. Individuals should be encouraged to email links and information to members of their individual network.

Possible ethical concerns of using viral marketing

An online presence on sites such as Facebook could be seen as an attempt to engage with children or adolescents, which some may see as unethical. It's unlikely that children could donate online as this would require a debit or credit card, but they could be encouraged to persuade their parents to donate – and to volunteer in shops.

The use of viral marketing and in particular social networking sites could also be seen to trivialise matters of life and death. It could also result in unwanted email ('SPAM') through the use of 'tell a friend' links.

28 Marketing action plan

(a)   **Changes at SX**

The changes at SX (increased use of technology, increased customer focus, new preparation and packaging equipment and more drivers) have implications for the marketing action plan. These implications are discussed below.

Product related issues relevant to the marketing action plan

SX sandwiches are currently perceived as fresh and high quality. Increased automation and packaging may require SX products to be more standardised (eg consistent sizes to allow automated packaging).

How these changes will affect coffee and fruit juice sales also needs to be considered. For example, could SX branded packaged juice be introduced? This may have other implications, for example antagonising other packaged juice suppliers who may attempt to influence retailers.

What are the sales targets/objectives (both in total and for different products – and across different market sectors)?

Place related issues relevant to the marketing action plan

Distribution is an essential element of the marketing mix for SX. To ensure freshness, products have to be delivered as soon as possible following production.

The earlier in the day products are delivered the more likely they are to sell (due to increased shelf time).

Satellite navigation software including vehicle positioning could be installed at the depot and in vehicles to allow delivery/driver tracking. Customers could be given the opportunity to access this information via an extranet.

How will distribution targets/objectives be set and how will they be measured? Asking drivers to gather feedback and increase sales is likely to reduce the number of deliveries each driver can perform.

Promotion related issues relevant to the marketing action plan

Increased automation and packaging may mean SX products need to be repositioned slightly – for example as good quality and good value. Home baked snacks may not be consistent with the increased use of food preparation equipment.

How will the new format products be promoted – is a launch required? If so, what should this entail?

Who should SX aim its promotion and brand awareness at (retailers, 'final customers' or both?) and what promotion channels are appropriate (eg radio, TV, newspaper, brochures, websites). Different channels may be required for different target audiences (eg trade magazines for petrol station operators).

What are the targets/objectives for promotion and how will they be measured? Isolating and measuring the effect of different promotional activities is difficult.

(b)   **Increased brand awareness** would have the following benefits for SX.

Product differentiation

Branding conveying a lot of information very quickly and concisely. This would help the general public to readily to identify SX's products, thereby helping to create customer loyalty and increase sales.

Advertising

Branding maximises the impact of advertising for product identification and recognition. Therefore SX would receive a greater return on its advertising investment.

Price differentials

Branding reduces the importance of price differentials between goods and would help SX to justify its premium prices.

Brand extension

Branding supports brand extension or stretching. This means SX could introduce other products to the brand range and 'piggy back' them onto the products already known to the customer.

Personal selling

A good brand eases the task of personal selling, by enhancing product recognition. This would help support the role of the driver in finding new outlets for SX's products.

(c)   The following **price setting strategies** may be followed.

Market penetration

The organisation sets a relatively low price for the product or service in order to stimulate growth of the market and/or to obtain a large share of it. This strategy was used by Japanese motor cycle manufacturers to enter the UK market. UK productive capacity was virtually eliminated and the imported Japanese machines could then be sold at a much higher price and still dominate the market.

Market skimming

Skimming involves setting a high initial price for a new product in order to take advantage of those buyers who are ready to pay a much higher price for it. A typical strategy would be initially to set a premium price and then gradually to reduce the price to attract more price sensitive segments of the market. This strategy is really an example of price discrimination over time. It may encourage competition, and growth will initially be slow.

Early cash recovery

Under this method the objective is to recover the investment in a new product or service as quickly as possible and achieve a minimum payback period. The price is set to facilitate this objective. After recovery, the product or service is 'milked' for as long as possible.

Product line promotion

This pricing strategy focuses on profit from the range of products which the organisation produces rather than treating each product as a separate entity. The product line promotion objective will look at the whole range from two points of view.

Recommendation. Given the circumstances, a policy of **market penetration** is recommended. As the market is price sensitive, lowering prices should increase sales. As unit costs fall as sales increases SX can afford to reduce its prices to achieve it.

The **lower prices** set could be enough to **put off the potential competitor** from entering the market.

Alternative approach

We recommend using the four strategies mentioned above as you can make lots of points on them. The following three strategies are equally valid but you may struggle to make enough points.

Cost-plus pricing. A firm may set its initial price by marking up its unit costs by a certain percentage or fixed amount.

Target pricing. A variant on cost-plus where the company tries to determine the price that gives a specified rate of return for a given output.

Price discrimination. Different prices are given to different buyers. However, the danger is that price cuts to one buyer may be used as a negotiating lever by another.

---

29 Consumer purchasing

> **Text reference**. Chapters 8, 9 and 10.
>
> **Top tips**. Don't worry if your answer to Part (a) is based around a different decision making process – there is no one single correct answer. If your answer is reasonable, logical and answers the question asked you will score well.
>
> In Part (b), you may have identified a wide range of factors. Again, don't worry if your answer does not match ours as many different answers could earn good marks on this question.
>
> **Easy marks**. Identifying benefits of marketing in Part (c).

Marking scheme

			Marks
(a)	1 mark per correctly identified stage in the decision making process	5	
			5
(b)	1 mark per relevant factor identified	4	
	1 mark per relevant point in support of each factor	max 6	
			10
(c)	2 marks for explaining 'marketing'	2	
	2 marks per relevant, explained benefit	8	
			10
			25

Our answer shows what we consider the most appropriate points to make. Other relevant points that answer the question would earn marks. However, irrelevant points that do not answer the question would not earn marks.

(a)   **Five decision making stages are identified below.**

 Need recognition

The customer perceives a want or a problem that must be satisfied

 Search

This is a search for information on solutions to the problem identified in step 1.

 Alternative evaluation

The search process identifies various ways in which the problem can be solved. These alternatives are evaluated.

 Purchase

The **intention to purchase** is translated into action unless unforeseen circumstances intervene to prevent or postpone the purchase decision.

 Evaluation

After purchase, the customer will use the product and continue to **compare performance** against expectations.

(b)   There are **four main groups of factors** that will influence a buyer such as Mr P.

Social factors

Social factors relate to social groupings which a consumer belongs to as well as trends in society which influence buying patterns. Social factors will include the buyer's peer group and the effect of mass media.

For Mr P the main social factors are his perceptions of the different makes of car and those of his peer group at the golf club regarding what is an acceptable car to drive. Other factors influencing the decision will include whether the car provides an appropriate status and image.

Cultural factors

Cultural factors include the values attitudes and beliefs held by people that help them function within society. Cultural factors change between different countries, eg smoking is accepted in restaurants in some countries but not in others. There are many different cultural factors such as religion, language, law and politics and social organisations. Depending on the beliefs and principles held in each of these areas, different individuals will make different purchase decisions.

Mr P may well be influenced by the look and feel of the car – hence the test drive to show him how the car drives. His environmental concerns may result in him choosing a car with low exhaust emissions.

Personal factors

Personal factors include things such as age, family including number and age of children, economic circumstances and lifestyle.

Family obviously affects Mr P – this is the main reason for purchasing a different car. Mr P's economic circumstances indicate he can afford a large car while other lifestyle benefits such as being able to transport his golf clubs easily will reinforce the decision by showing other personal benefits of a large car.

Psychological factors

The buyer will be also be influenced by:

- **Motivation** – that is how much the purchase needs to be made. The theories of Maslow and Herzberg discuss this area in more detail. Mr P will be motivated because his children will be reminding him of the need to change his car.

- **Perception** – that is the way purchasers view a specific product, which is in turn influenced by their past experience. For example, Mr P is interested in purchasing a Yotoda car, presumably because he thinks that is a good brand.

- **Beliefs** – the thoughts held about an object or brand. Mr P may well believe that some makes of car are more reliable.

(c) **Benefits of marketing to business organisations, consumers and society**

Marketing

Marketing is directed at satisfying needs and wants through exchange processes. The core concepts of marketing are needs, wants, demands, products, exchange, transactions and markets that will benefit the individual, consumers, organisations and society.

Managing demand

Marketers must be able to manage the level, timing and composition of demand from these different beneficiaries to satisfy their needs and wants. For instance IKEA and McDonald's have adopted the broader marketing concept on a global scale through understanding and responding to the changing needs of their customers.

Improve efficiency

Modern marketing is guided by a number of converging philosophies. The production concept holds that the consumer favours products which are available at low cost and that marketing's task is to improve production efficiency and bring down prices. The marketing concept holds that a company should research the needs and wants of a well defined target market and deliver the desired satisfactions, which is accompanied by long-run societal well being.

Customer retention

In marketing led organisations all employees share the belief that the customer is all important and that building lasting relationships is key to customer retention. A company's sales are derived from content existing customers and attracting new customers and this benefits the livelihoods of the employees and suppliers and their staff.

Customer loyalty and reduced price sensitivity

Successfully adopting a marketing approach should improve customer retention and minimise additional costs. A satisfied customer buys more, stays loyal longer, talks favourably to others, pays less attention to competing brands and is less price sensitive.

Benefits to consumers

The benefits described above result in higher quality products and service levels for consumers. For example, IKEA and McDonald's divert much of their energies to ensuring that customers repeatedly return to them satisfied and content with their offering.

Benefits to society

A society with a higher number of products and services that satisfy customer needs should be more efficient. Success breeds success, and financial success means increased taxation revenue to fund government services such as education and health.

30 Marketing, segmentation and ethics

Text reference. Chapters 8 and 9.

Top tips. There are several approaches you could have used to analyse CM's position, for example, a SWOT or PESTEL analysis. Watch how long you spend on Parts (a) and (b). They are 10 marks each so spend equal amounts of time on them.

Strong answers to part (a) will have substantial breadth to them. The scenario gives you plenty of potential issues to cover such as the competition, which creates challenges for the organisation, and an ethical dilemma, concerning marketing to children.

Easy marks. You should be able to think of five benefits of segmentation in Part (c) without too much trouble.

(a)   **Situation analysis**

Market position

CM has positioned its own brand products as premium brands, it is clearly spending considerable sums of money on television advertising, something economy or bargain brands do not do.

Target market

The company is **targeting children** as it is they who the television advertising and free gifts are aimed at. It is therefore taking a concentrated marketing approach since it is attempting to produce the ideal product for a single segment of the breakfast food market.

The targeting of children is increasingly being seen as unethical. A complete rethink of marketing strategy may be required.

Sales and competition

However, for all its efforts, sales have peaked, seemingly caused by increasing competition from a North American rival and possibly health concerns over levels of sugar and salt.

Marketing approach

CM has adopted a 'pull' approach to its marketing activities. TV advertising and free gifts are aimed at creating consumer demand for its cereals. However it is clear that this approach is not working. To counter the increased competition CM may need to consider a '**push**' approach. The aim is to persuade retailers to buy more of its goods than its competitors as increased shelf space means greater sales to consumers. This would be achieved by offering bulk discounts or other special offers to retailers just for stocking its products.

Threats

The sales problems may worsen if the **bad publicity** surrounding sugar and salt levels continues to grow. CM clearly faces a challenge to ensure its products remain acceptable. It could also be argued that CM has a responsibility to ensure its products are relatively healthy, particularly as they are targeted at children.

The main issue is should CM continue to sell foods high in sugar and salt? There is (currently) nothing **illegal** in what it is doing so why should it change? Children form the majority of CM's customers so pulling out of the market or stopping the advertising and promotion of such foods to children would cause it to lose most of its business.

The continued sale and promotion of its current products could lead to increased **adverse publicity** and this could (in the long-run) cause it to lose business. Fast food companies such as McDonalds have recently faced such challenges. However it is likely that this would only affect the main CM **branded** range, its generic supermarket 'own brand' product would be unaffected as consumers do not necessarily realise the manufacturer of such products.

Opportunities

Therefore in the near future it is quite possible that CM will have to research and produce '**healthy**' **alternatives** for its products. However, this will be expensive and could increase the cost of its new products when compared to its competitors.

Conclusion

In conclusion, CM clearly has a strong brand but faces strong competition and needs to handle the issue of social responsibility carefully. It may wish to wait to gain agreement between itself, its competitors and the food industry before spending money on developing healthy alternatives.

(b)   **CM** might **develop a marketing strategic plan** using the steps outlined below.

 Set its corporate objectives

CM should decide on a mission statement.

Using the mission statement, corporate objectives can be set. For example to become the number one selling brand of children's cereal.

 Carry out a marketing audit analysis

PEST analysis – CM should review the marketing environment for marketing opportunities and trends that may allow it to further meet its customers' needs and perceptions. It should also monitor its competitors' strategies.

SWOT analysis – CM should review its internal position (its strengths and weaknesses) and the general environment (for opportunities and threats).

By analysing its current internal position and the environment it operates in, CM can start to develop a plan that is relevant and realistic.

 Set its marketing objectives.

CM should set and prioritise what it wants to achieve based on its business objectives and given its current position.

Marketing objectives should be SMART – specific, measurable, achievable, real and timed. For example to achieve 10 million unit sales in the UK by the end of the next financial year.

 Devise an appropriate marketing strategy

CM should identify its broad perspectives and consider the following:

Marketing mix – CM should use the marketing mix to determine the correct strategy for product, place, promotion and price

Segmentation – should CM approach other segments such as adult cereals?

Targeting – should they just target children?

Positioning for the brand, should it remain a premium brand?

 Devise the tactics – plan the marketing mix

Pricing policy – will reducing price increase sales?

Product policy and **brand** – should it promote healthy eating or not?

Place or **distribution** – are there any alternative locations to sell the cereal?

Promotion (mix of advertising, sales promotion, public relations) – CM should consider whether it is wise to continue advertising its products on children's TV.

 Determine the implementation of the plan

How should the strategy and tactics be implemented to best effect?

(c) **Five benefits of market segmentation to CM**

It may identify new marketing opportunities

Segmentation creates a better understanding of customer needs and this may enable CM to spot new marketing opportunities. For example identifying children's favourite pop groups could result in CM including free gifts associated with them, rather than just TV characters.

Allows proportionate allocation of marketing budget

Segmentation allows the marketing budget to be allocated on the basis of segment size and likely returns from each segment. This will maximise the marketing benefit CM can achieve from its budget.

Promotes effective use of resources

CM needs to make effective use of all its resources if it is to remain competitive. Greater understanding of the market through segmentation will lead to improved allocation of resources since they can be targeted in a more effective way and better use can be made of them.

Domination of segments creates competitive advantage

Understanding customers within a segment and fulfilling their needs allows companies such as CM to dominate the segment. Domination allows the business to create economies of scale and other synergistic benefits such as improved competitive ability and ensures the business remains strong.

Improved responsiveness to customer needs

Effective marketing requires being responsive to the consumer. Segmentation increases this responsiveness as the business is far more in touch with its customers.

31 4QX

Text reference. Chapter 8.

Top tips. In Part (a), use the question requirement to structure your answer. There are two definite sections, 'explain the importance' and 'identify the influences'. The use of PESTEL or similar will assist in generating sufficient points for a good pass.

In Part (b), a process for estimating income is required. Think macro first (big picture) then consider the centre itself. This should generate sufficient points to score well. Strong answers will include many of the practical considerations provided in the scenario.

Easy marks

(a)   Use of an external theory (PESTEL) provides structure and helps gain easy marks.

(b)   Think about how demand and income could be estimated. There are a wide range of points that could be made here, ensure you link the points you make to income estimation.

Marking scheme

		Marks
(a)	Up to 3 marks for explaining the importance of the macro environment	3
	Up to 2 marks per correctly explained factor	<u>12</u>
		15
(b)	Up to 2 marks per correctly explained stage	
	(Otherwise one mark per valid point)	<u>10</u>
		<u>25</u>

Our answer shows what we consider the most appropriate points to make. Other relevant points that answer the question would earn marks. However, irrelevant points that do not answer the question would not earn marks.

(a)   **Importance of the macroenvironment**

It is essential for the centre to understand its **external (macro) environment** for the following reasons:

- To **monitor the actions of competitors** to ensure the centre remains competitive and anticipates or counters competitor actions.

- To **identify potential new customers** and **opportunities** to market its services.

- To **monitor consumer demand** and make appropriate amendments to its service provision where necessary.

The most **significant influences** in the **external environment** that are relevant to the centre include:

Political factors

Government tax incentives to keep the population fit and healthy. If the centre cannot obtain these incentives then other competitors may be able to provide enhanced services at lower cost (eg the female health and beauty facility).

Economic factors

The overall demand for leisure activities. A general fall in demand may indicate that the centre should be downsized to reduce costs or even closed.

Amount of disposable income available. An increase in disposable income could increase demand for leisure activities, although the centre already has an affluent surrounding population which may limit the effect of this factor.

Social/cultural factors

The cultural and social mix of the external population. This is particularly relevant with the centre wanting to expand its service provision to other groups – these groups need to be identified, targeted and their needs met.

Technological factors

An upgrade of the sports equipment will be required to attract and retain customers who may also expect online booking facilities.

New technology is required to integrate the pay-as-you go pre-pay cards into the centre's facilities.

Ecological factors

Two ecological factors should be considered. Firstly, attempting to limit damage to the area of outstanding natural beauty surrounding the centre. Secondly, attracting additional customers may increase vehicle pollution as public transport is limited.

Legal factors

Ensuring compliance with health and safety legislation, for example children needing supervision in the swimming pool. Breach of legislation could have significant negative impact on the hotel.

(b) **The centre's income potential** could be assessed as follows:

Prepare a macro-economic forecast

This would provide an estimate of the overall economic activity in economy where the centre is operating. This will provide an overall level of aggregate demand.

Prepare an industry sales forecast

This should include predictions as to what may happen to sales in the health and fitness industry using information from the macro-economic forecast.

Demand may be affected by government health initiatives. The centre may need to consider the likelihood of obtaining government grants and include these as a source of additional income.

Prepare a company sales forecast

This would be based on the centre's management forecast of the centre's market share. Market share will be affected by the use of the Old Town swimming pool and other fitness clubs opening in the town.

Sales (and capacity) will also be directly affected by the occupancy of the hotel and whether guests wish to use the centre (revenue will be affected if guests pay additionally for this facility). Revenue projections for the hotel must also be included as a variable within the centre's income forecast – pricing policy will impact on forecast revenue.

Prepare a demand forecast

The **forecast** needs to consider:

What customers are currently doing within the market (information from current sales performance and demand (if possible) for competing activities in the local Old Town.

Customer intentions in relation to using the products from the centre (information obtained from questionnaires from centre users, intentions of non-users by surveying the local population and partly from expert opinions). Information on possible alternative uses of the centre facilities will need to be included in this section.

What centre users have done in the past (eg a past sales analysis) to attempt to generate sales trends which can be used as a guide to future performance if possible.

Generate an income forecast

Finally, use this information to generate an income forecast. The income forecast is dependent on forecast demand and pricing levels.

Like all forecasts, the income forecast will be subjective and uncertain due to the uncertain nature of many of the variables. It will however provide a useful guide.

32 Objective test questions: Managing human capital 1

32.1 B Taylor believed individuals were motivated by material reward and that efficiency in the workplace was vital.

32.2 D The so-called 'psychological contract' is a notion that is based on the expectations the organisation and employee have of one another.

32.3 D CIMA's ethical guidelines require members to act responsibly, honour any legal contract of employment and conform to employment legislation.

32.4 A Job candidates are assessed at an assessment centre.

32.5 **Recruitment** involves employing people from outside the organisation. It includes finding applicants, communicating opportunities and information and generating interest.

Selection is the process of choosing who is offered the job. Selection involves procedures to choose the successful candidate from those made available through the recruitment process.

32.6 Herzberg identified **hygiene factors** as factors that don't motivate when present, but cause dissatisfaction if not present. An example is salary level. The argument is that employees who feel poorly rewarded could be demotivated, but that monetary reward (on its own) does not provide consistent motivation.

32.7 **Potential benefits to DES** are increased employee motivation and productivity, increased employee commitment, ability to attract high performing individuals, reduced absenteeism and reduced staff turnover.
Potential benefits to the employee include easier balancing of personal and professional priorities and feeling valued – which could lead to increased job satisfaction.

33 Objective test questions: Managing human capital 2

33.1 B   Induction is the set of activities designed to familiarise a new employee with an organisation.

33.2 B   The main risk of performance related pay is demotivation. The other problems can either be overcome or are simply not relevant to PRP.

33.3 D   Appraisal should be a participative, problem-solving process.

33.4 D   Charles Handy's 'shamrock organisation' consists of a three-leaf structure of core, contractual and flexible part-time employees.

33.5 **Advantages**

- Tailored to an organisation's specific requirements.

- Cost effective when provided by in-house staff.

Disadvantages

- Participants may be distracted by on-going work issues.

- More likely to cancel due to lack of a cancellation fee.

33.6 **Human Resource cycle**

- Selection process: obtain people with appropriate skills.

- Appraisal process: set individual performance targets in line with organisational goals.

- Training and development: fill any skill gaps and check the organisation retains appropriately skilled people.

- Reward system: to motivate and retain employees.

33.7 **Appraisal purposes**

- Reward review – measuring the extent to which employee bonuses or pay increases are deserved.

- Performance review – for identifying training and development needs and validating training methods.

- Potential review – planning career development by assessing the employee's long term capability.

The overall purpose of an appraisal system is to improve efficiency.

34 Corporate Upheaval

Text reference. Chapters 11 and 12.

Top tips. When answering each question part, plan out what you want to say in bullet points. Once planned, use the bullet points as headers and write a short paragraph on each.

There are many possible answers to each part so do not worry if your answers are different to those below. You will still earn marks if you have made relevant points.

Easy marks. Stating the levels of Maslow's hierarchy of needs in part (f).

(a)   **On-the-job training**

The advantages and disadvantages of on-the-job training include:

Advantages:

- Training is provided that is **relevant** to the job being undertaken.

- Training is '**just-in-time**' – that is specific queries are identified.

- Training can be given both **in and outside the office**.

Disadvantages:

- Training is **difficult** when the **employee is dealing with the client**.

- Where training is being carried out by a manager, they **may not have the appropriate training skills**.

(b)   **Benefits to the company**

Profit on sale

Being in the capital city, it is likely that ARi9's office building is worth a considerable sum of money. Therefore, selling it and purchasing a smaller building outside the capital is likely create a large financial gain for the company.

Ongoing costs

The costs of heating and maintaining a smaller building are lower than for a large building. Locating outside of the capital could mean a reduction in business rates.

Staff productivity

Staff productivity whilst in the office has already been identified as an issue. The open plan arrangement and crowded work stations have contributed to interruptions and other problems which mean staff are becoming less productive.

It is likely that allowing staff to work from home will help alleviate these problems and should increase staff productivity.

Attracting staff

Recruitment of new staff is also currently a problem for ARi9. There is considerable competition to attract talented individuals who live a short commute away.

Working from home may help attract these highly talented individuals to work for ARi9. They can choose to live in a location that they can afford and also working from home is often seen as a benefit by the employee.

Retaining staff

The same factors may help retain existing staff that are currently being lost when taking career breaks or maternity leave.

(c) **Costs of the proposal**

Equipment cost

The new IT equipment is likely to be expensive to purchase considering the numbers of staff which need to be provided with it.

Ongoing costs

There is also the ongoing cost of replacing the equipment every few years to keep pace with technology.

Reduced co-ordination

Having employees spread out in many locations makes co-ordinating them very difficult. However, provided ground rules are set and suitable technology is in place to enable the work to be done, problems due to lack of co-ordination can be reduced.

Reduced control

Managers will have less direct control over how an employee works. Problems such as poor employee output will only come to light over time and cannot easily be prevented or intercepted by a vigilant manager. Poor work by employees could potentially lead to a loss of clients.

Diluted culture

Employees will see less of each other if they work from home. This may dilute the organisation's culture and identity.

(d) **Benefits to employees**

Reduced cost of commuting

Employees currently have to pay high costs in relation to their commute into the office, in particular parking charges. These costs to the employee will be much reduced if they can work from home most of the time.

Reduced stress

Rush hour driving and few available parking spaces create stress for the employee even before they start work. This stress will be reduced if the employee has to visit the office less often.

Cost of housing

Employees can choose to live further from the office if they can work from home. This gives them scope to find housing which is cheaper in terms of mortgage or rent payments, giving them more money left over each month.

Balancing work and home life commitments

Employees all have personal lives and working from home allows them to strike an appropriate balance between work and home life. For example, the time saved on the commute could be used for other purposes such as taking children to school or other family commitments.

Privacy

Working in the office environment means that employees get very little privacy, for example, telephone conversations are easily overheard. Working from home will allow employees to enjoy as much privacy as they want as no other employees will be around them.

(e) **Problems for employees**

Loss of distinction between work and home

Some employees may prefer to keep their work and home life separate. Forcing them to work from home may be viewed as an unfair intrusion into their home life.

Risk of distraction

Employees may find it difficult to concentrate on work whilst in the home environment. Distractions such as television, or if children are around, could disrupt their work flow meaning they get less done.

Facilities available at home

Employees would have to provide a permanent area where the IT equipment can be installed. Not everyone will have sufficient space in their home for this purpose, or if they do, some may be unhappy to have a part of their home permanently dedicated to work.

Increased costs

Whilst employees may save money by working at home, some costs may rise. For example, electricity or heating bills will increase as the home is occupied for longer during the day. Home insurance costs will be affected as policies need to be amended to reflect the fact the home is being used as a place of work.

Lack of contact with colleagues

Many employees enjoy the social aspect to work. Colleagues often form strong friendships and see each other away from work. By working from home, this social interaction will be substantially reduced and some employees may suffer from isolation.

(f)　　The **hierarchy of needs** and its **relevance** to ARi9's teleworking scheme are as follows.

Physiological needs

These are basic survival needs, for example food and shelter, that individuals must meet to keep themselves alive. These needs will be unaffected by the teleworking proposal, as both before and after any change the employee would be earning money to pay for them.

Safety needs

These are needs for security, order, predictability and freedom from threat, ie that no physical harm will happen to the individual. Like physiological needs, they are unaffected by the teleworking scheme.

Love/social needs

These include the need for relationships, affection and belonging, ie social interaction. Under the teleworking scheme, individuals will be expected to work in isolation at home and therefore these needs are clearly affected by it. Employees who need social interaction will be demotivated by working at home.

Esteem needs

Esteem needs are almost at the top of the hierarchy. They include independence, recognition, status and respect from others. Clearly some of these needs will be affected by the teleworking scheme.

On the positive side, employees will now be virtually **independent** as they will be working alone, and therefore those employees who crave their independence will be better motivated.

However, some needs will be affected in a negative way. The increased distance between employees and managers mean it will be increasingly difficult for employees to gain the **recognition** they feel they deserve.

Self-actualisation

This is the fulfilment of personal potential, and as it represents the top of the hierarchy, will be unaffected by the teleworking scheme. Because it can never be satisfied it will always motivate an individual.

35 HR division and strategy

Text reference. Chapter 11.

Top tips. Before starting your answer for Part (a), consider what you will write for Part (b). There is potential for overlap in these two parts – but you will not score marks for making exactly the same point twice. The two parts are different; Part (a) covers the *role of the HR division* and Part (b) *aspects of the HR strategy*. In Part (b), start by thinking of areas that would be covered by the HR strategy – then think of how these may be affected by the recent changes at NS.

Easy marks. Stating the role of HR in Part (a).

Marking scheme

		Marks
(a)	1 mark for note format	1
	Up to 2 marks per role referenced to the scenario	12
		13
(b)	Up to 2 marks for explaining the aim of an HR strategy	2
	Up to 2 marks per change referenced to the scenario	10
		12
		25

Our answer shows what we consider the most appropriate points to make. Other relevant points that answer the question would earn marks. However, irrelevant points that do not answer the question would not earn marks.

OUTLINE NOTES: HEAD OF HR CANDIDATE INTERVIEW – HR DIVISION AND HR STRATEGY

To: Divisional director

From: Divisional accountant

Date: November 23 20X8

(a)   **Role of the HR division**

Following the new corporate initiative the HR division will have a wide ranging role. Some of the most important aspects of the role are explained below.

Strategy

The HR Division should take a strategic approach to employment, development and management of human resources at NS. It is important that all aspects of people/employment issues at NS are integrated. A long term perspective, rather than the short-term firefighting approach typical of personnel departments, should be taken.

Continuous improvement

The HR Division has a role to play in the empowerment and continuous improvement initiatives. The division could help set up quality circles to suggest improvements that ultimately result in improved service to customers.

Values system

The HR Division should represent the organisation's central value system or culture. At NS, all aspects of HR should be geared ultimately towards providing exceptional customer service – in line with the customer focus of NS. HR policies and procedures must be developed with quality (from a customer perspective) in mind.

Devising working arrangements

The changes at NS, and the need to improve customer service to policy holders is likely to mean longer operating hours in some areas. This is likely to require new ways of working, such as flexible shift patterns. The HR Division has an important role to play in devising these arrangements.

Internal marketing

As the change is quite substantial, NS may use an internal marketing campaign to get across the importance of customer focus to employees. HR will have a role to play in developing the marketing campaign, and in particular to advise the most appropriate methods of communicating the message.

Managing change

The HR Division also has an important role to play in managing the change process (eg staff consultation, 'selling' the change, possibly providing a 'champion of change'). It is likely that resistance to change will occur – the HR team have an important part to play in overcoming this (eg by rewarding compliance and emphasising the need for and benefits of the change).

(b) **HR strategy**

An HR strategy aims to ensure the people required to successfully implement an overall corporate plan are in place. The following aspects of the HR strategy will change significantly as a result of recent developments.

Recruitment and selection

The 'new NS' will require pro-active, customer focussed employees throughout the organisation. This will significantly impact the recruitment and selection strategy. A potential employee's technical skills are likely to be seen as less important – as these can be taught. The recruitment and selection process should aim to employ individuals with the personal traits/attitude required.

Training, induction and mentoring

NS aims to distinguish itself from the competition by providing superior customer service. This may require more employees (eg to reduce waiting times) and will also require all customer facing employees to be highly efficient and to deliver exceptional service. To be able to do this, employees must have a clear understanding of the role they perform and all associated procedures. This requires thorough training (including induction and possibly mentoring).

Appraisal

Employees should now be judged not only on their technical knowledge and proficiency but also on 'softer' areas such as displaying initiative and general attitude/helpfulness to both external customers and colleagues (internal customers). 360 degree appraisal could be considered.

Rewards

Employee reward schemes in the 'new NS' should encourage co-operation, initiative and a focus on customer satisfaction. A bonus system linked to customer satisfaction feedback should be implemented – this should include an individual element (to encourage initiative) and a team element (to encourage co-operation between team members).

Job design/job descriptions

Narrow job descriptions and strict task demarcation have no place in the new NS. Employees should now be encouraged to learn a wide range of skills to enable greater flexibility in the workforce. For example, employees should not specialise in one area – they should be skilled in all aspects such as dealing with new policy enquiries, policy renewals and claims handling.

36 Human resource plan and activities

> **Text reference.** Chapters 11 and 12.
>
> **Top tips.** As you read the scenario, highlight or underline areas which are relevant to the question. This will save you having to do this again on a second read through. For this to work, you must read the question requirements first.
>
> **Easy marks.** Stating the elements of an HR plan.

(a) **Elements of an HR plan**

Section 1. Strategic review

Overall business strategy will influence the HR strategy. It is necessary to establish what the strategy of the organisation is, so that the HR strategy can help this be achieved. The expansion of the tyre fitting service is a good opportunity, but has important HR implications.

Section 2. The current HR position

An audit of the existing staff and their skills is necessary to establish the current HR position. In this case, staff numbers are small so this will be a fairly simple exercise.

Section 3. The required HR position (taking into account the new way of working)

Any change in strategy has HR implications. The new ways of working should be documented and staffing requirements worked out.

In this case it seems likely that staff with tyre fitting and wheel alignment skills are required (whether through recruitment, training of existing staff or a combination of both). Additional staff may be required to cope with the co-ordination of the taxi service and reception work. Also, two drivers are required to replace the two who have just left.

Section 4. Action plan to move from the current HR position to the required HR position

The required position is then compared with the current position, and plans drawn up to 'close the gap' between the two positions. In this case it may be necessary to recruit people with the specific skills required (for example the use of wheel alignment equipment). They could then pass these skills onto existing employees – building a flexible, multi-skilled workforce.

> **Alternative answer**
>
> You may also have structured your answer under other headings such as **strategic analysis**, **forecasting**, **job analysis** and **recruitment and training**.

(b) The **important human resource activities** to which attention should be paid in order to get the most out of the workforce are the **reward system**, **appraisal system** and **working arrangements**.

Reward system

The reward system refers to how workers are compensated for the work they do. This includes wages, bonuses and any other rewards. The company might also make use of incentive payments to reward productivity. For example, taxi drivers could be rewarded by being entitled to a percentage of all fares in excess of a basic amount per week, tyre fitters may earn a bonus based on both the quantity of work completed and the quality (eg no customer complaints).

Appraisal system

Performance appraisal involves evaluating the performance of each employee including plans on how to improve their performance. The appraisal gives employees the opportunity to have some input into how they see their future career development – they may be content to continue in their current role which is not necessarily a bad thing. Appraisal may also help in decisions relating to promotion or poor performance. The process also helps identify training and development needs.

Working arrangements

Working arrangements will impact upon worker performance. Issues include shift patterns, team-work, priority setting and covering holidays and sickness. Health and safety is also an important consideration. Some of these issues are related to the reward and appraisal system – for example employees are unlikely to work as a team and help others if this would adversely impact upon their own recorded output, which in turn affects their bonus.

(c) **Recruitment policy and practice**

Policies are general guidelines that govern how certain organisational situations will be addressed. For example the human resource management department maintains policies that govern sick leave, and benefit options.

A typical recruitment policy might deal with the:

- Internal advertisement of vacancies
- Efficient and courteous processing of applications
- Fair and accurate provision of information to potential recruits
- Selection of candidates on the basis of abilities related to the position, without discrimination on any grounds

Changes to policies

Given the changes in the labour market over the past few decades and the move towards flexibility and multi-skilling, modern organisations have to be more acutely aware of gathering market intelligence as part of their manpower planning process.

Organisations need to therefore look at their overall priorities and requirements for labour and to put into place policies that recognise and meet any changes in the labour market.

There is also a need to focus not on the needs of sub-systems such as individual departments, but on the needs of the organisation and its future growth and development, particularly if the organisation has an international strategy in place.

Recruitment policy and practice

The selection of employees must be approached systematically. The recruiting officers must know what the organisation's requirements are, and must measure each potential candidate against those requirements. For example the selection policy may be to advertise all new posts externally with a view to introducing new blood into the organisation. In such a case the organisation's policy on selection will be evident to all members of the organisation whether they were internal or external applicants.

Although this policy may be unpopular with some members of the organisation, it clearly defines how candidates will be selected. Any organisation must however be aware that it should review and monitor both the recruitment and selection process in order to meet the challenges and changes that will affect the business.

37 Training and development

> **Text reference.** Chapters 4, 11 and 12.
>
> **Top tips.** Don't worry if you made different points to ours. Providing that they are relevant, you will earn marks. There is much you could say on each part but do not get carried away writing lots on one part at the expense of others. Give them all equal treatment.
>
> In Part (c) you can make use of the change management theories you studied in Chapter 4.
>
> **Easy marks.** Defining the types of flexibility in Part (a).

(a)   **Workforce flexibility**

Flexibility is about an organisation such as ZnZ being able to adapt and respond to changes in its environment. There are three types of workforce flexibility, **numerical**, **task** and **financial**.

Numerical flexibility

This concerns having an adequate number of suitably qualified or experienced staff available to perform tasks when required.

Task or functional flexibility

This involves ensuring the organisation has multi-skilled staff able to perform a range of tasks. This helps reduce overall staff numbers and provides cover in cases of absence.

Financial flexibility

This concerns an organisation being able to alter employee costs, or link their costs to output. It is often achieved through performance related reward systems.

Training and development

Training and development can improve ZnZ's numerical and task flexibility. Task flexibility is a result of skilling employees to being able to perform a number of roles. Numerical flexibility is improved as the number of staff trained or developed increases.

(b)   **Training and development**

Training involves planned learning events which are designed to help individuals achieve the level of knowledge, skills and competence to help them carry out their job effectively.

Development involves the growth or realisation of an individual's ability and potential through learning and educational experiences.

Benefits of training and development to ZnZ's employees.

Portfolio of skills

Employees become more attractive to potential employers and more promotable within ZnZ.

Psychological benefits

Employees feel they are of value to ZnZ due to its investment in them.

Social benefit

Training courses are social events and an employee's need for social interaction can be met through them.

Job satisfaction

Training helps ZnZ's employees improve their job performance and may also increase their job satisfaction.

(c)   There are a number of theories ZnZ's HR department and management could follow to aid the successful implementation of the career coach scheme. In this case, **Lewin's three stage model of change** is recommended.

Unfreeze

The first stage in implementing change is to **loosen up or 'un-freeze'** the current situation. If people are satisfied with the current state, they are unlikely to be motivated to change. The people that will mostly be affected by the career coach scheme will be those selected to act as coaches and these are the people HR and management should focus their attention on.

They need to **make selected employees receptive** to the scheme as on first glance it appears that they are just being given more work. The key role management should play is in explaining how the scheme might benefit them, for example acting as a coach will improve their management skills and therefore their prospects for promotion.

Move or change

The second stage of Lewin's three stage theory is to actually **make the change** – turning the selected employees into coaches.

The HR department should ensure that **resources**, such as time for staff training are made available as some employees may need to learn new skills.

Management's role in this stage is to reduce any residual resistance and build ownership of the new role by encouraging those involved to **participate** in the process. This will help motivate selected employees to help the scheme succeed.

Refreeze

After the scheme has been introduced, the new employee behaviours need to become **entrenched or frozen into place** to ensure that the coaches continue to perform their role. HR could introduce rewards such as pay rises or bonuses to those who act as coaches.

As part of the re-freeze process, management should introduce **feedback mechanisms** to ensure that they listen to any concerns coaches have and that they act on any as necessary.

(d)   **A systematic approach to training** could follow the following steps.

1.   Responsibility

A suitably qualified manager should be placed in charge of developing the training and development plan. The manager, probably from the HR department, will have the power to implement the programme and be responsible to the HR director for successful implementation.

2.   Extent of training

The individuals who need training will need to be determined. Training is to be focused on professionals within ZnZ. Given ZnZ employs a significant number of staff, there will be a large number of staff to train, with training focused on their role.

3.   Training Needs Analysis (TNA)

To determine the training requirement, the training gap must be determined. This will involve:

- Setting baselines for the skills to be acquired
- Determining which skills each individual has already acquired, and
- The difference between the two points established above is the 'training gap'
- Listing the training needs of each employee required to close this training gap

The training needs of individuals should be linked to organisational needs.

Some suitable training may be available from Continued Professional Development (CPD) carried out as part of membership of professional bodies (eg CIMA).

4.   Prepare outline learning programme

From the TNA, an outline learning programme can be developed for professional members of staff. This programme will again be mapped against organisational objectives.

Other benefits of training, such as meeting professional CPD requirements, will also be identified and the learning programme agreed by individual departments.

5. Training options/cost

Having identified learning requirements, different methods of training can be considered and the cost of each option obtained. Important decisions at this stage will include:

- Should internal/external training be used?

- Method of training (classroom/computer-based)

- Suitability of off-the-shelf programmes or need for bespoke training.

A total training budget can then be prepared and authorised.

6. Implementation and feedback

Finally, the training programme is implemented and after a suitable period of time, feedback obtained on its effectiveness. Feedback should relate to how well the objectives of the programme have been met.

38 Motivation and reward

Text reference. Chapters 11 and 12.

Top tips. You should be able to attempt Part (a) from your common sense even if your knowledge of appraisal systems is minimal – just make sure it is related to the scenario.

Herzberg's theory gives you a good structure to set out your answer to Part (b). We recommend splitting your answer between motivators and hygiene factors, you should then look for examples in the scenario for each.

Easy marks. There are few easy marks in this question. However you would gain credit for sensible factors suggested in Part (c).

Marking scheme

		Marks	
(a)	1 mark per relevant point in support of problems with appraisal systems	6	
	1 mark per relevant point in support of improvements	4	
			10
(b)	1 mark per relevant point (hygiene factors)	2	
	1 mark per relevant point (motivators)	2	
	1 per mark identified factor from scenario	6	
			10
(c)	1 mark per relevant factor identified		5
			25

Our answer shows what we consider the most appropriate points to make. Other relevant points that answer the question would earn marks. However, irrelevant points that do not answer the question would not earn marks.

(a) **Problems with appraisal systems**

A problem with many appraisal schemes is that they reinforce hierarchy, and are perhaps unsuitable for organisations where the relationship between management and subordinates is fluid or participatory.

Appraisal systems, because they target the individual's performance, tend to ignore the organisational and systems context of that performance. For example, if any organisation is badly led, no matter how able the employees, it is likely to be unsuccessful. Appraisal schemes focus on personal characteristics and performance, rather than the wider picture.

Effectiveness of appraisal systems

The effectiveness of an **appraisal system** could be hindered by:

- The **effort** line managers put into the appraisal process

- The **integrity** of line managers

- A tendency of line managers to **favour** people who have a similar personality and background

- A **lack of congruence** between what the organisation actually wants and the behaviours it is prepared to reward

The effectiveness of any appraisal system relies heavily on the **quality** and **reliability of assessment**. Variations in the consistency of reporting standards can quickly lead to a feeling of dissatisfaction and injustice.

Improvement to CQ4's appraisal system

To improve the appraisal system at CQ4, the new system should have the following characteristics.

It is not possible to apply a completely objective approach to every unique situation. The system should therefore always allow for at least a degree of discretion and personal judgement.

Although reviewing past performance is an integral part of an appraisal system, it is also important to concentrate attention on the changes required to bring about an improvement in future performance.

The HR department should learn from other organisations who have recognised the problems associated with performance appraisal and have taken steps taken to limit their detrimental effect.

For example:

- Systems that focus on performance rather than on the qualities of the appraisee, could increase the objectivity of the appraisal.

- Systems that incorporate appraisal within a wider, structured approach to the management of human resources.

(b) ### Herzberg's motivation-hygiene theory

Frederick Herzberg developed a two factor theory to analyse the causes of satisfaction and dissatisfaction of employees in the workplace. This research required 203 Pittsburgh engineers and accountants to recall events that made them feel good or bad about their work. He identified two factors that influenced their feelings – motivation and hygiene factors. The factors stem from two separate 'need systems' that individuals have (hygiene factors and motivators).

Hygiene factors

The first need is to avoid unpleasantness (hygiene factors). Such factors are unable to motivate individuals if present, however, their absence will cause dissatisfaction. Hygiene factors include salary, quality of supervision, interpersonal relations and working conditions.

Motivators

Secondly the need for personal growth (motivators). Motivators include factors such as status, recognition, achievement and growth. When these factors are present they are capable of motivating an individual's performance and effort.

Effect of hygiene factors and motivators

Herzberg noted that an absence of motivators results in employees focussing on hygiene factors for example, demanding more pay. If hygiene factors are addressed employees are more likely to focus on motivators.

The Chief Executive's initiatives

The two new initiatives from CQ4's chief executive address both the motivation and hygiene requirements of Herzberg's theory.

Motivators

- **Achievement** – from individual performance contract targets.
- **Recognition** – that SBU managers have a significant role to play.
- **Advancement** – of 'star achievers' to senior positions on a fast track scheme.
- **Responsibility** – SBU managers are to manage in the way they deem most appropriate.
- **Challenge and autonomy** – managers will become autonomous but will be assessed by their profitability.

Hygiene factors

- **Improved remuneration package** with bonuses linked to profitability.
- **Supervision of SBU managers** is reduced as 'central interference' is replaced by autonomy and responsibility.
- **Working conditions** should improve as the SBU managers can organise themselves in a way most appropriate to them.

The initiatives should improve the motivation of the SBU managers.

(c) **Factors** the **HR department** should consider when **redesigning** the **remuneration** and **reward package** of the SBU managers include the following.

Payroll budget

The HR department should ensure the package it offers is consistent with any budget or other restrictions in place.

Attractiveness to managers

Revised remuneration packages should be attractive and motivate the SBU managers.

Equity and relativity

The HR department should ensure the new packages offer equity (a fair rate for the job) and relativity (fair differential pay according to the economic conditions of the specific country the manager resides, as well as their status and competences).

Calculation of bonuses

Bonuses should be based on the results that an individual can directly influence if they are to be effective.

Quantifying performance

Whilst profitability is relatively simple to quantify through financial performance, non-financial performance such as innovation is harder to calculate.

Alternative approach

You may have also mentioned the following factors amongst others.

Measuring performance accurately

Performance measurement is often subjective and will include elements of personal judgement.

Maintaining staff morale

If targets aren't reached, staff morale is likely to suffer as a result of lower monetary rewards.

---

39 Multiple choice questions: General 1

39.1	D	Decision based software provides managers with the information and analysis tools to enable them to make decisions.
39.2	A	Web 2.0 applications include blogs and social networking sites.
39.3	B	Virtual teamworking is made possible by developments in communications and other technology, enabling people to work together even when they are not physically located in the same place.
39.4	C	The practical application of CAD and CAM technologies, rather than any general outlook or philosophy, are responsible for increased control over design and production using machinery.
39.5	B	By linking in to suppliers' systems, for example, a lot of paperwork and administration time (and cost) can be saved by the sharing of order processing and payment information via EDI.
39.6	B	A manufacturer with a production orientation concentrates upon production efficiencies and cost cutting because it believes that this will be enough to sell the product in whatever quantities can be manufactured.
39.7	A	The macro (external) environment exerts an influence over the organisation, rather than the other way around. It is beyond the organisation's control.
39.8	B	A non-governmental organisation (NGO) operates independently from any government and generally pursues some kind of social aim, such as Rotary International.
39.9	B	Examples include education and healthcare provided by governments.
39.10	B	The cognitive paradigm theory explains consumer behaviour as a rational process, from awareness to eventual purchase.

40   Multiple choice questions: General 2

40.1	A	Job enrichment involves adding new, more stimulating requirements to a person's job.
40.2	B	A total reward package brings together pay and non-pay elements and emphasises a positive organisational culture.
40.3	C	Organisational culture is not a spoke in Cousins' strategic supply wheel.
40.4	C	Customers participating directly in the delivery process is a feature of the service industry.
40.5	B	Sustainability is a long-term programme involving a series of sustainable development practices.
40.6	D	The four emerging world economies Brazil, Russia, India and China are sometimes referred to as the BRIC economies.
40.7	A	Off-shoring involves carrying out some operations in a different country.
40.8	B	Core competencies provide competitive advantage so should not be outsourced.
40.9	D	A service level agreement usually includes a definition of the level of service to be supplied.
40.10	B	Gross National Product is made up of Gross Domestic Product plus net overseas earnings.

41 Multiple choice questions: General 3

41.1	D	China is the largest of the BRIC economies.
41.2	B	Herzberg developed the two-factor content theory of motivation. One factor in the theory is motivators – these produce satisfaction in an individual when present.
41.3	C	The set of expectations between an organisation and its employees is known as a psychological contract.
41.4	B	Data redundancy refers to the duplication of data.
41.5	C	Aptitude testing is used during the selection process.
41.6	C	Promotion includes all marketing communications which let the public know about an organisation's products and services.
41.7	A	Economies of scale and manufacturing experience allow firms to reduce their costs and therefore compete successfully on price. Economies of scale, such as bulk discounts, mean organisations are able to purchase raw materials more cheaply. Organisations with extensive manufacturing experience know the most efficient and cost-effective methods of producing goods.
41.8	C	Stability might seem like a desirable feature in its own right, but it is covered by substantiality.
41.9	D	Predatory pricing involves setting a low price with the intention of damaging the competition.
41.10	C	A product life cycle chart plots sales volume against time.

42 Multiple choice questions: General 4

42.1	A	Kurt Lewin's ideas are based on the idea that change is capable of being planned.
42.2	C	The US, Canada and Mexico are the three members of the North American Free Trade Agreement (NAFTA).
42.3	B	Loss leaders are products that have a very low price set with the objective of attracting consumers to buy other products in the range with higher profit margins.
42.4	B	Victor Vroom's Expectancy Theory states that valence is the strength of an individual's preference for a certain outcome.
42.5	A	A widget is an example of a web 2.0 application.
42.6	C	The TQMEX model shows the relationship between quality management and other aspects of operations management. The answer must therefore mention these two areas, so C is correct.
42.7	A	Quality certification requires approval of such materials.
42.8	C	Rodger's theory relates to a person specification, so C is the correct answer.
42.9	B	The process of attracting suitable candidates is referred to as 'recruitment'.
42.10	B	The overall expectations an individual and organisation have of each other form a 'psychological contract'.

43 Multiple choice questions: General 5

43.1	A	Producing or purchasing items as they are needed is referred to as Just-in-Time (JIT).
43.2	C	These qualities focus on the person. A job description (option A) explains what is required in a job. Options B and D are part of an appraisal system.
43.3	D	At an assessment centre, candidates are observed and evaluated as they perform a variety of exercises.
43.4	A	Shareholders are connected stakeholders.
43.5	C	In the context of selection techniques, reliability means the achievement of consistent results.
43.6	A	Reck and Long's positioning tool is strategic (The strategic positioning Tool).
43.7	B	Plan-Do-Check-Act (PDCA) is a cycle that breaks continuous improvement down into four stages.
43.8	B	On-line testing and user acceptance occurs after implementation. Logic testing is done before any software is written.
43.9	C	The 5-S model describes operations management practices of structurise, systemise, sanitise and self-discipline. It does not describe internal analysis or a form of six sigma.
43.10	A	Corrective work, the cost of scrap and materials lost are examples of internal failure costs.

44 Multiple choice questions: General 6

44.1	A	TQM aims to eliminate the costs of poor quality – not just reduce them. It is not possible to eliminate all quality-related costs without ceasing production. TQM does not aim to reduce the workforce – although changes in working methods may be required to improve quality.
44.2	B	Fewer (preferably no) internal failures means less time lost correcting problems and therefore more time engaged in production. The other options are false; internal failures cause delays in delivery, improving process quality should reduce the testing required and inspecting finished goods is expensive as it means re-producing sub-standard production rather than focusing efforts on producing high quality output first time.
44.3	D	The marketing strategy follows the business planning process – it does not drive the company objectives (A) or productive capacity (B). C is incorrect because it fails to consider the requirements of the consumer.
44.4	A	Perfective maintenance is aimed at extending or improving a system. It is usually requested by users.
44.5	A	Taylor assumed that workers are rational so would try to obtain the highest remuneration for the least effort.
44.6	A	Kaizen is originally a Buddhist term but was adopted by the Japanese (and now by other nations) to represent continuous improvement. The other options may involve or imply some elements of continuous improvement but have different meanings.
44.7	A	The usual course of action to reduce inflation is to raise interest rates as this makes borrowing more expensive and reduces overall demand in the economy.
44.8	D	The other options do not refer to recognised, formal supply sourcing strategies.
44.9	D	Schein developed the concept of 'social man'.
44.10	B	Professional accountants must not be party to anything which is deceptive or misleading. This is specified in CIMA's Ethical guidelines and goes further than simply 'not telling lies'.

45 Multiple choice questions: General 7

45.1	B	Penetration pricing involves setting a relatively low price for a product in order to increase the organisation's share of the market.
45.2	A	Expert systems allow general users to benefit from knowledge and techniques of human experts.
45.3	D	Rodger's seven-point plan consists of: circumstances (background), attainments, disposition, physical make-up, interests, general intelligence and special aptitudes.
45.4	B	Content theories, such as Maslow's Hierarchy of Needs, assume motivation is directed at fulfilling personal needs.
45.5	A	Porter's value system reflects the importance of adding value at all stages in the supply chain – from the first supplier in the chain to the end-user or customer.
45.6	D	ABC inventory management focuses on the most expensive items as a priority as their value justifies the extra administrative effort.
45.7	C	Duplicating data is known as data redundancy.
45.8	C	A product oriented organisation focuses on product development and features.
45.9	C	Teleworking means working away from the organisation's premises, usually from home .
45.10	C	Induction involves familiarising an individual with the organisation after they have been selected for a position and have accepted the role.

46 Various topics 1

		Marks
(a)	1 mark for each relevant explained point	5
(b)	1 mark for each relevant explained point	5
(c)	1 mark for each relevant explained point	5
(d)	Half mark for identifying each P and 1 mark for each explanation - max overall 5	5
(e)	1 mark for each relevant explained point	5
(f)	1 mark for each relevant explained point	5
		30

Our answer shows what we consider the most appropriate points to make. Other relevant points that answer the question would earn marks. However, irrelevant points that do not answer the question would not earn marks.

(a)

> **Text reference.** Chapter 2
>
> **Top tips.** Note that this is NOT a question about the decision about whether, or what, to outsource. The organisation has already made that decision – your answer needs to focus on HOW to go about it. The examiner has stated that 'accuracy, brevity and clarity' are called for in all Section B answers.
>
> **Easy marks.** Make the point that this is a 'total' outsource - an external supplier is to provide the entire IS/IT service. Think about the effect on the organisation's current staff, and how the relationship with the vendor company is to be managed.

An organisation that has decided to outsource its IS function needs to address the flowing issues.

Budget

A budget should have been set as part of the decision on whether or not to outsource. Now that the decision to outsource has been made, the budget should be reflected in the service level agreement and control should be exercised over expenditure.

Communication with staff

Communication with existing staff is essential to ensure all are aware of what this means for them and the organisation. Some staff may be offered positions with the organisation the function is outsourced to, others may be made redundant.

Negotiating with a range of vendors

The vendors who are invited to tender for the contract must be reputable and able to 'fit' with the organisation's culture and operations.

Choosing the appropriate vendor

The service provider and the organisation must establish an effective working relationship. For this reason, it is vital to make the right choice of outsourcing vendor. Factors such as organisation culture need to be considered when entering into such a close and critical relationship.

Drawing up the contract/service level agreement

A key factor when negotiating with external vendors is the contract. The contract must state clearly the obligations and responsibilities of both parties. It should specify minimum levels of service and the penalties for failure to meet these standards. Such standards might include response time to requests for assistance/information and deadlines for performing tasks

Timescale, handover and exit strategies

Timescales must be clearly set out, for example how the transition to the outsource company would be handled and how long the contract would last. Organisations should avoid tying themselves into a long term outsourcing agreement if requirements are likely to change. Arrangements for an exit route, such as a move back in-house, should be considered.

(b)

Text reference. Chapter 4

Top tips. Use your own experience as an employee to consider where IS and IT could be applied. How did you find your current job? Perhaps you used a jobs/recruitment website, where the company was able to reach huge numbers of candidates by placing one advertisement online. Or look at the definition of human resources management in Chapter 4 of the Text; 'the process of evaluating an organisation's human resource needs, finding people to fill those needs, and getting the best work from each employee...' How can IS/IT help with each of these?

Easy marks. The various activities performed by the human resource function have grown in scope and influence. Think about each of these functions, and how IS and IT might help each one.

The information systems within an organisation should complement and support other functional areas, one of which is human resources. Human resource (HR) management includes the activities of recruiting, training, developing and rewarding people.

HR planning. Planning processes are assisted by the use of IT, for example **spreadsheets** or **specialised packages** to construct budgets and the use of the Internet and the web to gather information required to formulate HR strategy.

Recruitment and selection. IT can be used in the advertising of job vacancies, perhaps using a third party jobs website – able to reach large numbers of potential candidates cheaply and quickly. Organisations can also advertise vacancies on their own corporate **intranet** and **website**.

Technology allows the recording and monitoring of information relevant for **appraisal**. IT can also be used to identify skills and performance gaps, for example a skills **database** could be maintained to enable the organisation to record the skills held within the organisation.

Training and development ensure skills remain up-to-date, relevant, and comparable with the best in the industry. Training content and material will often be delivered using technology such as **DVDs** and web-based training courses.

The reward system should motivate and ensure valued staff members are retained. At the basic level, **payroll** operations in most businesses use a system of direct bank transfer of salaries – IT systems are essential for this, as well as the capturing of all payroll-related information (needed for income tax returns for example). IT may also be used to gather information to establish and compare salary and reward levels.

A **human resources page** or section within the organisation's intranet provides an easily accessible source for HR policies and procedures. This could include employment manuals, job descriptions, grievance procedures, payroll dates and other general information.

(c)

Text reference. Chapter 8

Top tips. Distribution is one of the four elements of the classic marketing mix. There are many channels available and different types of promotion will apply to each one.

Easy marks. Think about the definition of distribution: 'getting the right products to the right people at the right time'. The main distinction between different types of distribution channel is whether they are direct or indirect.

A manufacturer's **promotional activity** will vary dependent upon the sort of distribution channel that operates.

One way of classifying distribution channels is as zero level, one level and two level. Promotional activity for a manufacturer would differ depending upon the type of channel.

A manufacturer operating a **zero level channel** would sell direct to the final customer. Promotional activity would focus on the final customer.

Promotional activity **aimed at the final customer** is sometimes referred to as **'pull marketing'** as it attempts to pull the customer towards the product. Examples include for example empowering customers to purchase direct using e-commerce or encouraging purchase at a 'factory shop' attached to the production facility. Often, pull marketing involves heavy expenditure on advertising and consumer promotion to encourage purchase.

A manufacturer operating a **one level channel** would sell to retailers who in turn sell to final customers. The manufacturer may conduct promotions directed at the final customer and also at retailers (to encourage them to source products from them rather than other manufacturers).

A manufacturer operating a **two level channel** would sell to a wholesaler, who in turn sells to retailers, who in turn sells to final customers. The manufacturer may conduct promotions directed at wholesalers (to encourage them to source products from them rather than other manufacturers) as well as at the final customer.

One and two level channels are examples of **indirect distribution**. Promotional activity for indirect channels should include an element of pull marketing (to stimulate final customer demand) and also **'push marketing'**, which is **aimed at intermediaries**.

Push marketing attempts to push the product from supplier down the distribution chain. This typically involves advertising in trade publications, trade promotions, promotional stands at trade conferences and competitive trade discounting.

(d)

> **Text reference.** Chapters 8 and 9
>
> **Top tips.** The four elements of the marketing mix are product, price, place and promotion. The mark allocation is a clear indication that the extended marketing mix is not required here.
>
> **Easy marks.** Getting the elements of the marketing mix correct will be a large step on the way to a strong answer.

A marketing mix for an online company selling branded sportswear is suggested below. It is important that the elements of the mix are coordinated and consistent, and tailored appropriately for the identified target market.

Product	The product is a branded sportswear range promising quality and durability. It offers high quality clothing for dedicated sports people including elite, high profile athletes. The brand values are quality, innovation and performance.
Price	High prices reflect a premium position in any market, whether the product is sold traditionally or online. The customers are serious athletes who rely upon the strong brand name and expect high quality, and are prepared to pay for it. 'Loyal' customers may be able to benefit from discounts.
Place (distribution)	The website is the place of business, which could lead to cost savings that could be passed on to the customer. Orders can be sent directly to the customer (anywhere in the world, potentially) within 24 hours of placing the order – this requires a well stocked warehouse. Use of specialist courier firms will ensure a high level of service. A scale of delivery charges will need to be developed.
Promotion	The website will need to be innovative, attractive (lots of pictures) and easy to use. Search Engine Optimisation is important, so the site appears prominently (first page) when a user searches for 'sportswear' or related terms. Advertising may also be embedded in related sites, such as those promoting large sporting events or lifestyle-related activities. 'Stalls' could be held at major events (such as the London Marathon) and sponsorship of events at grass roots level could be considered (eg youth football competitions). Word of mouth recommendation will also be important.

(e)

Text reference. Chapters 11 and 12

Top tips. Think about how your own organisation advertises vacancies internally.

Easy marks. The use of a notice board and the company intranet are fairly obvious points to make.

There are a number of internal options available to an organisation wishing to fill a job vacancy. These internal options should be cheaper than involving a recruitment agency, but will require more internal time and effort.

Nevertheless, there is no reason why internal methods cannot be used for recruitment, shortlisting and selection.

Possibilities include:

- Internal advertising using company notice boards, the company intranet, e-mail messages or newsletters to attract applications from suitable candidates (whether looking for promotion or a sideways move).

- Speaking to employees (utilising 'the grapevine') to identify suitable internal candidates without advertising the position. Care should be taken to ensure internal HR policies and relevant employment legislation are complied with.

- Advertising the vacancy using the organisational website. Many company websites have a 'Jobs at X' area where interested candidates can browse the jobs on offer and even make an application without the need to apply via a recruitment agency.

- Contacting previous applicants whose details have been held (with their permission) with a view to future vacancies.

- Training existing employees to expand their skills making them suitable for a wider range of positions.

(f)

Text reference. Chapter 11

Top tips. Use Herzberg's two factor theory to structure your answer. This theory holds that, in general, financial incentives are in some ways less important to maintaining a well-motivated workforce than other factors such as job satisfaction.

Easy marks. Encouraging good social relationships should be a relatively easy point to make to gain a mark.

In the context of human resource management, motivation is an employee's desire to perform their role.

Herzberg developed a 'two-factor theory' of motivation. This distinguishes between factors that motivate (motivators) and other factors that he believed don't actually motivate but can cause dissatisfaction (hygiene factors). Hertzberg saw salary as a hygiene factor, not a motivator.

An organisation looking to motivate through non-financial means should focus on **improving motivating factors**.

1. **Recognition.** Outstanding employee performance can be rewarded in a variety of non-financial ways. The organisation could establish schemes such as 'employee of the month' to recognise exceptional performance. It is important that such a scheme be properly and fairly managed.

2. **Job redesign.** Job redesign aims to improve performance by building more interest, variety, challenge and collaborative working into jobs, all of which might motivate employees.

3. **Job enlargement and rotation.** Job enlargement increases the width of the job by adding extra tasks. Job rotation allows for a little variety by moving a person from one task to another. Introducing variety can reduce boredom and increase motivation.

4. **Promotion and/or increased responsibility.** Additional responsibility often motivates as it makes someone feel valued and respected. This could be achieved by adding elements of planning and control to a role.

Reduce the dissatisfaction caused by hygiene factors. If hygiene factors are currently causing dissatisfaction (and by implication reducing motivation), the situation could be improved by addressing issues such as the following.

1. **Social satisfaction**. By encouraging social relationships, good working relationships and strong work teams can be formed. Employees will enjoy coming to work if they feel that they are working with people they know and get on with.

2. **Regular, meaningful communication**. Employees like to feel important enough to be kept informed about the organisation they work for.

3. **Consistent leadership and management**. A responsive and approachable, yet strong and consistent, management team is more likely to motivate employees than one that is perceived as distant and 'out of touch'.

4. **Encourage employee pride**. The company might seek to enhance its status among current and potential employees, and the wider community, by seeking out awards such as a listing in rankings such as 'The Best 100 Companies to Work For'.

47 Various topics 2

(a)

Five benefits a collaborative process of Human Resource planning might bring to an organisation are explained below.

Improved staff motivation and morale

Communicating and collaborating with staff across the organisation demonstrates a willingness to listen, and shows employees their opinions matter. This should improve staff motivation and morale.

Enable a consistent approach to be taken across the organisation

By collaborating widely, across departmental boundaries, the process should enable an organisation-wide policy to be developed. This in turn helps provide a sense of unity and a shared organisational culture.

Emphasise the importance of people and their development

The focus on human resources emphasises the value and importance the organisation places on its people. The process should also help define staff training and development needs required for the organisation to meet future objectives.

Establish future human resource needs

The human resource planning process aims to ensure the right people (with the right skills) are in place to enable the organisation to operate efficiently and effectively. The plan may identify a future under or over supply of people in particular areas, which will need to be dealt with.

Encourages a strategic perspective and agreed priorities

In order to plan effectively for Human Resources, planning in other areas will be required, for example an overall strategic plan. The overall strategic plan drives the HR strategy and plan. The collaboration process should result in the establishment of common ground and agreed priorities.

(b)

Internal failure costs result from inadequate quality, where the problem is identified before the transfer of the item or service from the organisation to the customer. Types or examples include:

- The cost of **materials scrapped** due to inefficiencies in stockholding procedures
- The cost of **materials and components lost** during production or service delivery
- The cost of **output rejected** during the **inspection process** (scrapped)
- The cost of **re-working** faulty output
- The cost of **re-inspecting** reworked output

The **significance** of internal failure costs for an organisation with a reputation for quality is that although these costs are best avoided, they are seen as preferable to external failure costs. Incurring these costs internally, before the product or service reaches the customer, prevents damaging the organisations reputation. The organisation should still aim to reduce internal failure costs, perhaps through a quality assurance program.

(c)

SERVQUAL is a method used to measure quality in service organisations.

Features of SERVQUAL

 (i) **Customer focussed.** SERVQUAL focuses on the customer, particularly the gap between a customer's expectations and their actual experience.

 (ii) **An emphasis on quality.** By implementing SERVQUAL (or its off-shoot RATER) an organisation demonstrates its commitment to quality in service delivery.

 (iii) **A formal framework.** SERVQUAL provides a comprehensive framework to measure customer expectations and experience. The version of SERVQUAL in use since the 1990's emphasises the role of the employee delivering the service and the tangible environment, for example facilities, equipment and staff appearance.

Benefits of SERVQUAL

 (i) **Results highlight areas for change.** Areas where gaps appear between customer expectations and the service received ('service gaps') require action, for example refined processes or staff training.

 (ii) **Improved customer satisfaction and retention.** Closing service gaps results in improved customer satisfaction and retention.

 (iii) **A customer and quality focussed culture.** Emphasising the importance of quality and implementing a formal quality framework helps permeate a customer and quality-focussed culture throughout the organisation.

(d)

Five key issues for a manufacturing organisation considering adopting **Six Sigma** are identified below.

Training

The introduction of Six Sigma will require the training of staff regarding the aims and practical workings of the programme, including the procedures surrounding the measurement of output.

Establishing the measurement metrics

Six Sigma aims to eliminate defects. To implement Six Sigma, an organisation must decide what constitutes a defect (from the customer's perspective) and be able to measure output to establish the frequency/rate at which defects occur.

Ensure the expected benefits outweigh costs

As with any initiative, Six Sigma should only be implemented if the benefits (for example reduced reworking, improved customer satisfaction and retention) outweigh the costs of implementing the program (for example changes to working practices).

Cultural shift

To be effective, Six Sigma requires a commitment to quality and the elimination of waste and defects across the whole organisation. A cultural shift may be required before adopting Six Sigma or planned for as part of the implementation.

Senior management involvement and commitment

Six Sigma represents a philosophy based on the elimination of defects with the ultimate aim of 'customer delight'. Senior management must 'set the tone' by emphasising the importance of quality and communicating and demonstrating their commitment to the Six Sigma philosophy.

(e)

Text reference. Chapter 2.

Top tips. Read and think about the requirement carefully to establish what the examiner is getting at. 'A wider group of stakeholders' than shareholders should have you thinking of Corporate Social Responsibility (CSR).

Easy marks. Explaining the benefits of a proactive CSR program will earn good, relatively easy marks.

The concept that a business with shareholders has responsibilities to a wider group of stakeholders and to society as a whole is known as **Corporate Social Responsibility (CSR)**. An important aspect of CSR is that companies behave ethically, in a fair and just way.

Five reasons why a company might act in a socially responsible way when considering a policy decision are explained below.

Interdependence of business and society

The state of society as a whole impacts upon trading conditions and results. Therefore, it is in a company's best interest to act in a way that contributes to a sustainable, stable and prosperous society.

Necessity - customers demand it

Customers now expect companies to act responsibly. Failing to do so is likely to result in customers moving elsewhere. For example, focussing solely on shareholder returns could lead to a decision to outsource production to an unscrupulous operator that fails to comply with minimum wage requirements. However, customers may boycott the company if this information reaches the public domain.

Taking a wider perspective produces better balanced decisions

Focussing exclusively on shareholder interests tends to encourage a short-term, solely financial perspective. Taking into account the interests of a wider group of stakeholders is likely to encourage a wider, longer term perspective and result in better balanced decisions.

Staff productivity, development and retention

It makes business sense to take into account the interests of employees. Flexible working practices and encouraging a reasonable work life balance is likely to result in improved employee commitment and retention.

External relationship building

An important aspect of business success is building mutually-beneficial relationships with key stakeholders, for example suppliers and customers. Decisions that consider only the needs of shareholders may harm important supplier and customer relationships.

(f)

Text reference. Chapter 1.

Top tips. Organisations make plans based on assumptions relating to market conditions, regulations and laws. Think about the effects of changes to these factors.

Easy marks. Identifying political instability and the potential for this to cause economic instability will earn some marks.

The nature and possible effects of **five risks** relevant when an organisation is considering doing business in a country that has a government and political system it is unfamiliar with are identified below.

Political instability

Organisations are able to plan and operate more effectively in a stable trading environment. The risk of instability can make long-term planning difficult, and unforeseen political changes could have adverse effects, for example favouring local producers.

Unfamiliar with pressure groups and lobbyists

Failing to understand the motivation, methods and influence of political lobbyists could result in conduct that offends, for example employing an excessively high proportion of ex-pates. The effect of this could be to create a backlash, for example a boycott.

Unexpected changes to economic policy

There is a risk that the government will pursue unfavourable economic policies, for example increasing taxation rates. The effect of this would be to make the venture less profitable.

Lack of understanding of political processes

Political processes may differ from those the organisation is used to, and may also change at short notice. For example an organisation may commit resources to a planning application only to find the government agency's requirements change.

Totalitarian government

There is the possibility that the current government, or a future government, could implement totalitarian policies, for example state appropriation of assets. This could result in the loss of the funds invested in the project.

48 Various topics 3

Top tips. Use short, clear paragraphs in your answer to make it easier for the marker to award you marks.

(a) **Benefits of databases** include:

- **Reduced data duplication/data redundancy**. Having a centralised pool of data reduces the chance of data duplication and redundancy. For example, stock and customer information are held and maintained centrally.

- **Provision of tailored reports**. Databases should facilitate more flexible reporting. For example, procurement managers should be able to produce reports on slow moving products by different types of supplier.

- **Ease of access to information for staff**. Databases should enable staff to find data quickly (eg to answer customer queries).

- **Reduced IT maintenance costs**. As data is maintained centrally, maintenance (eg checking data accuracy, adding new types of data) should be an easier task.

- **Enhanced security**. One centralised database is easier to protect than data spread across many locations.

(b) The **benefits of effective management information systems** (used by all grades of managers) include:

- **Provision of timely information** enabling managers to take informed decisions as and when required (from daily stock re-ordering to assessing weekly or monthly staffing requirements).

- **Reducing inventory holding costs** by enabling Just-in-Time.

- **Providing competitive advantage** as customers are provided with effective customer service (eg monitoring customers to identify their requirements in advance).

Other **benefits, relating to executive information systems** (used at senior manager or board level) includes:

- **Provision of summary, company-wide data** enabling directors/senior managers to identify key areas for further investigation and action.

- Allow the **monitoring of competitors** (eg active review of website changes) to ensure the organisation is aware of and can react to (or anticipate) changes in the competitive environment in a timely basis.

(c) **Issues to consider** when **transferring** from **business to business** (B2B) trading to **consumer trading** (B2C) include:

- **Payment methods**. B2C trading will normally mean customers pay for goods immediately, B2B normally allows payment on account. Facilities for on-line payment will be needed on the website.

- **Web-enable databases**. For example, inventory databases need to be accessible to customers. B2C customers will expect to see stock availability prior to placing orders.

- **Database web search**. Company websites should include search facilities that allow customers to find products they require.

- **User-friendly website**. B2C customers require a clear, well presented, easy to navigate site. Investment in the website may be necessary.

- **Regular price reviews**. The Internet allows for easy comparison between supplier prices. Companies may need to review prices charged compared to competitors on a regular basis to ensure competitiveness.

(d)   The **effectiveness of staff training** events can be assessed by:

- Requiring attendees to complete **course assessment sheets** after the training is completed.

- Requiring delegates to **complete tasks at the end of the event** that test the skills taught.

- Requiring delegates to **complete tasks some time after the training event** to demonstrate retention of relevant skills.

- Having the **trainer complete an assessment** that identifies gaps in knowledge provision or deficiencies in the skills of delegates.

- A **critical review by human resources staff** to ensure training objectives have been met.

(e)   **Advantages of using specialist providers** to deliver a training programme include:

- **Specialists focus on a relatively narrow area** so should deliver high quality training; employee trainers may not have these skills.

- **External trainers should have in-depth knowledge** of the applications being trained; again employee trainers may not have this knowledge.

- **External trainers are less likely to be distracted** by other work commitments.

- **Combining external trainers'** expertise with **employee trainers'** knowledge of the business should 'cover all bases' (eg allow the inclusion of business specific examples in the training material).

- **External trainers could pass on their knowledge to employee trainers**, who will then be able to support staff post-training.

(f)   The **development** of the use of **quality circles** could be encouraged by:

- **Rewarding the circle** for suggestions that are implemented (eg a share of any savings made).

- **Providing a budget and support** to run the quality circle in terms of room provision, refreshments, staff to take minutes etc.

- **Ensuring management are supportive** and prepared to act on useful suggestions from the circle.

- **Providing an explanation** as to why **suggestions not implemented** were rejected.

- **Management asking the circle** for **suggestions** and **comments** on specific issues and problems facing the company, without anticipating the outcomes.

49 Tracey plc

> **Top tips.** The answer format specified is 'briefing notes'. This implies focussed, concise and clear. Bullet points are acceptable but ensure you provide explanation. To pass each part make about five explained points.

(a)   A set of procedures is necessary to control the change from the old to the new database. The **Systems Development Life Cycle** provides an appropriate model.

The key stages are:

- **Feasibility study** – ensure that the proposed database can be used.

- **Systems investigation** and **analysis** – obtain details of the current system to ensure no functionality is missed in the new system

- **Systems design** –the new system is designed

- **Systems implementation** – changeover from old to new database

- **Review** – check that the new database is working correctly

(b)   **Benefits of the database**

- **Promotion** – including advertising, public relations and building a brand image. The database will show how each potential customer heard of Tracey plc and identify which promotional activity is most effective.

- **Product** – marketing will assist product design by identifying features customers would like. The database will contain customer 'wish lists' assisting this function.

- **Price** – product pricing. External links to the Internet will enable the marketing department to find prices of similar products to assist with Tracey plc's pricing.

- **Place** (distribution) – how the product will reach the customer.

Unfortunately, no additional detail will be kept – but as Tracey distributes via mail order only this won't cause any operational problems.

(c)   **Use of the new technology** in marketing will enable the company's marketing efforts to be targeted more effectively. For example:

- The **type of marketing** that was previously effective in making the customer contact will be recorded. Future marketing expenditure will be directed into the more effective forms of advertising.

- **Links** can be determined between **geographical location** and **products purchased**. Special offers can be directed at specific groups of people to encourage overall increases in sales eg. patio tubs for small inner city gardens or summer houses for larger country gardens.

- **Customers** who have not purchased from Tracey plc for a while may be **identified** and **targeted**.

- The **product(s) bought** by a customer will be **recorded** and the information used for 'linked' offers (eg purchase of a greenhouse followed by an offer on greenhouse shelves).

- **Feedback** can be held and **reviewed** to ensure that products meet **customer requirements**. Where appropriate, production specifications can be changed.

(d)   **Marketing information** can be used to **determine production strategy** – as long as the company accepts the necessary operations strategy. Tracey plc could become **marketing orientated** – based on the following principles.

- Tracey plc needs to satisfy customer needs.

- Needs can be satisfied using an appropriate marketing mix, which the marketing department can provide.

- The operational department will set performance indicators to check appropriate goods are being produced.

- Production and product features will be based on customer requirements.

(e)   **Organisation structure**

- The new database enables any person in the marketing department to enter and access data. Previously only the marketing manager was able to use the database.

- The organisational structure of the department will be 'flatter' – that is the manager will now control 20 sales and marketing staff rather than 5 assistant managers controlling 4 staff each.

- The span of control of the marketing manager is therefore wider – the manager will be in charge of more people.

Organisational culture

Sales and marketing staff will have access to the new database. Changes to culture include:

- Learning new technology and data access/retrieval skills – support for learning needed.

- Staff will work with less supervision – support is needed to encourage own decision making.

Top tips. Where possible tie your answers into the scenario. This is particularly important in Part (f).

(f)   A **job competence** refers to a capacity that leads to behaviour that meets the requirements of a specific job. Specific skills for the new data controller will include:

- Personal – ability to relate to other people (specifically managers in different departments)

- Personal – ability to influence managers to conform to Tracey plc data standards

- Intellectual – understanding of data requirements

- Intellectual – understanding of the functionality of hardware and software

- Work-based – experience with data control issues in other companies

- Intellectual – ability to see strategic data requirements for the company (not just one department)

- Intellectual – ability to plan for change and implement new systems

50 Zodiac plc

> **Top tips.** MRP is not an overly large part of the syllabus – but this question shows how even a small topic can be used for this type of question. Prepare and be aware just in case an 'unexpected' topic crops up in the exam.
>
> As with all Section B questions, aim for five explained points per part and ensure your answer is related to the scenario.

(a) The **feasibility** of the new **Material Requirements Planning system** can be analysed as follows:

Technical feasibility

The requirements must be technically feasible. The use of a computer system to run MRP, as well as EDI and an extranet is feasible – the technology exists and is widely used. Links will also be required to the production and customer ordering systems, although again there does not appear to be any technical reason that these cannot be achieved, both use standard software.

Operational feasibility

The MRP system must fit in with the current operations in Zodiac. The system may require a change in responsibilities, with the production controller losing authority to order stock.

Social feasibility

The new MRP system has to be acceptable to the staff in Zodiac or changes made to ensure it is accepted eg training and the possible redrawing of job specifications.

Ecological feasibility

The new system should be as environmentally friendly as possible. EDI will reduce paper usage, and hopefully stock wastage will be reduced as only the required amount of stock will be purchased.

Financial feasibility

A cost benefit analysis will be needed to ensure that benefits outweigh the costs. This will have to be carried out carefully as many benefits will be intangible.

(b) **Benefits** of a **Materials Requirements Planning** system include:

Reduced stock holding

Stock will only be re-ordered when necessary and then taking into account past usage. This should ensure a more appropriate amount of stock is ordered compared to the current 'guess' by the production controller.

Better customer service

There will be fewer production delays due to stockouts of materials. Stock will be re-ordered on a timelier basis.

Improved information on delivery times

Linking the MRP system direct to suppliers means that details of delivery times can be sent electronically back to Zodiac plc.

Better time management

The production controller will spend less time having to produce 'emergency' orders, allowing more time to control the production activity itself.

Improved facilities utilisation

The amount of warehouse space required to store stock will be reduced allowing for alternative use of this space.

(c)   **Questions to assist the board regarding outsourcing.**

Is the system of strategic importance?

Strategic IS are not normally outsourced because they can require a high degree of specific business knowledge which the outsourcing company may not possess. However, a standard MRP system could be outsourced, even though it is important to the running of the business; the outsourcing company should have knowledge of this system.

Can the system be relatively isolated?

Systems that have limited interfaces with other IS are more easily outsourced. The MRP will have links to production and ordering, potentially limiting the ability to outsource it.

Can the outsourcing agreement be managed effectively?

In other words, does Zodiac know enough about MRP to be able to monitor the outsourcing company? The answer is probably 'no' so Zodiac will need to hire at least one specialist to understand MRP and manage the relationship.

Are requirements likely to change?

If the MRP will be replaced in the near future then a long term agreement would be inappropriate.

(d)   **Customer**

- New customers acquired – increase in long run with better customer service

- Customer complaints – fall with better fulfilment

- Delivery speeds – overall increase due to fewer stockouts

Internal operations

- Quality control rejects – may not change because production unaltered

- Productivity – should increase with fewer production stoppages resulting from fewer stockouts

Innovation and learning

- Training days – more needed to understand the MRP system

- Average time taken to develop new clothing fashions – probably unchanged because no change to CAD/CAM

Financial

- Return on capital employed – should increase with fewer production stoppages

- Revenue growth – should increase with better customer service

- EPS – increase with better ROCE and profits reported and better image/brand name

(e)   **Market segmentation** means subdividing a market into distinct and homogenous subgroups or customers where any subgroup can be selected as a target market with a distinct marketing mix. Market segmentation is likely to be beneficial to Zodiac for the following reasons:

- Clothes for male and female customers tend to be different. Segmenting the market in this way will also require specific marketing activities to attract each segment.

- The marketing budget can be allocated to each market segment and the return from each segment analysed to assist future investment.

- The product range can be designed to meet customer needs. For example, segmenting the market by age as well as gender will allow Zodiac to target specific fashions at different age groups.

- Zodiac may decide to try and dominate one market segment eg clothes for females aged 25 to 40 and attempt to gain specific competitive advantage in that segment.

> **Top tips.** These are standard steps in an appraisal system which are applied to the scenario in the question. If you look for opportunities to apply textbook knowledge, you will find your answers have a ready-made structure to them.

(f)   The steps in an **appraisal system** are described below.

 Identification of criteria for assessment. The main criterion appears to be quality of the production system, although other criteria such as ability to manage junior staff can also be used.

 Preparation of an appraisal report, either by the management accountant, the production controller or both individually for comparison.

 Appraisal interview. Exchange of views concerning work, setting targets for the next appraisal etc.

 Review of assessment by assessor's superior. To ensure that there is no prejudice in the report. The CEO may be the appropriate person for this job being senior to the management accountant and in charge of running the company.

 Prepare and implement action plan to achieve improvements and actions agreed.

 Follow up and **monitor** the **plan**.

51 Hubbles

> **Top tips.** The question requirement asks for 'a slide outline and brief accompanying notes of two to three sentences'. A slide outline is in effect a list of headings, usually one or two main headings and a number of sub-headings. Keep your notes brief – this will help your time allocation and keep your answer focussed.

(a)

> **Sales orientation v marketing orientation**
>
> Companies with a **sales orientation**
>
> - 'Let's sell what we've made'
> - A focus on advertising, selling and sales promotion
>
> Companies with a **marketing orientation**
>
> - 'Let's make what the customer wants'
> - All employees, and the organisation as a whole, have a 'customer focus'

Notes. Hubbles' emphasis on 'selling' implies that not enough effort has been made to establish what customers want. If Hubbles produces items that 'strike a cord' with customers, the products should 'sell themselves'.

> **Top tips.** In Part (b) think of ways in which Hubbles can become customer focussed. You might have thought of other examples.

(b)

> **A marketing orientation for Hubbles**
>
> - Find out what customers want – **market research**
> - What (and how) are **competitors** supplying?
> - Compare customer wants with all items currently on the market – **any gap** is an opportunity
> - Establishing **a true marketing orientation** will require new ways of working, commitment from staff at all levels and a change of culture
> - Some staff may not be suited to the new way of working and may have to leave; others will require information and **training**

Notes. Adopting a marketing orientation will require Hubbles to change how and why decisions are taken. The driving force behind Hubbles' products, markets, prices, and communication must be customer needs. All staff at all levels must see their roles in the context of how Hubbles satisfies or delights customers.

(c)

> **The traditional components of the marketing mix**
>
> - **Product** – the totality of what the customer purchases including product characteristics
> - **Place** (distribution) – how the customer accesses or purchases the product
> - **Promotion** – customers must be aware of the product and what it offers
> - **Price** – linked to perceptions of quality and value for money
>
> Recent thinking recognises the importance of a fifth component
>
> - **People** – the people involved in producing and bringing the offering to customers are crucial

Notes. The marketing mix is a framework that enables organisations to structure their thinking in a way that focuses on the customer. After Hubbles has devised a customer-focussed strategy it will be in a position to develop an appropriate marketing mix to achieve the strategy. This will require Hubbles to meet or exceed customer needs and expectations in all areas of the marketing mix.

(d)

Hubbles and the marketing mix

- **Product**. Identify what products customers want and focus production on these.

- **Place**. Make it as easy as possible for customers to purchase Hubbles products. Ensure widespread distribution; offer on-line sales with next day delivery.

- **Promotion**. Get the message out that Hubbles has listened and has changed. Likely to require advertising campaigns using different media to target groups.

- **Price**. Revise pricing strategy to match the new products. Decide the balance between competing on style and quality or on price.

- **People**. Reorganise along customer-focussed lines. Encourage customer-focussed culture through training programmes, incentives and staff empowerment.

Notes. Hubbles must develop a marketing mix that precisely matches the needs of potential customers in the target market. Research the market for data relating to the age, income, sex and educational level of target market, preferences for product features and attitudes to competitors' products.

(e)

Human resources helping purchasing

- **Recruiting** – ensuring people employed are suited to the role

- **Job design** – establishing clear responsibilities

- **Development and motivation** – developing training, appraisal and reward/incentive programmes that result in capable, motivated staff

- **Discipline and conflict resolution** – providing a framework to limit the possible adverse effects of misconduct and conflict

---

Notes. HR issues are important in all departments, including purchasing. The purchasing department plays a crucial role at Hubble in the procurement of materials and finished goods for sale, supplier selection and relationships, and price negotiation. HR must ensure the purchasing department has people with the right attitude and skills to perform these tasks.

(f)

The purchasing department and organisational performance

- **Supplier selection, links and relationships**. Establishing supplier selection criteria, quality standards, extranet links, electronic data interchange (EDI)

- **Supplier contract negotiation**. Guaranteed delivery times and quality enables Just in Time (JIT) production methods to be used

- **Co-ordinating purchasing activities** to maximise discounts

- **Relationship management** to encourage mutual co-operation and benefits with suppliers – possible development of a supply network

---

Notes. The purchasing function is now recognised as being crucial to organisational success, particularly in relation to the creation of value and in supply chain management. Purchasing policies that build close relationships with trusted suppliers should result in higher quality – which customers demand. Effective purchasing policies therefore help meet customer needs which is key to achieving organisational goals.

52 OK4u

> **Top tips**. Look for opportunities to break the requirements down into smaller parts. For example in part (a) you could break your answer down into ethical and managerial failings. This will give a structure to your answer and help you identify points to make under each heading from the scenario.

(a) **Ethical failings**

Making late orders and threatening financial penalties

OK4u made late orders to its fashion suppliers and used the threat of financial penalties to force them into meeting tight deadlines. Putting suppliers under such pressure is unfair and bad business practice by OK4u. This resulted in suppliers having to sub-contract out work in order to keep their own costs down and to get the work completed in time to avoid paying penalties.

Not researching where new suppliers source their products

Companies which follow ethical policies usually look into where new suppliers source their products very carefully and even stipulate that they should avoid using sub-contractors that themselves do not meet certain ethical standards. OK4u did not make such investigations. This failing contributed to the unfavourable newspaper investigation.

Managerial failings

CEO trying to manage everything

OK4u's CEO is also the founder. Despite the rapid growth the company went through, he still attempted to run the business by himself. This was a mistake as he could not devote enough time to all business areas and should have brought in a management team to help him run the organisation. A purchasing director would have had the time to look into the new suppliers in more detail and may have been able to identify the ethical problems before they became a problem.

Choosing to increase sales by discounting

Reducing prices is not the only way to increase sales. Promotions and advertising could also have a similar effect and OK4u should have looked into using them. The use of such methods would not have put pressure on the suppliers to reduce costs and may have prevented them from using sweat shop labour.

Claiming it follows ethical policies

Despite claiming to follow ethical policies, there is no evidence of such policies being implemented by OK4u's management. It appears that the company's claims are just for marketing purposes and are not backed up by managerial action. This is a major failing as had management implemented such policies then many of the problems that OK4u has faced could have been avoided.

> **Top tips**. Reasonable suggestions in Part (b) will earn good marks. However, be careful to manage your time and avoid writing too much.

(b) **Measures to restore public confidence**

Appoint a social responsibility director

The CEO should appoint a director with responsibility for corporate ethical and social responsibility policies. For added public confidence a well known or respected figure could be awarded the role.

Develop an ethical or social responsibility policy

The director should develop ethical or social responsibility policies which are comprehensive and sincere.

Gain senior management support for the policy

Senior management should be seen by the public to be supportive and enthusiastic for the policy otherwise they will question its merits.

Train and support employees in following the policy

Ethical or social responsibility policies are ineffective unless they form part of the corporate culture and are implemented by employees in their working lives. Therefore training and support should be given to all to achieve this.

Publicise the steps the company has taken in developing and following its policy

The public must be made aware of the changes that the company has made. To be successful it is important for the company to be sincere. If the policy appears to be for marketing or 'damage limitation' purposes then the publicity could backfire and damage the company further.

As part of this, a public apology should be issued with a statement that in future all suppliers, including sub-contractors, will sign up to a code of conduct.

(c) **Delivering excellent customer satisfaction**

Marketing

Brand design

OK4u was known for good product design and broad appeal which established it as one of the country's favourite high street brands. Branding sets customer expectations in areas such as image, price, service and values. Customer satisfaction is achieved by meeting or exceeding such expectations.

OK4u should therefore reassess its brand image to ensure it is sending out the right expectations to customers so they are not disappointed when they visit the shops.

Pricing

Generally customers will be satisfied if they feel that they have received value for money (even if the product or service is priced higher than competitors). This is not just in terms of the product purchased but is also related to the service received and corporate branding.

OK4u should therefore review its price setting strategy to ensure it is in line with customer expectations. It may be that the discounting policy followed should be abandoned as it may cheapen the value of the brand.

HRM

Culture

It is important that nothing OK4u's customers experience when they visit one of its shops contradict the corporate culture, expected, in particular, the new ethical stance. All employees must be seen to embody the ethical culture. This is because customers may be attracted to OK4u because of its ethical policies and much of their satisfaction will come from knowing they are supporting an ethical company.

Training

Staff training is important, especially in relation to sports equipment. Much customer satisfaction will be achieved by providing expert advice on which products are most suitable for an individual's needs.

OK4u should therefore ensure all staff receive suitable training on all products sold in order to provide excellent levels of advice.

Operations

Stock availability

An aspect of the company's initial success was that it never had any 'stock outs'. Customers are unlikely to be happy if they make a special trip to one of OK4u's stores to find that it has sold out of the one item they need. Good operations management will monitor stock and reorder levels and schedule deliveries before goods run out.

Customer service

Staff should focus their attention on providing good service to the customer. Measures of customer service could be taken and targets for satisfaction levels set, by which staff performance can be analysed.

(d)   **Evaluation of strategic relationship with suppliers**

Sports equipment and clothing suppliers

The suppliers of sports equipment and clothing are all personally known to OK4u's CEO, and some are close friends. This enabled strong relationships to develop over time which have been of great benefit to the company. The main benefit of this was excellent logistics, which meant that an appropriate level of stock was kept on the shop floors and the elimination of stock outs.

Fashion clothing suppliers

The suppliers of fashion clothing were previously unknown to OK4u. Soon after the relationships were formed, problems began. The supply contracts were tightly negotiated by OK4u. The company was able to pass on the costs of the discounting campaign to the suppliers. On top of this, the company pressured suppliers with tight deadlines and financial penalties for not meeting them.

These issues have created poor strategic relationships between OK4u and the fashion clothing suppliers. This resulted in the ethical problems and adverse publicity that the company has experienced.

(e)   **Analysis of OK4u's past year using the basic marketing mix**

The basic marketing mix includes the variables product, price, place and promotion.

Product

The company began the year selling products which it was well known for, sports equipment and clothing. This was clearly what the customer wanted as the business was successful. However, it then began to sell products that the customer did not associate with it, fashion clothing, and this caused sales to drop.

Price

To counter the fall in sales, OK4u decided to discount its products. The discounts did make the fashion clothing more attractive to customers and sales picked up.

Place

As well as shops, place includes the logistics of a company. OK4u began the year with close relationships with suppliers of its core business. These logistics worked well as the shops were always well stocked. However, a lack of close relationships between OK4u and the fashion suppliers meant poor logistics between them. It is likely that OK4u's late ordering was caused by a lack of a suitable ordering and distribution system between them.

Promotion

At the beginning of the year, OK4u was well promoted. This was largely the result of allowing local managers to be imaginative when setting up shop displays and the use of promotion in the local area.

However, all that changed with the adverse newspaper and television reports. This created adverse publicity and rather than inspiring desire to use OK4u's shops, it actually drove customers away.

(f)   **Purpose of an appraisal system**

Performance appraisal is 'the regular and systematic review of performance and the assessment of potential with the aim of producing action programmes to develop both work and individuals.'

The general purpose of any assessment or appraisal system is to improve the efficiency of the organisation by ensuring that the individual employees are performing to the best of their ability and developing their potential for improvement.

Objectives of an appraisal system

To **establish what the individual has to do in a job** in order that the objectives for the section or department are realised.

To **assess an individual's current level of job performance**. This can be used both as a base line against which performance can be measured in future, as a means of deciding how the individual has improved since the last performance appraisal and to identify weaknesses and training needs.

To **assess the level of reward** payable for an individual's efforts, eg, in merit payment systems.

To **assess potential**. At the organisational level this permits career and succession planning. At the individual level it permits appraiser and appraisee to assess the most effective development plans for the appraisee.

MOCK EXAMS

174

CIMA
Paper E1 (Operational)
Enterprise Operations

Mock Exam 1

Question Paper		
Time allowed:	Reading time	**20 mins**
	Answering question paper	**3 hours**
This paper is divided into three sections		
Section A	**Answer ALL sub-questions in this section**	
Section B	**Answer ALL of the six short answer questions**	
Section C	**Answer BOTH of these questions**	

DO NOT OPEN THIS PAPER UNTIL YOU ARE READY TO START UNDER EXAMINATION CONDITIONS

SECTION A – 20 marks

Question 1

1.1   Where there is a price leader in a market, a cut in price will normally prompt:

   A   A cut in price by competitors
   B   An increase in price by competitors
   C   Maintenance of the original price by competitors
   D   Competitors moving into other product areas   **(2 marks)**

1.2   In terms of market positioning, concentrated positioning means to:

   A   Target a single market segment with a specific product
   B   Target the whole market with a single product
   C   Target each market segment with a distinct marketing mix
   D   Target a single market with a range of products   **(2 marks)**

1.3   The primary tool governments use when following a policy of export-led industrialisation is:

   A   Import quotas
   B   Import tariffs
   C   Interest rate cuts
   D   Currency devaluation   **(2 marks)**

1.4   What does the UK stock exchange combined code recommend regarding the remuneration of directors?

   A   Remuneration should be sufficiently high to retain directors
   B   Directors should agree their remuneration collectively
   C   Directors should not receive bonuses
   D   Directors should not be involved in setting their own remuneration   **(2 marks)**

1.5   Explain the difference between push and pull marketing.   **(4 marks)**

1.6   Explain the difference between a job description and a person specification. **(4 marks)**

1.7   Explain what an expert system is.   **(4 marks)**

                                                                     (Total = 20 marks)

SECTION B – 30 marks

Answer ALL parts of this question

Question 2

The PTR Company designs and manufactures a wide range of ladies' and men's clothes from a large factory. Overall, about 650 different clothes are produced ranging from shirts and blouses to skirts and trousers. Much of the company's success can be attributed to the adoption of lean principles of production – in particular the concept of employee empowerment. However the Chief Executive Officer is not convinced that a just-in-time system of production that has recently been introduced is running as effectively as it should.

The range produced depends on the time of year; the country PTR operates in has particularly cold winters but warm and humid summers meaning that the style and variety of clothes sold vary over the year. Because of the different fabrics required for different weather and changes in fashion from year to year, the fabrics used to manufacture the clothes are rarely used for more than 6 to 8 months.

The Chief Executive Officer has recently learnt that it is cheaper to produce clothes in another country. However, he is reluctant to suggest this to the other directors as PTR has been owned by the same family for the last 60 years, and has a good reputation as a caring employer within the community.

Inventory is managed by a continuous inventory system. Orders are placed by PTR's computerised production system which automatically places orders with PTR's suppliers when inventory reaches the re-order level. The production system monitors usage for the last six months and automatically raises an order via an electronic link at the economic order quantity for that particular stock line.

Details of production of each line of clothing are is entered into the company's Executive Information System (EIS) on a daily basis. The EIS then produces comparison reports of production of each line for the last 12 months, including recommendations for amendments to production according to the time of year. The directors monitor production in terms of ensuring that appropriate cloths are being produced for the time of year. The EIS contains no other data.

Clothes are sold to a variety of different customers from teenagers to business people and a few senior citizens. Fashions vary greatly, and PTR sometimes has difficulty identifying target markets. However, the PTR maintains a good brand name, and consequently the Company is able to charge premium prices in most markets.

Required

Use a separate page of your answer book for each part.

(a)   Explain how the continuous inventory system might work against PTR's just-in-time (JIT) production system.   **(5 marks)**

(b)   Explain the meaning and possible benefits of employee empowerment.   **(5 marks)**

(c)   Recommend changes to the EIS, clearly showing how the changes will benefit the directors of the company.   **(5 marks)**

(d)   Explain the benefits of market segmentation to the PTR company and suggest three ways of segmenting the market for PTR Company.   **(5 marks)**

(e)   Explain how societal, economic, technological, and legal factors could affect a clothes manufacturing company such as PTR.   **(5 marks)**

(f)   Suggest reasons why the PTR Company may not want to move production facilities to another country.

(5 marks)

(Total = 30 marks)

SECTION C – 50 marks

Answer BOTH questions

Question 3

Banking services within the country of Everland are provided exclusively by a few well established banks, all offering broadly similar 'traditional' banking services. Overall, the industry performance is viewed from within as satisfactory and historically all banks have maintained stable profits and employment levels. Marketeers would describe the industry as being classically 'product oriented'. The profile of senior Everland bank officials and managers is of well qualified professionals, possessing long banking industry experience and considerable financial skills. Within the combined workforce other business skills (in, for instance, HR or marketing) are noticeably lacking.

In the external environment, the government will soon pass new legislation that will effectively break the oligopoly-type position of banks and open the market up to other providers. Senior bank officials, however, are unconcerned, feeling that banks are in 'reasonable shape' to face any new challenge.

You work for the Everland Banking Advisory Group (EBAG), an independent body, and have been asked to analyse the banking industry in the country of Utopia to identify lessons that might be learnt. Your investigation reveals that since the sector opened up to more competition, a much wider range of financial institutions offer banking services. Despite this, banks in Utopia have all prospered over the past few years. This is thanks to wide-ranging changes in how they operate, the products and services they offer and their organisational structures. You identify some significant trends within the banking industry of Utopia, including:

- The use of marketing techniques;

- A clearer focus on customers (who have become increasingly more demanding);

- A new generation of bank employees, many with commercial backgrounds;

- Banks now exhibiting a strong sense of ethical and social responsibilities towards customers.

Required

(a)   Identify the main threat to Everland banks and discuss the types of change that they could be making in order to survive and prosper.   **(13 marks)**

(b)   The importance of ethics and social responsibility in all areas of business has attracted increased attention in recent years. Discuss (with examples) the main ethical and social responsibility issues that face marketers within the banking sector.   **(12 marks)**

(Total = 25 marks)

Question 4

QW9 is a large insurance company. The industry conditions are very competitive and QW9 is under constant pressure to achieve higher standards of customer service and improve profitability for shareholders.

You have recently taken up a post in QW9's central project and technical support team working directly for the Director of Strategy, who is also relatively new to the organisation. In an initial briefing with you, the Director explains that he has met with most senior managers and discussed their feelings on the strengths and weaknesses of the company. He has concluded that there are a number of areas that need to be addressed, including two from the area of human resource management, namely, performance related rewards and performance management.

- *Performance related rewards*. QW9 experiences difficulty in recruiting staff even though it pays comparable salaries to its rivals. Senior managers do not feel that there are problems with either staff morale or the external image of the company The Director of Strategy explains that although QW9 offers a number of benefits to its employees beyond basic pay, this is not made explicit enough either internally or externally. The Director has so far identified a good pension scheme, flexitime, personal insurance cover at reduced rates, a subsidised canteen and a social club. You have also heard it said that the balance between a professional and personal life is a distinguishing feature of being an QW9 employee. It is the Director's view that all benefits should be examined and a 'total reward package' approach should be progressed. This would draw together all the financial and non-financial benefits (including working practices, development opportunities and the challenge of working for QW9 itself) into an integrated package which would be available to all employees.

- *Performance management*. A formal performance appraisal system supported by standardised procedures and paperwork has operated for a number of years. The scheme has clear organisational objectives centred on staff development and improved performance rather than as a basis for paying individual annual bonuses. It is, however, not well regarded by either managers or staff and its objectives are not being met. Senior managers complain about the time that is taken up with the process. Exit interviews are conducted whenever someone leaves QW9, and a review of a sample of recorded comments indicates staff feelings on the scheme very clearly: 'appraisal is just a paper exercise', 'a joke', 'a waste of time and effort'.

Required

(a)   Discuss the advantages and disadvantages of QW9 developing a 'total reward package' approach.

(14 marks)

(b)   State three areas, relevant to the design of a total reward package scheme, that QW9 should investigate.

(3 marks)

(c)   Explain the possible reasons why the objectives of the formal appraisal system are not being met.

(8 marks)

(Total = 25 marks)

(Total for Section C = 50 marks)

END OF QUESTION PAPER

Answers

DO NOT TURN THIS PAGE UNTIL YOU HAVE
COMPLETED MOCK EXAM 1

A plan of attack

Before the three hours writing time starts, you are allowed 20 minutes to read through the paper. Use this time wisely – in effect it gives you an extra 20 minutes to gain the marks you need to pass.

What should you do in this 20 minutes?

We recommend you spend the first ten minutes of reading time scanning the paper and identifying the main topic areas covered.

The second ten minutes, we suggest you simply **start working through the Section A questions** – by **writing your answers on the question paper**. These answers can then be transferred **very carefully** to your answer booklet when the exam starts. Remember though, you **must not write in your answer booklet during the reading time**.

Using the time in this way should mean that later in the exam, when you reach Section C, you have sufficient time to read both questions carefully and plan your answers to them.

Turn back to the question paper now, and we'll sort out a **plan of attack** for Mock exam 1.

First things first

It's usually best to **start with the multiple choice** and **objective test** questions (ie do Section A first). You should always be able to do a fair proportion of these, even if you really haven't done as much preparation as you should have, and answering even a couple of them will give you the confidence to attack the rest of the paper.

Allow yourself 36 minutes to do the objective test questions - no more.

The next step – Section B

Attempt Question 2 immediately after you've completed Section A. You've got to do this question so there's no point delaying it. The question is split into sub-parts. In this mock exam, the parts are all based on a single scenario. CIMA reserve the right to use this format in Section B of the real exam, although to date Section B questions have not been based on a scenario.

Read the scenario carefully, then take a look at the question requirements.

- Part (a) requires you to use your knowledge of inventory management and JIT – and to apply this knowledge to PTR's production system.

- Part (b) is a general question on employee empowerment.

- Part (c) requires suggestions that relate specifically to the EIS at The PTR Company. Don't just make general points – your answer must be realistic in the context of the scenario.

- Part (d) draws upon the marketing area of the syllabus. Suggest three reasonable points.

- Part (e) covers PEST factors – with legal specified rather than political. Your answer must be relevant to the situation faced by The PTR Company.

- Read part (f) carefully. The key word in the question is 'not'.

Section C

Once you've done Sections A and B, you are required to answer two longer questions available in Section C.

- **Question 3**. You must spot the key threat in the scenario and make reasonable suggestions in Part (a). In Part (b) use your understanding of ethical and social issues and apply it to the banking sector. Don't be afraid to draw on 'real-world knowledge gained from wider reading and media coverage.

- **Question 4**. Part (a) could be answered using text book knowledge of reward packages, but your answer to Part (b) must be related to the scenario. The same applies to part (c) – don't provide general reasons for appraisal system failure, your points must be relevant to the scenario.

General advice

Don't forget that all questions in the E1 exam are **compulsory**.

No matter how many times we remind you....

Always, always **allocate your time** according to the marks for the question in total and for the parts of the question. And always, **always follow the requirements** exactly.

You've got spare time at the end of the exam.....?

If you have allocated your time properly then you **shouldn't have time on your hands** at the end of the exam. If you find yourself with five or ten minutes spare, however, **go back to any parts of questions that you didn't finish** because you ran out of ideas or time. A fresh look may spark new thoughts.

Forget about it!

And don't worry if you found the paper difficult. More than likely other candidates would too. If this were the real thing you would need to **forget** the exam the minute you leave the exam hall and **think about the next one**. Or, if it's the last one, **celebrate**!

SECTION A

Question 1

1.1   A   Price leadership normally involves all prices in a market moving in the same direction.

1.2   A   B and C are examples of undifferentiated positioning and differentiated targeting, while D is incorrect as it refers to a range of products.

1.3   D   Currency devaluation is used to make exports cheaper and more competitive. It also reduces imports by making them more expensive.

1.4   D   The UK stock exchange combined code states that directors should not be involved in setting their own remuneration.

1.5   **Push marketing** involves transferring goods to wholesalers and retailers – who then sell the goods. 'Push' requires wholesalers and retailers to accept these goods.

   Pull marketing involves influencing consumer attitudes to create demand for a product – wholesalers and retailers then seek supplies to satisfy this demand.

1.6   **Job description**: explains the overall purpose of a job and the main tasks carried out within that job.

   Person specification: defines the personal characteristics, qualifications and experience required by the person carrying out that job.

1.7   An **expert system** is a form of DSS that allows users to benefit from expert knowledge or information. They are based around a database that contains specialised data and rules on how to use or interpret it according to a set of given circumstances.

SECTION B

Question 2

> **Text reference.** Chapters 5, 7, 8, 11.
>
> **Top tips.** This is a 'typical' scenario question with a mixture of knowledge reproduction and knowledge application required. Ensure you relate the points you make to the scenario.
>
> **Easy marks.** Some marks are available for demonstrating your knowledge of systems theory, your understanding of market segmentation, and a grasp of PEST factors.

Marking scheme

		Marks
(a)	1 mark for each relevant explained point	5
(b)	1 mark for each relevant explained point	5
(c)	1 mark for each relevant explained point	5
(d)	1 mark for each relevant explained point	5
(e)	1 mark for each relevant explained point	5
(f)	1 mark for each relevant explained point	5
		30

Our answer shows what we consider the most appropriate points to make. Other relevant points that answer the question would earn marks. However, irrelevant points that do not answer the question would not earn marks.

(a) **Continuous inventory systems**

Continuous inventory systems continually monitor inventory levels. When levels fall below a predetermined amount an order is sent to replenish it. A minimum buffer stock is held regardless of demand. In PTR's case, inventory is ordered once stock levels are at the re-order level.

Just-in-time production systems

Just-in-time is an approach to operations planning and control based on the idea that goods and services should be produced only when they are needed – neither too early (so that inventories build up) nor too late (so that the customer has to wait). JIT is also known as 'stockless production' and may be used as part of a lean production system. In its extreme form, JIT systems seek to hold zero inventories.

Continuous inventory systems and JIT production.

PTR's continuous inventory system works against the JIT philosophy that goods should only be delivered when needed because of the holding of buffer stocks. This explains why the Chief Executive Officer believes the JIT system is not working as efficiently as it should.

(b) **Empowerment**

The concept of **empowerment** means allowing employees to take the decisions required to do their jobs. Empowerment reflects the view that those performing a task are best placed to decide how it is performed.

This ideal contrasts markedly with traditional ideas of **top-down management**, in which management is seen as being best qualified to make almost all decisions. The traditional model inhibits decision making at lower levels in an organisation's hierarchy.

Empowerment reflects the need for **flexibility** to react to changing conditions. This is achieved by empowering employees at all levels to take **decisions** on aspects of work that relate to themselves, cutting out the red tape of hierarchical command structures. This has been an important theme in developments such as **quality circles**, **just in time production** and **continuous improvement** programmes. Empowerment therefore plays an important role in devising and spreading best practice.

To be effective, empowerment must be **embraced** by management and staff at all levels of the organisation.

(c)   The **main problem** with the **EIS** at present is it appears to be **focused on the analysis of operational data**, which is more of a Management Information System role. To be useful to the directors, the EIS needs to be **focused at the strategic level** of the company, providing summary information for decision making at this level.

Specific changes that could take place include:

- The initial summarisation of data can take place within some MIS. **Only summaries** of clothes being produced along with unusual variances for management attention actually **need to be transferred to the EIS**. A drill down feature can produce additional detail.

- Over time, the EIS can **accumulate data** on the **sales potential** of different types of clothes, and different fashions. This information can be used to **forecast potential demand** helping the PTR Company to provide an appropriate product range.

- As the **current EIS is inward looking** only, details of customer demands and fashion requirements are not known. Information from **customer surveys**, **fashion trends** from magazines and appropriate **web sites** could be **input into the EIS**.

- **Competitor information** is also not available from the EIS. Links can be provided to competitors' websites to show the types of product they are marketing.

(d)   A **market segment** is a group of customers with **common needs**, **preferences or characteristics** who will respond in similar ways to a given set of market stimuli.

The **benefits of segmenting the market** for PTR include it would enable PTR to identify those groups of customers who are most likely to purchase its products. Marketing activities can then be directed at those groups saving time and effort of attempting to market all clothes types to all people.

Methods of segmenting the market for PTR include:

- By **age** – younger customers are likely to prefer different clothes to older customers.

- By **income** – people with more disposable income are likely to purchase more expensive clothes.

- By **sex** – some clothes are nearly always worn by one sex eg skirts for ladies and ties for gentlemen.

- By **occupation** – some jobs require certain clothes (eg suits for accountants).

(e)   **Societal factors**

For any product to be sold, it must be socially accepted within the market place. In designing and manufacturing clothes, the PTR Company undertakes market research to determine what types of clothes are acceptable, bearing in mind that acceptability will vary between countries as well as within one country. For example, wearing shorts to work in an office in some countries such as Australia may be acceptable, but not in the UK.

Economic factors

Clothes sales may be affected by the amount of income available within society, interest rates affecting the cost of borrowing for PTR and business and personal taxes affecting both price (eg VAT or similar sales tax) and disposable income. Most of these factors the PTR company will have little or no control over.

Technological factors

Improvements in production machinery including Computer Aided Design will change the cost of production of clothes. The use of Internet technology may provide PTR with a new sales channel and ability to reach more customers, both in its home country and abroad.

Legal factors

These relate to legislation regarding the **supply of goods**. PTR will have to ensure that the quality of clothes is acceptable to limit the amount of legal returns and any consequent bad publicity.

(f)   Reasons why PTR may not want to move production facilities include the following.

Social concerns

PTR has the image of being a responsible employer, implying that it treats its' staff well and possibly assists the local community in some way. Moving the production facility would result in making many workers redundant and therefore result in adverse publicity, damaging the responsible employer image.

Family members

The company appears to have been run by the same people for a significant length of time. This implies that the directors and/or shareholders feel some social ties or responsibility to their workers. Moving production may therefore go against their individual morals.

Distances involved

No information is provided regarding the location of the suppliers for the PTR company. However, moving the production facility may result in an increase in the distance that supplies have to be transported, as well as the finished goods back to the home country. These costs may exceed the savings in labour.

Integration of other sections of supply chain

It is also not clear whether the R&D, admin and other departments would be required to move. Having R&D and production in two different locations may make it difficult to monitor production and ensure that clothes are manufactured as expected by R&D staff.

SECTION C

Question 3

Text reference. Chapters 3, 8, 9, 10 and 12.

Top tips. In part (a), resist the temptation to provide a general discussion about not responding to environmental change. Ensure your discussion is relevant to banks in Everland.

In part (b), don't be afraid to draw on knowledge of the banking industry gained from media coverage. Try to avoid being overly political or controversial – provide a logical, reasoned discussion.

Easy marks. The identification of the main threat (legislation).

Marking scheme

			Marks
(a)	Explanation of main threat (legislation)		2
	Maximum of 3 marks per relevant explained change referenced to the scenario	(Max)	<u>11</u>
			13
(b)	Up to 2 marks for each relevant, well-explained point		<u>12</u>
			<u><u>25</u></u>

Our answer shows what we consider the most appropriate points to make. Other relevant points that answer the question would earn marks. However, irrelevant points that do not answer the question would not earn marks.

(a) **Threat to Everland banks**

Everland banks have enjoyed an oligopoly-type position over the years (a small number of service providers have dominated the market with little competition). The new legislation presents a threat as it aims to weaken them and introduce competition into the market.

Changes that should be made

The banks of Everland need to make changes to their marketing, organisation, human resources and information systems in order for them to improve their customer focus and to survive.

Marketing changes

Products should be designed to meet customer needs. Market research is required to determine what the needs are.

Market segmentation should be considered to focus certain products on specific groups.

The use of customer service questionnaires or other methods of analysing satisfaction levels should be investigated to monitor how well customer needs are being met.

Organisational changes

Structural changes should be made that reflect the need to provide improved customer service. For example, setting up of a customer services department.

The strategic importance of marketing should be reflected by the inclusion of a marketing department, headed by a marketing director to co-ordinate resources and activities.

Human resources

Marketing and customer service professionals should be recruited at the expense of traditional bankers.

A broad range of skill sets and experience should be brought in by employing staff from markets outside banking.

Recruitment, selection and promotion policies should reflect the new skills/experience mix. Senior management must also reflect this diversity to counter the lack of marketing, HR and customer service experience.

Training should be given to promote customer focus and new marketing techniques.

Information technology systems

Systems should be updated to focus on the need for customer focus and quality of information.

New systems may be needed to monitor marketing and customer satisfaction.

Systems should allow feedback from customers and marketing campaigns to be available to senior management who can use it to make strategic decisions.

Systems should allow awareness of customer needs such as ethical behaviour or social responsibility to filter out to all staff.

(b)   **Ethical issues** facing marketers in the banking sector include:

Providing appropriate lending and support to businesses and households

In times of recession, banks have an important role to play in supporting recovery. Businesses require access to funds to enable them to survive in the short-term and invest for the medium and long terms. Banks that are excessively risk averse can hinder economic recovery.

Reasonable, transparent and understandable charges

Banks have been criticised in recent times for levying excessive, punitive charges on customers. Charges should be transparent and in some way related to what they are charged for. In the past, some banks have levied unjustly high charges on customers who exceed agreed lending levels.

Marketing and selling responsibly

Banks should not encourage customers to take services that they do not need or are inappropriate. For example, income protection insurance should not be automatically added into personal loan repayments.

Corporate social responsibility describes a range of obligations that an organisation has towards external stakeholders and to society as a whole. Issues marketers in the banking sector may face include:

Providing essential services in rural areas

Banking is an many ways an essential service. A local bank in a rural areas provides a convenient, accessible service for local individuals and businesses. Some believe banks have a responsibility to provide good geographical coverage, rather than only operating branches in 'busy' locations.

'Green' policies

All areas of business are now expected to follow green, sustainable policies where practical. Many banks offer 'paperless banking'.

Ethical investment

Some banks make a point of marketing themselves as ethical, and only provide funding for projects that meet their ethical standards.

Encourage a culture of financial responsibility and saving

Banks have been accused of lending excessively and recklessly in the recent past (for example 120% mortgages). Many in society believe banks should be encouraging a culture of financial responsibility and saving.

Question 4

Text reference. Chapters 11 and 12.

Top tips. Analyse this question carefully. Strong answers to Part (c) will discuss several substantive reasons which are clearly linked to the scenario.

Easy marks. General advantages and disadvantages of 'total reward packages'.

Marking scheme

			Marks
(a)	Up to 2marks for explaining 'total reward package'		2
	Up to 2 marks per relevant advantage	(Max)	6
	Up to 2 marks per relevant disadvantage	(Max)	6
			14
(b)	1 mark per valid area		3
(c)	1 - 2 marks per valid point referenced to the scenario		8
			25

Our answer shows what we consider the most appropriate points to make. Other relevant points that answer the question would earn marks. However, irrelevant points that do not answer the question would not earn marks.

(a)   **Total reward package**

A '**total reward package**' comprises monetary and non-monetary, motivators offered to staff. These packages recognise that individuals are all different and may not be motivated by money alone. The key principle is that employees can pick and choose what benefits they receive rather than everyone receiving the same. Employees can tailor their remuneration packages to suit their needs at any given time

Advantages to QW9

Carrington (2004) identified a number of other **advantages** of such schemes that are relevant to QW9.

They make a positive statement about the culture of the organisation.

Organisations that offer total reward packages are often seen as forward thinking and caring about the needs of their employees. This will not only further aid recruitment, but will **boost the overall image of the organisation** within the market place as it demonstrates an investment in its people.

The creation of a more inclusive rather than a 'them and us' attitude.

Staff morale and attitude may improve at all levels because the package of benefits is available to all rather than a select group of (possibly) senior employees.

Improved recruitment and retention as a result of employer branding.

Being seen as a good employer will further assist recruitment and retention of staff. Recruitment is improved as QW9 may become considered as a 'good place to work' making it more competitive when attracting new staff. Retention is improved as employees find that their needs (financial and otherwise) are met so why would they want to move?

Disadvantages to QW9

It may not be a success

Whilst total reward packages have worked for many companies, there is no guarantee that QW9's scheme will also be a success. The company will run the risk of the scheme failing. Failure may cause problems such as loss of the company's image – exactly the opposite of what was trying to be achieve.

It may not solve the problem

It appears that the main reason for introducing the scheme is to solve the problem of poor recruitment. However, this problem may not be caused by a lack of a total reward package. It is possible that other causes such as choosing inappropriate recruitment methods are to blame. Therefore, introducing the scheme may not resolve the issue.

It may cause organisational stagnation

Staff may become 'too comfortable' and even complacent about their jobs. Employees with a satisfactory total reward package may not push themselves further as there would be few other benefits to be achieved. Reduced staff turnover limits the amount of fresh blood being introduced into the organisation, resulting in fewer fresh ideas and reduced competition for higher status jobs.

(b)   QW9 should **investigate** a number of important areas that are relevant to the **design** of the total reward package. These areas are:

- What benefits are already on offer and what other benefits could be offered.
- What employees think about current and potential benefits.
- The costs and consequences of the new scheme.

(c)   > **Tutorial note.** This answer is more detailed than you need for eight marks as it shows a range of possible answers. Four well explained points is enough to earn full marks here.

Limited information is available regarding QW9's appraisal system. However, it is clear that the organisation has taken a **formal approach** using standardised forms with clear objectives for staff development and performance improvements.

Problems with the system can be considered under two headings, firstly inherent problems with the design and implementation of the system, and secondly problems concerning its operation.

Design and implementation problems

The system may have been **poorly designed** in the first place. For example, it may be based on systems used by other organisations and no thought given to whether it is suitable for QW9.

The design of the system may have reflected the needs of the organisation at an earlier time but is **no longer relevant** because the company has '**moved on**'.

There may have been a **lack of consultation** and **communication** with senior managers when the system was being developed. They may view it as being imposed on them and therefore are not interested in making it work.

Appraisal schemes should provide **benefits** which justify the cost and effort put into them. Senior management comments such as 'a waste of time and effort' indicate that there is an imbalance between what is put into the scheme and what comes out. This may have been caused by the system being put into place because one was thought to be needed rather than as a true method of improving staff development and performance.

Operational problems

Senior managers may have **insufficient time** to conduct the appraisal process properly. This may reduce the scheme into a form filling exercise just to meet HR requirements, missing the point of the scheme and its objectives.

The scheme focuses on staff development needs. Invariably this means **additional departmental training costs** that will have an impact on the profits each manager makes. Therefore, it is not necessarily in the interest of some managers to have large numbers of staff undergoing training. This of course is a short-sighted view as training should in the long-run improve profitability, but managers may not wish to wait for such benefits to materialise.

The scheme is **not linked to annual bonuses**. Employees are likely to act in a manner that maximises their bonus, which may be at odds with the objectives of the appraisal system.

Standard procedures indicate a **bureaucratic** or mechanical approach to appraisals. Senior mangers will be faced with a large volume of identical paperwork that needs to be processed in addition to their existing work load. There is likely to be a temptation to rush through the process with not much thought to the objectives just to get it done.

Appraisal schemes often involve **subjective judgements** and **opinions** by senior managers over their staff. There is a risk that employees are not assessed correctly or consistently meaning that some staff who do not require training are offered it whilst others that need help to improve their performance are not.

Alternative approach

Other advantages and disadvantages that you might have mentioned include:

Advantages

Attract suitable potential employees

QW9 operates in a competitive industry and must attract the highest quality staff to achieve high standards of customer care. However it is having problems attracting suitable applicants. By packaging all the benefits on offer and communicating it effectively in recruitment literature, QW9 may resolve this problem.

Improve staff motivation

Pay is not always a motivator and therefore it is important to offer a range of benefits that meet a diverse range of motivational needs. For example, flexitime allows staff to maintain a healthy work life balance which will maintain interest and motivation in the job for a long period.

Disadvantages

It ignores other factors

The scheme ignores some other important factors concerning staff welfare and motivation. Those in highly stressful roles will still be stressed and employees working in under staffed departments may not be able to take full advantage of benefits such as flexitime.

Staff dissatisfaction

Not all staff will be happy with the benefits on offer and many may just prefer more money. Those who do not want the benefits on offer may feel left out and leave the organisation.

CIMA
Paper E1 (Operational)
Enterprise Operations

Mock Exam 2

Question Paper		
Time allowed:	Reading time	**20 mins**
	Answering question paper	**3 hours**
This paper is divided into three sections		
Section A	**Answer ALL sub-questions in this section**	
Section B	**Answer ALL of the six short answer questions**	
Section C	**Answer BOTH of these questions**	

DO NOT OPEN THIS PAPER UNTIL YOU ARE READY TO START UNDER EXAMINATION CONDITIONS

SECTION A – 20 marks

Instructions for answering Section A

Each of the sub-questions numbered from 1.1 to 1.4 inclusive, given below, has only ONE correct answer, worth two marks.

Question 1

1.1   A collection of separate companies each with a specific expertise who work together to compete for bigger contracts than would be possible if they worked alone is known as a:

    A   Virtual team
    B   Virtual supply chain
    C   Virtual company
    D   Virtual network   **(2 marks)**

1.2   What is the sourcing strategy where one buyer chooses between several sources of supply known as?

    A   Single
    B   Multiple
    C   Delegated
    D   Parallel   **(2 marks)**

1.3   According to Caroll and Bucholtz which type of corporate social responsibility is desired rather than required of businesses?

    A   Economic
    B   Ethical
    C   Philanthropic
    D   Legal   **(2 marks)**

1.4   What category of quality cost is a cost arising from inadequate quality, during the production process?

    A   Internal failure cost
    B   External failure cost
    C   Appraisal cost
    D   Prevention cost   **(2 marks)**

Each of the sub-questions numbered **1.5** to **1.7** below require a brief written response. Each sub-question is worth 4 marks.

Each response should be in note form and should not exceed 50 words.

The following short scenario relates to Questions 1.5 - 1.7.

GUG produces a range of men's and women's watches. The company does not undertake any market research but prefers to concentrate on producing products for the lowest possible cost and then marketing them accordingly.

The company does use market segmentation and its marketing plan involves targeting each watch at a particular segment and then persuading that segment that the watch is the 'ideal' product.

1.5   Describe the 'marketing mix'.   **(4 marks)**

1.6   Explain the extent to which GUG is 'sales oriented'.   **(4 marks)**

1.7   Explain which marketing approach GUG appears to be taking (differentiated, undifferentiated and concentrated marketing).   **(4 marks)**

(Total = 20 marks)

SECTION B – 30 marks

Answer ALL parts of this question

Question 2

The Kyrano Company manufactures and sells electronic games. Customer data is currently held on four different computer systems, representing the four main areas of business of hand held game consoles, radio controlled cars, train sets and a new division selling electronically operated lights. Almost all sales are made by mail order, direct to individual customers.

Product development is rapid, with individual products progressing through the whole product life cycle in a minimum of 6 months and a maximum of 18 months.

The new management accountant has recommended that a new centralised database is established to maintain all customer data. However, there is also the recognition that existing systems have been in place for more than 12 years, so there is likely to be some resistance to change within the company. There is also the issue that there is no formal IT department and so a database programmer will have to be hired to write the new database.

The new database will provide a significant amount of statistical information on customers including sales history, average customer spend etc. with the option to obtain additional reports based on geographical area, demographic breakdowns such as purchases for different age groups and demand for each product.

Required

To assist in selling the new database to the Board of Kyrano, prepare a slide outline along with brief accompanying notes or two to three sentences, for each of the management accountant's points identified below.

Use a separate page of your answer book for each part.

(a)   State the benefits of using a database to manage the customer data in the Kyrano Company.   **(5 marks)**

(b)   Outline methods of reducing employee resistance to the new system.   **(5 marks)**

(c)   With reference to the product life cycle, explain how recording demand in the new database assists with product pricing.   **(5 marks)**

(d)   List the contents of a job specification (an outline of the position) for the database programmer.**(5 marks)**

(e)   Explain how a quality plan can be used to monitor development of the database.   **(5 marks)**

(f)   Explain how the new database can be used to provide data for marketing activities.   **(5 marks)**

(Total = 30 marks)

SECTION C – 50 marks

Answer BOTH questions

Question 3

Titan plc provides insurance services to individuals including car, house and personal accident insurance. Potential customers telephone Titan's call centre to ask for insurance quotes. The quotes are provided by call centre staff using a computer system to record quotes provided.

The computer system is relatively slow and will be replaced with upgraded hardware and software using a new expert system to assist call centre staff in providing quotes. Staff will enter information such as address, telephone number and driving licence details into the expert system which will then provide a quote based on those details. Call centre staff have no knowledge of the new system and additional assistance will be needed in using the system while talking to potential customers.

Required

(a)   Explain the steps in a training plan, relating your answer to Titan plc where possible.   **(15 marks)**

(b)   Describe the meaning and purpose of a post-implementation review and briefly describe three measures the directors of Titan plc could use to quantify the success of the upgraded hardware and software.

(10 marks)

(Total = 25 marks)

Question 4

The Zarni Company produces computer games for the PC market. It is based in the USA and its employees include 60 programmers, 20 strategic games advisors and 10 marketing managers. The company has been trading for 5 years, with turnover growing at the rate of 400% per annum in the last two years due to the success of its two games 'black shift' and 'Z force'. However, none of the company's games have reached the number one position in the games league tables. The company currently has a 12% market share in its target markets.

The company is considering producing a series of games based on black shift, with each game being given a different colour name (eg yellow shift, blue shift...). The average cost of producing one game has increased by 300% in the last two years as a result of the additional details and features now expected by customers. The standard customer of Zarni is aged between 18 and 35, and predominantly male.

There are at least six other similar games companies in the USA, with significant, if declining, competition from the Japanese market. The latter tends to rely on older platform style games featuring characters such as 'chain' and 'mule chimp'.

The games market in the USA is relatively stagnant, although other markets such as South America and on-line gaming are growing rapidly. Zarni has little experience in these segments.

Required

(a)   Explain how you would evaluate the commercial attractiveness of market segments.   **(10 marks)**

(b)   Prepare a situation analysis and strategic marketing plan for the Zarni Company.   **(15 marks)**

(Total = 25 marks)

(Total for Section C = 50 marks)

END OF QUESTION PAPER

Answers

DO NOT TURN THIS PAGE UNTIL YOU HAVE
COMPLETED MOCK EXAM 2

202

A plan of attack

Before the three hours writing time starts, you are allowed 20 minutes to read through the paper. Use this time wisely – in effect it gives you an extra 20 minutes to gain the marks you need to pass.

What should you do in this 20 minutes?

We recommend you spend the first ten minutes of reading time scanning the paper and identifying the main topic areas covered.

The second ten minutes, we suggest you simply **start working through the Section A questions** – by **writing your answers on the question paper**. These answers can then be transferred **very carefully** to your answer booklet when the exam starts. Remember though, you **must not write in your answer booklet during the reading time**.

Using the time in this way should mean that later in the exam, when you reach Section C, you have sufficient time to read both questions carefully and plan your answers to them.

Turn back to the question paper now, and we'll sort out a **plan of attack** for Mock exam 2.

First things first

It's usually best to **start with the multiple choice** and **objective test** questions (ie do Section A first). You should always be able to do a fair proportion of these, even if you really haven't done as much preparation as you should have, and answering even a couple of them will give you the confidence to attack the rest of the paper.

Allow yourself 36 minutes to do the objective test questions. No more.

The next step – Section B

Attempt Question 2 immediately after you've completed Section A. You've got to do this question so there's no point delaying it. The question is split into sub-parts. In this mock exam, the parts are all based on a single scenario. CIMA reserve the right to use this format in Section B of the real exam, although to date Section B questions have not been based on a scenario.

Read the scenario carefully, then take a look at the question requirements.

- Part (a) requires you to state the advantages of databases and to apply this knowledge to the Kyrano Company.

- Part (b) covers resistance to change – remember the theories you have studied that cover change and resistance to change.

- Part (c) requires application of the product life cycle. Don't just make general points – your answer must be realistic in the context of the scenario.

- In part (d), ensure the job description is realistic.

- Part (e) requires application of quality plan knowledge.

- Think about part (f) carefully, you should be able to think of enough uses for customer data and opportunities to exploit it.

Section C

Once you've done Sections A and B, you are required to answer the two longer questions in Section C.

- **Question 3**. To earn the marks on offer in Part (a) you are required to outline a training plan. Again, ensure your answer relates to the scenario.

  Part (b) requires a general explanation of post-implementation review. Ensure your three suggestions are relevant to Titan plc.

- **Question 4**. Part (a) requires you to take a commercial point of view. Ensure you focus on commercial aspects, which generally means financial results and/or financial potential.

  In part (b) you are required to produce a situation analysis that identifies issues in the scenario which will affect Zarni.

General advice

Don't forget that all questions in the E1 exam are **compulsory**.

No matter how many times we remind you....

Always, always **allocate your time** according to the marks for the question in total and for the parts of the question. And always, **always follow the requirements** exactly.

You've got spare time at the end of the exam.....?

If you have allocated your time properly then you **shouldn't have time on your hands** at the end of the exam. If you find yourself with five or ten minutes spare, however, **go back to any parts of questions that you didn't finish** because you ran out of ideas or time. A fresh look may spark new thoughts.

Forget about it!

And don't worry if you found the paper difficult. More than likely other candidates would too. If this were the real thing you would need to forget the exam the minute you leave the exam hall and **think about the next one**. Or, if it's the last one, **celebrate**!

SECTION A

Question 1

1.1   C   The text describes a virtual company.

1.2   B   The definition refers to the use of multiple suppliers.

1.3   C   Philanthropic responsibilities such as charitable donations are desired rather than required of businesses.

1.4   A   Internal failure costs include the cost of materials or components lost or scrapped in the production process, re-working costs, and losses from selling faulty output at reduced prices. The other categories of quality costs are appraisal costs (or inspection costs), prevention costs and external failure costs. Appraisal costs are the costs of checking finished goods. Prevention costs are costs incurred prior to making a product or delivering a service, to prevent substandard production. External failure costs are costs arising from inadequate quality, where the problem is identified after the finished product or service has been delivered to the customer.

1.5   The '**marketing mix**' is the range of decisions and elements of marketing that achieve the maximum impact for a product or service. This mix of elements traditionally includes **price**, **place**, **product** and **promotion**. 'People' is sometimes added as a fifth element, particularly in services marketing.

1.6   '**Sales orientation**' usually occurs where a company produces a product without first establishing what the customer needs are. This exactly describes GUG's approach, GUG focuses on trying to sell the low cost watches it has produced.

1.7   **Differentiated marketing** – applying a different marketing mix to each segment the product is marketed at.

Undifferentiated marketing – applying a single marketing mix to all segments.

Concentrated marketing – targeting one market segment with the 'ideal' product for that segment.

GUG is therefore taking a **concentrated approach**.

SECTION B

Question 2

Text reference. Chapters 3, 4, 6, 8, 9, 10, 12.

Top tips. In an exam situation, if you are asked to produce slides keep them simple. Each slide is essentially a list of headings – with the main heading as the slide title. Be careful to avoid making purely generic points – always relate your answer to the scenario.

Easy marks. The job specification is a simple proforma.

Marking scheme

		Marks
(a)	1 mark for each relevant explained point	5
(b)	1 mark for each relevant explained point	5
(c)	1 mark for each relevant explained point	5
(d)	1 mark for each relevant explained point	5
(e)	1 mark for each relevant explained point	5
(f)	1 mark for each relevant explained point	5
		30

Our answer shows what we consider the most appropriate points to make. Other relevant points that answer the question would earn marks. However, irrelevant points that do not answer the question would not earn marks.

(a) **Slide 1**

Benefits of database

Reduction in data redundancy – customer data held once only

Reduced storage costs – only one system to maintain

Data integrity – no inconsistencies between databases

Privacy – Data kept secure in one location

Notes to slide one.

Existing databases amalgamated into one reducing duplication of data and computer hardware. Inconsistencies (eg different delivery addresses) removed by using only one database. Security enhanced by applying good controls in one location only.

Top tips. In Part (b) you may have based your answer on other change management theories.

(b) **Slide 2**

Overcoming resistance to change

Provide forum for discussing weaknesses of old system

Education – focus on benefits of new system

Participation in system design

Negotiation and agreement on system functionality

Notes to slide two

Employees need to be involved in change, hence providing an initial forum and then inviting user participation in design. Where appropriate, the benefits of the system will have to be 'sold', particularly if employees do not want or resist change. Some form of negotiation may be necessary to provide employees with other benefits if they accept change.

(c)   **Slide 3**

Product pricing – database benefits

Introduction – High price to cover development costs

Growth – Fall in price reflecting increased competition

Maturity – Further fall in price – niche marketing

Decline – Sell below cost

Notes to slide three

Product life cycle information available from demand for discontinued products. The stage of each product in the life cycle can be determined, and from this an estimate made of the most appropriate price. Given rapid product development, it will be important to identify when a product is in decline so as to sell off stocks and concentrate production on newer products.

(d)   **Slide 4**

Job specification

Job title – database programmer

Reporting to – management accountant

Key task – write customer database (more detail available in the Job Description)

Required skills – knowledge and experience of database programming needed

---

Notes to slide four

The job specification sets out the purpose of the job and the key attributes required to fill the position. The lack of any formal IT department or hierarchy means that the programmer will report to the management accountant. We must ensure the appointee has the necessary technical knowledge to write the database.

(e)   **Slide 5**

Quality plan

1.   Establish standards for the database and method of writing

2.   Agree methods of monitoring quality

3.   Compare database production against specification

4.   Control actions – test database – where below standard implement remedial work

5.   Amend plan where necessary

Notes to slide five

A quality plan is necessary because Kyrano Company has no experience in database writing; the programmer must therefore be monitored in some way. The idea of setting standards and then monitoring development against those standards is not unusual. Comparing actual outputs to agreed outputs helps us monitor development without having to understand database design in detail.

(f)   **Slide 6**

Use of new database – marketing

Segmentation analysis – identify target markets by age or geographical area

Purchasing history – send details of new products; repeat purchases

Sales history – identify popular products for new investment

Marketing effectiveness – type and amount of spend against product type

---

Notes to slide six

The database will provide additional detail on individual products sold. Data will be analysed to identify types of purchase allowing marketing to be directed at specific market segments. Sales of different product types can also be tracked over time to ensure that new products are developed to meet customer requirements.

SECTION C

Question 3

> **Text reference.** Chapters 4 and 12.
>
> **Top tips.** Start Part (a) by writing down the steps you will include in your plan, with sufficient space below each step to flesh out your answer.
>
> Don't worry if your steps aren't the same as those shown in our answer – a wide range of answers would have scored well on this question.
>
> The general sequence; determine, plan, implement and evaluate, should be followed.
>
> You may be able to draw on your own experience in your answer to Part (b).
>
> **Easy marks.** Reproducing a standard planning sequence provides a framework for your answer and earns a few marks.

Marking scheme

		Marks	
(a)	1 mark per valid point regarding developing a training plan generally	10	
	1 mark per relevant reference to scenario	5	
			15
(b)	Up to 2 marks for explaining 'post-implementation review'	2	
	Up to 2 marks for explaining the purpose of such a review	2	
	Up to 2 marks per relevant measure referenced to the scenario	6	
			10
			25

Our answer shows what we consider the most appropriate points to make. Other relevant points that answer the question would earn marks. However, irrelevant points that do not answer the question would not earn marks.

(a) **Training plan for Titan plc**

   1. **Determine training needs**

      Training needs may be satisfied either by training existing employees or by recruiting new employees with specific training skills. In the case of Titan, the change is incremental indicating that in-house training will be appropriate.

   2. **Identify training objectives**

      In other words, Titan must specify the knowledge, skills and competences that have to be acquired. This is easier for technical training where skills match a specific computer system, as in Titan. Identifying objectives is more difficult where 'soft' skills, that is personnel skills, are involved as they are more difficult to define. For example, telephone skills can be taught, but these will have to be refined over time as experience is gained of working with people.

   3. **Develop criteria against which to measure performance**

      Training will normally be checked to determine that it has met the training needs. This means identifying criteria to measure the training against. In terms of Titan, criteria such as number of customer queries handled or average waiting time can be used.

4.   Determine current levels of proficiency

This information is required to target training to meet specific skills gaps in the organisation. In Titan, for example, staff are already familiar with computer systems but not with the specific expert system. Training on the general use of computers therefore is not required – but training on the expert system is.

5.   Arrange training

This step simply involves production of training material, booking training rooms and communicating the time and purpose of training to participants.

6.   Implement training

Carry out the training. The content and delivery must be clear and appropriate for trainees. The delivery method should be appropriate, for example a mixture of face-to-face and online delivery.

7.   Evaluate the training

Performance criteria have already been set in step 3. Improvements in skills will be checked at the end of training, using questionnaires or skills based testing. Evaluation should be repeated after a few weeks to check that skills have been retained.

(b)   **Post-implementation review**

A post-implementation review usually takes place a few months after system implementation is complete. The purpose of the review is to receive feedback from users on how well the system is working and to check that the objectives of the project have been met. The review normally takes the form of a meeting between the management and users.

Review purpose

The review will investigate both the procedures used throughout the project and the systems that have been produced. The purpose of doing this is to identify what features of the project went well, and what went wrong or badly, so that future projects will avoid these problems.

In reviewing the objectives of the project, the review will also check whether or not the business benefits expected from the project have been achieved. Where benefits have not been achieved, or other objectives of the project have not been met, the review may also recommend remedial action to ensure that the required benefits are obtained.

Measures of success for hardware or software.

(i)   **Number of errors reported**

A log can be maintained, either by individual users or the management, of the **number** and **type** or **errors** found in the system. The actual error rate provides an indication of the quality of programming and the effectiveness of the different stages of testing.

(ii)   **Number of quotations processed**

The original **software specification** will indicate how many quotes should be processed. Comparing the specification with the **actual** number processed will provide information on the usefulness of the system (if the system is not useful then presumably it will be used less than expected). A small number of quotes being processed could also be indicative of poor programming or inadequate hardware specifications, so further analysis may be needed to determine which of these is relevant.

(iii)   **Number of change requests**

Users may request changes to the system, either where that system did not meet their **original requirements**, or where the system as implemented does not meet their **expectations** in some way. Changes requested due to initial specifications not being met provides some measure on the quality of the design and testing processes. Changes requested because the software is not meeting expectations may indicate weaknesses in this method of obtaining data for initial specification.

Question 4

Text reference. Chapters 8, 9 and 10.

Top tips. When reading through the scenario information, underline points that seem significant (eg growth of 400%, market share 12% etc). Then, ensure these factors are taken into account with your plan.

In Part (a) you needed to go beyond a basic explanation of segment validity by looking at commercial attractiveness – hence 'actionability' and evaluation'. You might have come up with other ideas.

Easy marks. In Part (b) start by heading up your plan and writing the headings you will use (with enough space for the material you will add).

Marking scheme

			Marks
(a)	Up to 2 marks per relevant measure of segment attractiveness		10
(b)	SWOT analysis – half mark per issue identified	5	
	Strategic marketing plan appropriate structure, up to 2 marks	2	
	1 mark per relevant point made in plan	8	
			15
			25

Our answer shows what we consider the most appropriate points to make. Other relevant points that answer the question would earn marks. However, irrelevant points that do not answer the question would not earn marks.

(a)   **Market segment attractiveness**

There are a number of methods to evaluate the **commercial attractiveness** of market segments. We need to understand the performance within each segment and how effective the targeting and positioning has been from our efforts. To be useful, market segments must have the following characteristics:

Measurable

How easy is it to ascertain the actual attribute within each segment? The size, buying power and profiles of the segments need measuring. For example, how measurable is a segment based on the enjoyment of computer games? Is current sales levels a sufficient measure?

Accessibility

The market segment needs to be reached effectively and properly served. For example, how are males aged 18-35 best reached? To be cost-effective, marketing and advertising needs to use methods in-tune with the target market.

Substantiality

The market segments need to be large enough and have sufficient profit potential to be attractive propositions. A segment should be the largest possible homogenous group worth pursuing with a tailored marketing programme.

Profitability

Do the identified customer needs cost less to satisfy than the revenue they earn? Ultimately, unless a segment is profitable (either now or in the future), there is no point pursuing it.

Stability

There is a need to understand the **potential** for each segment to **grow**, to assess current **competitor activity** and the likelihood of future targeting by other businesses of particular segments. There may also be changes in **tastes**, **lifestyles** and **aspirations** that need to be considered.

(b)

> **Top tips.** Your situation analysis should really be a SWOT analysis as there insufficient information for PEST.

Situation analysis

The current situation is presented below, in SWOT format.

Strengths	Weaknesses
High growth	Lack of Number One game
Good reputation	Increasing production costs
Opportunities	**Threats**
Expansion into South America	Lack of experience with new markets
Expansion into online gaming	USA based companies
Produce brand of games	Declining threat from Japan

Strategic marketing plan

1. **Executive summary**

   This document sets out the marketing plan for the Zarni Company for the year end 20X7. The main goals for this period are:

   - Produce a top selling game

   - Increase market share

   The main recommendations for this report are:

   - Authorise increased marketing budget

   - Investigate other markets

2. **Situation analysis**

   - Completed above.

3. **Objectives and goals**

   The company needs to continue to grow to support increased expenditure on games manufacture. Growth targets are set at:

   - Market share of 15%

   - Sales growth of 450%

   - Net profit of 10%

4. **Marketing strategy**

   The company's main target market of 18 to 35 year old males will be maintained. However, additional information is be obtained on the South American games market. This will be easier to access than online gaming using the assumption that the company's existing products can be sold there.

5. **Strategic marketing plan aims**

   The marketing plan for the next 3 years is:

   - Produce a 'shift' game every year.

   - Focus marketing activities on building the brand name of 'shift'.

   - Investigate, and where appropriate, enter new markets.

6. **Tactical marketing plan aims**

    In the next year the company will:

    - Investigate the South American market.

    - Produce the next 'shift' game – research needed on the most appropriate colour.

7. **Action plan**

    Marketing mix strategy

    - Product – produce the 'shift' required

    - Price – target $49

    - Place – distributed via wholesalers as previous games

    - Promotion – continue existing promotion in gaming magazines

    - People – employ five new programmers

    - Processes – investigate South America

8. **Budget**

    An initial budget of $550,000 to be set for marketing activities including advertising.

9. **Controls**

    Any expenditure over $40,000 to be authorised in advance by the Financial Accountant.

CIMA
Paper E1 (Operational)
Enterprise Operations

Mock Exam 3

Question Paper		
Time allowed: Reading time Answering question paper		**20 mins** **3 hours**
This paper is divided into three sections		
Section A	**Answer ALL sub-questions in this section**	
Section B	**Answer ALL of the six short answer questions**	
Section C	**Answer BOTH of these questions**	

DO NOT OPEN THIS PAPER UNTIL YOU ARE READY TO START UNDER EXAMINATION CONDITIONS

CIMA

Paper E1 (Operational)

Enterprise Operations

Mock Exam 3

Mock Paper		
Time allowed / Reading and planning Writing / answering question paper		20 mins 3 hours
This paper is divided into three sections		
Section A	Answer ALL sub-questions in this section	
Section B	Answer ALL of the six short answer questions	
Section C	Answer BOTH of these questions	

DO NOT OPEN THIS PAPER UNTIL YOU ARE READY TO START UNDER EXAMINATION CONDITIONS

SECTION A – 20 marks

Instructions for answering Section A

Each of the sub-questions numbered from 1.1 to 1.10 has only ONE correct answer worth two marks.

Question 1

1.1 Which one of the following is NOT a benefit of corporate governance?

    A   Improved access to capital markets
    B   Stimulation of performance
    C   Enhanced marketability of goods and services
    D   Prevention of fraudulent claims by contractors   **(2 marks)**

1.2 Corporate political activity is normally undertaken in order to

    A   Secure policy preferences
    B   Make the world a better place
    C   Further an environmental agenda
    D   Understand the external drivers on an organisation   **(2 marks)**

1.3 Political risk analysis is conducted by a company considering international operations and normally focuses on the

    A   World economy generally
    B   Relations between the USA, Japan and Europe
    C   Political and cultural differences between the home and target country
    D   Industrialisation of the target country   **(2 marks)**

1.4 Efficient regulation of companies is said to exist if

    A   The total benefit to the nation is greater than the total cost
    B   There is greater integration of the world's economies
    C   Greater innovation takes place by all businesses
    D   The effect on businesses is neutral   **(2 marks)**

1.5 The basis of the stakeholder view is that

    A   Only shareholders are legitimate stakeholders
    B   Only creditors and shareholders are legitimate stakeholders
    C   Persons, groups and organisations with an interest in the organisation are stakeholders
    D   Only members that an organisation officially recognises are stakeholders   **(2 marks)**

1.6 Which ONE of the following is not an approach to systems implementation?

    A   Parallel running
    B   Phased changeover
    C   Matrix operation
    D   Pilot testing   **(2 marks)**

1.7   Which ONE of the following is not normally associated with outsourced IS solutions?

    A   Ensuring contract compliance
    B   Assembly and maintenance of a suitably skilled workforce
    C   Preparing formal tendering documents
    D   Invoicing, processing and payment   **(2 marks)**

1.8   A necessary product/service requirement to meet the Japanese interpretation of 'quality' is

    A   To comply with all safety standards
    B   To cost no more than necessary
    C   To meet a design brief
    D   To meet customer expectations   **(2 marks)**

1.9   Process design can best be improved by

    A   An organisational restructure to reflect functions not processes
    B   Improved checks on suppliers
    C   Adopting a strategy of continuous improvement
    D   Improved quality control   **(2 marks)**

1.10 Collaborating with its suppliers may bring a company added value because it can

    A   Strike a harder bargain with its suppliers
    B   Work with a supplier to improve quality and reduce costs
    C   Avoid transaction costs
    D   Introduce price competition amongst suppliers   **(2 marks)**

(Total = 20 marks)

SECTION B – 30 marks

Answer ALL parts of this question

Question 2

(a)   Briefly **explain** FIVE reasons for the growth in outsourcing by organisations. **(5 marks)**

(b)   **Describe** FIVE ways in which emerging economies have benefited as a result of foreign direct investment in their countries by multinational enterprises. **(5 marks)**

(c)   Certain organisations have been transformed by information and communication technology (ICT). Briefly **explain** FIVE significant ICT changes using retail organisations as an example. **(5 marks)**

(d)   **Describe** FIVE forms of waste within manufacturing organisations that lean process improvement aims to eliminate. **(5 marks)**

(e)   'Lean' thinking was first developed with manufacturing organisations in mind. **Describe** FIVE examples of ways in which these waste elimination principles might be applied to improve efficiency in service organisations (such as hospitals and offices). **(5 marks)**

(f)   **Describe** the key aspects of a programme to implement Total Quality Management (TQM) within a manufacturing organisation. **(5 marks)**

(Total = 30 marks)

SECTION C – 50 marks

Answer BOTH questions

Question 3

The country of Bigland has a democratically elected government which determines broad national policies. Local services such as education, social care and environmental services are the responsibility of the elected local government for the regions. These regions are funded by a combination of local taxes and government grants. The largest region is Middleregion, which is about to develop a new workforce strategy for its many local government employees. Recently it has received a report from its external auditor into its overall arrangements for achieving value for money. The external auditor has made three recommendations relevant to human resources (HR):

- There needs to be greater clarity over the distinctive roles carried out by both Middleregion's Human Resources Department and line managers in developing and implementing HR practices.

- A new workforce strategy is a good initiative but planning will need to take account of a changing environment and be relevant to local conditions.

- Middleregion should consider moving to more electronically-based HR processes and systems (e-HR). e-HR includes using technology to improve HR services, such as recording and monitoring systems, automating administrative tasks like recruitment, and communicating HR information on the intranet.

Required

(a) **Discuss** the contributions of both Middleregion's Human Resources Department and line managers in developing and then implementing HR practices.   **(10 marks)**

(b) **Explain**, with examples, how Middleregion should plan a new workforce strategy that takes account of a changing environment and is relevant to local conditions.   **(10 marks)**

(c) **Explain** the costs Middleregion should take account of when considering moving to e-HR.   **(5 marks)**

(Total = 25 marks)

Question 4

The DD drinks company was founded over one hundred years ago by a deeply religious family and has been recognised as being a good employer ever since. The company has a long history of supporting sporting events as part of its stated commitment to help promote healthy lifestyles. DD has a corporate social responsibility (CSR) commitment to behave ethically while helping improve the quality of life of society generally. A percentage of DD's profits are also allocated to a number of local charitable causes every year.

Using secret natural ingredients, DD has grown to become the world's leading manufacturer and distributor of non-alcoholic drinks. The company has an extremely strong brand and its drinks are sometimes sold alongside 'own brand' alternatives which it manufactures and packages on behalf of a few large supermarket chains. Own brand drinks sell more cheaply than DD branded products, are less costly to produce (they avoid expensive labelling and promotion) but sales remain low. DD spends heavily on displaying some of its ever-expanding product lines on television, normally before and after popular programmes aimed at children and teenagers. For the first time this year, DD is also spending an equal amount on online advertising. Following the pattern of its major rivals, DD has recently sought celebrity endorsements for its products. Focus group research indicated that the endorsement by a controversial rapper Mr TT would appeal to its target market segment. When this was announced there was criticism from religious and political groups because of the music's association with exploitation of females, violence and bad language. One newspaper editorial accused DD of 'endorsing immorality'. In response, DD decided not to use Mr TT in its campaigns and admitted that it had made an error of judgement in a press statement.

Now a further problem has arisen. An international health 'watchdog' body has reported that DD's products contain high levels of sugar and, if drunk excessively by children, they can lead to long term gum and tooth decay. DD has yet to respond to the report.

Required

(a)   **Discuss** the implications of DD's activities on its ethical stance and CSR position.   **(10 marks)**

(b)   **Explain** the role that the basic marketing mix and branding have in DD's positioning to appeal to its target market segment.   **(10 marks)**

(c)   **Discuss** the likely benefits of DD's increased use of the internet for marketing purposes.   **(5 marks)**

(Total = 25 marks)

(Total for Section C = 50 marks)

END OF QUESTION PAPER

Answers

DO NOT TURN THIS PAGE UNTIL YOU HAVE
COMPLETED MOCK EXAM 3

A plan of attack

Before the three hours writing time starts, you are allowed 20 minutes to read through the paper. Use this time wisely – in effect it gives you an extra 20 minutes to gain the marks you need to pass.

What should you do in this 20 minutes?

We recommend you spend the first ten minutes of reading time scanning the paper and identifying the main topic areas covered.

The second ten minutes, we suggest you simply **start working through the Section A questions** – by **writing your answers on the question paper**. These answers can then be transferred **very carefully** to your answer booklet when the exam starts. Remember though, you **must not write in your answer booklet during the reading time**.

Using the time in this way should mean that later in the exam, when you reach Section C, you have sufficient time to read both questions carefully and plan your answers to them.

Turn back to the question paper now, and we'll sort out a **plan of attack** for Mock exam 3.

First things first

It's usually best to **start with the multiple choice** and **objective test** questions (ie do Section A first). You should always be able to do a fair proportion of these, even if you really haven't done as much preparation as you should have, and answering even a couple of them will give you the confidence to attack the rest of the paper.

Allow yourself 36 minutes to do the objective test questions. No more.

The next step – Section B

Attempt Question 2 immediately after you've completed Section A. All questions are compulsory, and question 2 is possibly less demanding than questions 3 and 4 (as in this exam at least, there isn't a scenario to consider in question 2). The question is split into six independent sub-parts.

- Part (a) tests your knowledge of outsourcing. Your answer should refer to how technology and other factors have made outsourcing possible and attractive.

- In (b), benefits such as providing employment should spring to mind as soon as you read the requirement. Other benefits, for example taxation and building confidence in the economy, may require more thought.

- For (c), think about the technology used when you visit retail outlets such as supermarkets.

- Book knowledge alone should prove sufficient points to score well in part (d).

- Part (e) requires some thought to apply your knowledge of lean techniques to a service environment. Remember that elimination of waste is key.

- Part (f), as with part (b), requires little more than the reproduction of the appropriate book knowledge.

Section C

Once you've done Sections A and B, you are required to answer the two questions in Section C. Almost all Section C questions will require you to relate the points you make to the organisation and situation described in the scenario.

- In **question 3** part (a), think about the different roles played by a 'general' HR department and the narrower focus of local line managers.

  In part (b), don't be thrown by the use of the term 'workforce strategy'. Even if you haven't seen this term before, you should be able to connect it with human resources strategy and human resources planning.

  Part (c) should be relatively straightforward, think about the costs associated with any IT system – for example hardware, software, maintenance and training – and also the specific costs such as maintaining the employee database.

- **Question 4**. In part (a) remember that an ethical stance means trying to 'do the right thing' in the eyes of society as a whole.

Part (b) provides an opportunity to apply your marketing-mix, branding and positioning knowledge to the DD's situation.

In (c), there is potential to discuss social networking, web 2.0 and viral marketing.

General advice

Don't forget that all questions in the E1 exam are **compulsory**.

No matter how many times we remind you....

Always, always **allocate your time** according to the marks for the question in total and for the parts of the question. And always, **always follow the requirements** exactly.

You've got spare time at the end of the exam.....?

If you have allocated your time properly then you **shouldn't have time on your hands** at the end of the exam. If you find yourself with five or ten minutes spare, however, **go back to any parts of questions that you didn't finish** because you ran out of ideas or time. A fresh look may spark new thoughts.

Forget about it!

And don't worry if you found the paper difficult. More than likely other candidates would too. If this were the real thing you would need to forget the exam the minute you leave the exam hall and **think about the next one**. Or, if it's the last one, **celebrate**!

SECTION A

Question 1

1.1 D Corporate governance focuses to a large extent on preventing directors from abusing their power. Prevention of fraudulent claims by contractors is not a major benefit of good corporate governance. The other three options are.

1.2 A Corporate political activity aims to secure policy preferences.

1.3 C Political risk analysis focuses on the political and cultural differences between the home and target country.

1.4 A Efficient regulation of companies exists if the total benefit (of regulation) to the nation exceeds the total cost.

1.5 C Under the stakeholder view, the people, groups and organisations with an interest in the organisation are viewed as stakeholders.

1.6 C 'Matrix operation' is not a term associated with systems development or changeover.

1.7 B If the Information Systems function is outsourced, the organisation does not need to assemble and maintain a suitable IS workforce in-house.

1.8 D A key focus of quality under the Japanese approach is customer satisfaction, which relies on meeting customer needs and expectations.

1.9 C Process design often benefits from the use of kaizen (continuous improvement).

1.10 B Closer relationships with a supplier can help improve quality and reduce costs.

SECTION B

Question 2

Text reference. Chapters 1, 2, 3 and 6.

Top tips. Parts (a) - (e) all specify that five points are required. This makes it clear that the examiner requires one substantive point per mark in this question.

Easy marks. Reproducing basic 'book knowledge' will earn many of the marks on offer in these six sub-questions. If a part requires application of knowledge, such as part (e), ensure you phrase your answer in such a way that makes it clear how the points you're making relate to the situation described.

Marking scheme

		Marks
(a)	1 mark for each relevant explained point	5
(b)	1 mark for each relevant explained point	5
(c)	1 mark for each relevant explained point	5
(d)	1 mark for each relevant explained point	5
(e)	1 mark for each relevant explained point	5
(f)	1 mark for each relevant explained point	5
		30

Our answer shows what we consider the most appropriate points to make. Other relevant points that answer the question would earn marks. However, irrelevant points that do not answer the question would not earn marks.

(a) Five reasons for the growth in outsourcing by organisations are:

Focus on costs

We're currently in tough economic times. During these times organisations tend to focus on costs. Outsourcing facilitates accurate prediction of costs and budgetary control. The outsource provider should enjoy economies of scale that enable them to provide a cost-effective service. This links with competitive rivalry as if other organisations save money by outsourcing you may have no choice but to follow suit.

High outsource service provider standards

In areas that require specialised knowledge, the external provider is likely to have access to a much larger pool of expertise than would be possible in-house. This access to expertise should result in a higher quality service than could be provided by in-house staff.

The need for flexibility

Contract permitting, outsourcing provides the flexibility to scale resource use up or down depending upon demand. The same level of flexibility is more difficult to achieve through the use of in-house employees.

Developments in technology and an increasingly global approach to business

In many areas, for example call centres and data processing, developments in information and communications technology have made it feasible to use outsource suppliers based overseas (for example, India).

Need to focus on core competencies

The growth in outsourcing has been fuelled partly by the need for businesses to focus their efforts and resources on their core competencies. To establish or preserve competitive advantage, an organisation should focus on what it is they do that other businesses don't or can't do as well. This has encouraged the outsourcing of 'administrative' tasks such as payroll.

(b)   Five ways in which emerging economies have benefited as a result of foreign direct investment in their countries by multinational enterprises are:

Job creation

Foreign direct investment by multinational enterprise creates employment opportunities for the local population. Even if some senior management are expatriate, a large proportion of jobs in the venture are usually taken by the local population.

Taxation revenue and infrastructure improvements

The government should benefit from increased domestic taxation take, for example through income tax paid by local employees. This revenue could be used to improve the local infrastructure, making the country more able to support increased commercial activity.

Spread of expertise

Foreign direct investment often funds ventures that involve both local and expatriate staff. This facilitates the spread of expertise and good practice that benefits the local economy.

Stimulate the local economy

The domestic economy should benefit from wages earned by employees based in the home country. Much of this income will be spent locally, benefiting local businesses and encouraging economic growth.

Raise confidence and encourage other foreign investment

By investing in the foreign country the multinational enterprise is demonstrating confidence in the local country and its business environment. This can encourage further investment by other multinational enterprises.

(c)   Five significant ICT changes for retail organisations are:

Electronic payment

The proportion of retail transactions paid for using cash and cheques has dropped significantly over the past two decades. Electronic payment is becoming the norm, utilising technology such as 'chip and pin' and new contactless payment systems.

Online sales (e-commerce)

Even traditional 'high street' retailers now do a significant proportion of their business online. Integration between the website and physical retail outlets is becoming increasingly important, with in-store pick-up often offered now for orders placed online (as well as the delivery option).

Customer database analysis and loyalty schemes

Computerised inventory and sales systems enable retailers to capture huge amounts of transaction data. This has led to improved inventory control and store design (enabling items often purchased together to be arranged closer together). Customer loyalty cards enable the database to include purchaser-specific data, facilitating targeted marketing offers.

Self-service checkout terminals

Many retailers (for example supermarkets) have introduced self-service checkouts that utilise barcode scanning and point of sale payment technology. The technology has made it feasible for untrained members of the public to process their own transactions.

Price comparison websites

There are now many price comparison sites on the web, including sites covering retailers (for example supermarkets and electronic products). These sites make it significantly easier for consumers to identify the best deals. Retailers have responded to this challenge with 'price matching' schemes.

(d)   Five forms of waste within manufacturing organisations that lean process improvements aim to eliminate are:

Inventory holdings

The purchase and holding of unnecessary raw materials, work in process and finished goods is wasteful. A lean process is characterised by minimal inventory holdings at each stage of the production process (as in Just In Time).

Unnecessary waiting or idle time

Lean process improvements aim to eliminate delays that add time to the process without adding value. For example, if employees are required to wait for a previous step in the process to complete, this is wasteful. It may be possible to redesign the process in a way that eliminates this.

Transport or motion delays

Lean process improvements aim to identify and eliminate actions that do not add value. Part of this involves ensuring the production layout is efficient and based on work flow, to remove unnecessary transportation or movement of goods and people.

Defective units

Defective production requires re-work or is written off, so is extremely wasteful. Lean process improvements would focus on defect prevention (rather than inspection and rework) by building quality into the process.

Unnecessary or over-processing

Lean techniques aim to identify and eliminate unnecessary steps or procedures (non added value work). This involves analysing a process and thinking 'if this wasn't done, would the impact be significant?'. The ultimate test of whether an activity is necessary is the impact removing it would have on the customer.

(e)   Five examples of ways in which lean waste elimination principles might be applied to improve efficiency in service organisations such as hospitals and offices are:

Reduce waiting times

Time spent waiting, whether by customers (patients) or employees, is inefficient. For example, lean techniques could be applied to improve flexibility in a hospital accident and emergency department to **reduce patient waiting time** (the aim being a balance between capacity and demand).

Eliminate non-value adding activities (ensure all who are allocated hospital beds do need them)

If a resource is being consumed by an activity that adds little value, this is inefficient. In the context of a hospital, lean techniques could focus on identifying patients that are currently allocated a hospital bed, but whose condition could **just as effectively be treated as an out-patient**. This would leave more bed nights available for patients that definitely require on-site care.

Raise standards to reduce complaints

Dealing with complaints **consumes resources without adding to output**, so is wasteful. Lean waste elimination principles could be applied to **improve hospital processes** and raise quality standards. For example introducing more flexibility in working patterns could reduce staff 'idle time' and patient waiting time. This would **improve patient satisfaction** and reduce the number of complaints.

Job redesign

Waste elimination principles could be applied to enable an office worker to work more efficiently. This could involve **giving an employee the authority to take action**, within agreed limits, to **keep work moving**. For example, the authority to approve transactions that meet certain criteria may be extended to a wider group of people to reduce the chance of this causing a delay.

Focus on workflow

Office layout could be based on **how work flows through the department**. Likewise with hospitals, for example the accident and emergency department could be redesigned to better reflect **how patients move through the system** (for example having the initial assessment area immediately next to the patient reception and registration area).

(f)   Five key aspects of a programme to implement Total Quality Management (TQM) within a manufacturing organisation are:

Senior management commitment

Successful implementation of TQM requires an acceptance that **everyone** in the organisation is responsible for improving processes and systems. It is especially important that **senior management are committed** to the implementation and that they display this commitment.

Clear implementation strategy

Implementing TQM requires thorough planning and a **clear implementation strategy**. One of the first steps should be to **explain to staff why TQM is being implemented**, the benefits it will bring, why their commitment is important and how the implementation will be conducted. How the implementation processes and procedures will be **documented** is also important.

Establish a TQM steering committee or similar

As with all organisation-wide initiatives, it is important to establish a team that spans the whole organisation **to ensure a co-ordinated approach** is taken. This committee or team also provides a focal point for TQM queries to be fed to, and a mechanism to cascade information to all areas of the organisation.

Training

Employee participation is an essential element of TQM. **Training** will be required to ensure employees are able do what's expected of them. For example, training may be required in process mapping, creative problem solving techniques and in the operation of **quality circles**.

Reporting - monitoring and feedback

An important part of the implementation will be the setting of appropriate **quality standards** and establishing **systems to monitor results** against targets. A process is required to report **feedback** and for the modification of standards and targets if required.

SECTION C

Question 3

Text reference. Chapters 3, 11 and 12.

Top tips. Read the requirement for part (a) carefully. Ensure your answer covers both the development and the implementation of HR practices.

Don't be surprised if occasionally you see a term in the exam you have not seen before, for example 'workforce strategy'. Use the term itself, and it's context, to decide what's required. Planning 'a new workforce strategy' could be interpreted as 'planning a new HR strategy' or 'producing a new HR plan' - either of these interpretations are fine for answering this question. So, for part (b), you may find it helpful to refer to a HR planning model to provide a structure for your answer. Our answer is based on Mullin's model. You may have used a different model, or no model at all. The points you make within the answer are what earn marks. The model, if you use one, simply provides a framework that helps you cover relevant areas.

In (c), start by thinking about the costs associated with any new system implementation (hardware, software, changeover, training, maintenance etc) then apply them to the scenario.

Easy marks. Part (c) should prove relatively straightforward as even explaining generic systems development costs will earn marks.

Marking scheme

		Marks
(a)	Up to 2marks per valid point referenced to the scenario	10
(b)	Up to 2marks per valid point referenced to the scenario	10
(c)	Up to 2marks per valid point referenced to the scenario	5
		25

Our answer shows what we consider the most appropriate points to make. Other relevant points that answer the question would earn marks. However, irrelevant points that do not answer the question would not earn marks.

(a) **Middleregion's HR department** should focus on developing a high level HR strategy that can be applied by managers to meet their needs and employees the needs of employees. The strategy should enable staff to effectively deliver education, social care and environmental services.

Middleregion's HR department should develop policies and practices covering the key areas of HRM. Devanna identified four key aspects of HR, discussed below.

- Effective recruitment and **selection** practices are important to ensure Middleregion obtains people with the qualities and skills required. Succession planning is also important.

- The **appraisal** system should enable targets to be set that contribute to the achievement of the overall strategic objectives of Middleregion. It should also identify skills and performance gaps and provide information relevant to reward levels.

- Effective **training and development** practices are required to ensure employee skills remain up-to-date, relevant, and comparable with (or better than) other public and private sector organisations.

- The **reward system** should motivate and ensure valued staff are retained.

A key influence on the HR practices developed would be the **structure or hierarchy** in place. The trend is towards flexible, flatter structures, with teams often built around specific initiatives or projects. HR planning and practices need to take into account the need for **flexibility** and constant **environmental change or uncertainty**.

The HR department should also ensure HR practices are **co-ordinated**. Devanna points out that the overall **performance** of the organisation depends upon each of the four components and how they are co-ordinated.

The contributions of Middleregion's **line managers** is more likely to be in **implementing** HR practices developed by the HR department.

The strategy developed by the HR department should allow **some flexibility** to line managers, enabling them to ensure procedures are appropriate for local conditions and to the service being provided.

Another key contribution of line managers is to provide **effective leadership**. Part of this involves ensuring individuals are clear about their role and responsibilities. It also involves **motivating** employees, and **supporting** them to ensure they have the **resources required** to do their job.

If high quality employees are to be retained by Middleregion, it is important they have opportunity for **career progression** and **development**. Line managers play an important part identifying individuals for progression and providing the opportunities they need.

To help **staff retention**, line managers could consider the implementation of **job enlargement** (adding additional tasks) and **job enrichment** (increasing responsibility) schemes to help employee **motivation** and prevent staleness.

Line managers should also **encourage teamwork**, this is always important, but even more so in project-based teams

(b)   Middleregion requires a workforce strategy that takes account of a changing environment and is relevant to local conditions.

The **workforce or HR planning process** should follow the steps outlined below (based on Mullins).

Step 1 Start with the corporate strategic objectives

The starting point for workforce strategy is the overall objectives of the organisation. It is these objectives that the organisation's people are tasked with delivering.

Middleregion's strategic objectives should ensure the efficient and effective delivery of education, social care and environmental services.

To take into account the changing, volatile environment, strategic objectives should be reassessed regularly, for example every year (ie **shorter planning time frame**).

Step 2 Design the organisation structure

Middleregion's organisation structure should be designed to enable strategic objectives to be delivered. To provide **flexibility**, a relatively flat, **project-based** structure is likely to be required to deliver education, social care and environmental services.

There may be potential for some employees to work **across different functional areas** at different times. For example a project manager may be equally able to manage an education project as a social work project (given sufficient specialist expertise within the project team).

Step 3 Develop HR plan

The strategic HR plan includes forecasts of human resource **supply** and what is required to deliver organisation objectives (ie the organisation's HR **demand**).

The plan aims to ensure Middleregion has the right number of people, with the right skills, in place at the right time.

People and / or skill shortages must be identified and a plan to **match demand with supply** drawn up. In some areas there may be an over supply of resource, perhaps requiring redundancies or retraining.

Succession planning, particularly for senior positions should be considered.

Step 4 Develop HR management action plan

The HR action plan puts the strategic HR plan in to operation. It includes **operational plans** for recruitment, selection, training, development, redeployment and redundancies.

It's important that staff motivation, career progression, and salaries are considered as these impact both performance and retention.

To provide **flexibility**, line managers should aim to develop a **multi-skilled workforce** in which employees are able to be switched from task to task depending upon demand. **Job rotation** can help increase workforce flexibility. Flexible working practises should be introduced.

External factors such as demographics and population trends are important when assessing demand for Middleregion's services. Population characteristics and trends will differ in different towns and cities throughout Middleregion. **Local information** must be collected to enable local conditions to be taken into account.

Step 5 Exercise control over the plan

Once the HR plan has been established, **performance** must be **monitored and reported**. For example, actual numbers recruited, leaving and promoted should be compared with planned numbers. Action may be required to correct any imbalance.

Actual pay, conditions of employment and training should be compared with assumptions in the HR plan. Neglecting these areas may cause excessive **staff turnover**. Periodically, the HR plan itself should be reviewed and revised to reflect **changed objectives** and changes in the environment.

(c)   The costs Middleregion should take account of when considering moving to e-HR include **development** costs, **implementation** costs and **running** costs. The cost of the system will depend on the range of HR tasks moving to e-HR.

Development costs include the costs associated with systems analysts **establishing system requirements** and costs associated with **software development**. It may be possible to purchase an existing system 'off the shelf' or one in use by another government region. Developing a new system from scratch would be the most expensive development option.

Implementation costs would include costs of new **hardware**, costs associated with **system changeover** (for example file conversion) and user **training costs**. Ensuring that existing HR records are transferred accurately to the new system may require some 'human' checking, which can be expensive. Training may be able to be provided through online tutorials, which are significantly cheaper than face-to-face sessions.

Running costs include **maintenance** costs, software-leasing costs, hardware-leasing costs, system **security** costs, **database administration** costs and on-going **user support**. Effective security is important when dealing with sensitive data, such as salaries. Users should have access to both online and telephone support – there will be a cost associated with this regardless of whether support is delivered by in-house staff or outsourced.

It is possible the move to e-HR will result in some **redundancies**, so there may also be **redundancy costs**. For example e-HR systems can effectively monitor sickness absence and accurately monitor and promote action to support equality and diversity in the workforce. Fewer people will be required to monitor and record this data.

The costs of moving to e-HR should be balanced against **existing HR costs that may be reduced or eliminated** when the new system is introduced. An effective e-HR system can free up HR staff to work on tasks that support the new workforce strategy.

Question 4

Marking scheme

		Marks
(a)	Up to 2marks per valid point referenced to the scenario	10
(b)	Up to 2marks per valid point referenced to the scenario	10
(c)	Up to 2marks per valid point referenced to the scenario	5
		25

Our answer shows what we consider the most appropriate points to make. Other relevant points that answer the question would earn marks. However, irrelevant points that do not answer the question would not earn marks.

(a)   Some of DD's activities have implications for its ethical stance and CSR position.

Aiming television advertising at **children** and teenagers could be seen as unethical and irresponsible. Children do not have the ability to make reasoned judgements. Encouraging children to drink **potentially unhealthy products** will be seen as unethical by some, and contradicts DD's commitment to 'behave ethically while helping improve the quality of life of society generally'. Targeting teenagers is less controversial, as teenagers understand the concept of advertising and should be able to make an informed decision.

Whilst **supporting sporting events** and promoting healthy lifestyles could be seen as ethical, it could also be seen as unethical. By trying to establish a link between healthy activities and its possibly unhealthy products, DD could be seen as hypocritical and be accused of **misleading the public**, particularly children.

The celebrity endorsement of Mr TT has caused concern. Mr TT's association with exploitation of females, violence and bad language **does not fit with DD's ethical, responsible image**. However, Mr TT appears to appeal to teenagers, DD's target segment.

Involvement with Mr TT exposes what seems to be a fundamental **mismatch** between DD's squeaky clean ethical and CSR position and the attitudes of a key target market (teenagers). Whether DD should be overly concerned about the people offended by their association with Mr TT is debatable, as these people probably don't buy DD's products.

The admission by DD that using Mr TT was a mistake will have positive and negative repercussions. The back-down may limit damage to DD's ethical, responsible reputation, but to a large extent the damage to their reputation has been done. By ending it's association with Mr TT, DD may have **lost credibility** with a key target market, teenagers. This could damage sales, for example teenagers may start an online campaign in support of Mr TT and start a boycott of DD.

It isn't clear from the scenario how long has elapsed since the health watchdog report stating that DD's products have high sugar levels and linking them to gum and tooth decay was released. It is essential that DD **responds promptly and honestly** to the report. It may be necessary to introduce 'low sugar' products to better reflect the current expectations of society.

One aspect of DD's activities that should help **support its ethical, socially responsible stance** is the donating of a percentage profits to a number of local charitable causes every year. However, if the products themselves are seen as unhealthy and DD appears to be **misleading the public**, this will outweigh the positive public sentiment generated by the donations.

(b)   Market positioning involves designing the company's offer and image so that it occupies a **distinct** and **valued** place in the target customer's mind.

DD's main **target market** appears to be **children and teenagers**, as most advertising targets this group. The marketing mix (product, price, promotion, place) and branding play an important role in DD's positioning to appeal to children and teenagers.

The '**product**' includes the drink itself, the packaging and the 'package of benefits' the consumer gets from the purchase. The taste, ingredients, any health benefits (or adverse effects) and physiological benefits such as feeling part of a particular social group are relevant. The social aspect is particularly important for teenagers who generally seek social acceptance and want to be seen as 'cool' or 'hip'.

DD's **pricing** strategy is typical of that found in the soft drink sector. DD's premium products are branded as DD offerings. DD produces other, cheaper products that are branded in a different way, for example supermarket own brands. Price is used to reinforce customer perceptions of quality – the implication is that a DD branded drink must be higher quality as it is more expensive. Teenagers, even those who are relatively cash poor, are often prepared to pay a premium price to buy-in to the brand culture (if they identify with it).

Promotion has proved to be problematic for DD. The target market of teenagers identify with **personalities such as Mr TT** whose image seems at odds with DD's highly ethical, socially responsible public image. To retain credibility with a key target market (teenagers), DD may need to consider **relaxing its ethical stance** and **trusting the public** to understand that a relationship between DD and with Mr TT does not mean DD endorses violence and the exploitation of women. The alternative would be to perhaps **target a different market segment**, such as the over 20s. This would probably require product development (perhaps a sports rehydration drink) and some market repositioning, which carries risk.

Place refers to how the product is distributed and how it reaches its customers. Soft drinks are generally purchased at **supermarkets**, other **convenience stores** and from **vending machines**. The **support of the large supermarket chains** is vital to ensure an effective route to market (supermarket shelf space is highly sought after). Teenagers are increasingly using supermarkets, particularly the smaller 'local' or 'metro' stores located in town and city centres.

Branding is important in the drinks industry. Effective branding can result in a drink becoming associated with a **certain attitude and lifestyle**. This breeds **brand loyalty**, and explains why people are often prepared to pay more for a branded drink than they will for a supermarket 'own brand' product that they may actually struggle to taste the difference between in a blind tasting. Branding requires extensive, effective advertising, so is **expensive**. Effective spending on branding is an investment in future sales.

(c)   The likely benefits of DD's increased use of the Internet for marketing purposes include the following.

Increasing online advertising should enable DD to **spend less on television advertising**

The Internet provides DD with the potential to **establish a community and to spread its message** using e-mail and social networking tools such as Facebook (to go 'viral').

The Internet provides **interactivity, speed (instant feedback) and convenience** (including access via mobile devices). Potentially, DD can reach people anywhere, anytime. This is particularly true of teenagers, who tend to be early adopters of technology such as the mobile web (and fans of web 2.0 with users interacting and collaborating with each other).

DD can use the Internet to **forge relationships** with other organisations, both commercial and charitable. For example, the DD website could host music quizzes with electronic iTunes vouchers as prizes. Links to charities could also be provided, free of charge, to reinforce DD's ethical, responsible position.

DD could also launch a **mobile application** ('get the DD app'). To appeal, this must be credible and offer something more than just DD marketing material. For example, a deal with a record label could be struck which allowed limited streaming of music videos through the DD app.

Notes